Marianne Thamm

Hitler, Verwoerd, Mandela and me

A memoir of sorts

TAFELBERG

Tafelberg
an imprint of NB Publishers,
a Division of Media24 Boeke (Pty) Ltd.,
40 Heerengracht, Cape Town 8001
P.O. Box 879, Cape Town 8000
www.tafelberg.com

The publication of this book was made possible by
the generous support of

LAN℗YE

Copyright © 2016 Marianne Thamm

Cover design: Doret Ferreira
Cover photograph: Georg Thamm
Other photographs: Thamm family collection, unless otherwise indicated
Book design: Nazli Jacobs
Editor: Alison Lowry
Proofreader: Russell Martin

Printed by *paarlmedia*, a division of Novus Holdings

First edition, first print 2016

ISBN: 978-0-624-07520-2
Epub: 978-0-624-07521-9
Mobi: 978-0-624-07522-6

For G, L and K – who made me real
like the Velveteen Rabbit

MR TOLMIE WORE the expression of a man accustomed to dealing with the bereaved. His forehead appeared set in a permanent compassionate frown, his mouth downturned but not unfriendly. His gaze was firm but soft.

Wearing his ill-fitting but respectable dark suit, he had learned to lean in – not too close – comforting those who required the services of the Doves funeral home. This was a grey-bricked, single-storey building tucked away in a semi-industrial area near the railway station in Somerset West, Cape Town.

The stack of reading matter in the reception area provided a fascinating insight into the undertaking business. Sitting with my father Georg on a puckered couch waiting for Mr Tolmie to finish off a phone call, I flipped through the latest National Funeral Directors Association newsletter.

The ads were more intriguing than the thuddingly dreary reports from regions about who had been promoted to what. I learned that in 1997 a fully functional multi-storey crematorium was going for around R3 million. It seemed like a sizeable amount, but the good news, of course, should you choose to invest in this line of business, was that you would never run out of custom. The dead are always with us, no matter how bad the economy. The dead need the living to dispose of them – at a cost.

When Mr Tolmie did emerge from his office – soundlessly, thanks to the industrial grey wall-to-wall carpet – he displayed all the appropriate connecting gestures. A sympathetic nod, a hand gently guiding the shoulder of a bereaved family member, in this instance my father, into his office, with its cheap mass-produced desk and triad of maroon upholstered office chairs clustered around it.

Accompanying my father was the least I could do. At the funeral home he clutched a neat brown envelope containing all documents required. Funeral policy, my mother's old black South African identity book with its marriage certificate. He was dressed formally in a light grey suit – it was a sweltering day – with a white shirt, open at the collar, and a pair of polished black slip-ons. Beside him I probably appeared, well, at least to Georg's mind, disrespectful in my casual jeans, T-shirt and sneakers. But there we were.

Georg had long prepared for this moment. Typically German. Everything in order to feed the bureaucratic machine that cranks up – birth, marriage, death. There was no thwarting him and he was happy to obey and oblige.

"Yes, ID, I haf it here. Yes, death certificate, I haf arranged."

It was, I later realised, an instructive occasion for the day to come when I would perch, alone, on one of those very same chairs in the same office arranging my father's funeral (although *sans* Mr Tolmie, who would have moved on by then: "Nervous breakdown" according to the receptionist). But that was still some way off.

When he spoke it was clear Mr Tolmie was either deaf or hard of hearing. His voice was pitched a little too high, the tone just too regular and linear, without the lilts, pauses and cadences that imbue language with its subtleties, its meanings. Perhaps that was why he needed to convey his condolences more through facial expression and body language.

Somewhere in the quiet building my mother's corpse lay chilling in a communal mortuary fridge, still wearing the nightie she had been dressed in the night before when she succumbed to a massive heart attack. She died a month short of her seventy-second birthday.

In a plastic bag I had packed a (highly flammable) Crimplene patterned brown slax suit my mother had bought in the 1970s and which she had treasured for years. It was one of her favourite outfits. The slax suit, a pair of sandals, clean underwear (she would have wanted that).

Crimplene was a miracle 1970s fabric, no need to iron, dries in minutes – great for the busy mother and housewife. One of those wonder substances of the twentieth century every stay-at-home mom came to love, like MSG and tartrazine.

Shuffling some papers, Mr Tolmie began.

"First we need four death certificates and these would be R300 each," he announced in his now distinct monotone, eyes lowered, pen hovering over a form.

"But four? Vye four? Ve already haf von from ze doctor who came to ze home," protested my father in his thick German accent. The accent had never softened, despite his living in South Africa for over 50 years.

"Well, the second doctor has to verify what the first doctor wrote and the third doctor verifies this and so on," Mr Tolmie slowly explained, using his hands to make himself clearer, no doubt, and the gesture perhaps a left-over from signing.

My father shot me an irritated look. I knew what it meant. This was all a money-making scam, he was thinking. And he was determined to pay as little as possible. It's the white culturally alienated secular thing to do. Get the dead buried or preferably cremated as soon as possible in the cheapest coffin available. Pine or, even better, cardboard. Wait, there's a wrapped-in-linen option? How much? No use wasting any money on what no longer matters.

Spending money on a funeral was as bad, my father believed, as buying a new car.

THE NEWS OF my mother's death, when it came, arrived as I had always imagined it would. The phone call, the tense 40-minute journey on the N2 highway from Cape Town to Somerset West where my father insisted on locating himself. My mother had spent the last fourteen years of her life mute, paralysed and confined to a wheelchair in a "home", named after some minor Nationalist politician. The home was around the corner from where Georg lived.

She had had a stroke at the age of 58 which had rendered her speechless. She would have preferred to have died but didn't. Modern medicine stepped in. I was in my mid-20s and lost, in an instant, the source of all benevolent light, love and emotional nourishment that a Portuguese mother is capable of offering. And that, believe me, is a lot. Enough to warrant years of therapy to undo the potentially harmful residual narcissism that being loved unconditionally brings with it. Being loved by a Portuguese mother, my Portuguese mother, was tantamount to being offered a lifelong store of unreasonable self-esteem. I am the mistress of my universe because of Barbara Maria Da Palma Fernandes Thamm.

When I do come to doubt myself, it is thanks to Georg. Mow the entire lawn and he will be sure to emerge into the sunlight, survey the task and notice the one patch that had escaped the blades and that stood now traitorously upright bending in the breeze.

"You didn't mow over zere," he would remark, gesturing in the direction of the scraggly tall grass.

And now we had come to cremate Barbara. She was Catholic, devout but culturally so. She seldom attended mass. A crucifix hung above her single bed in our Pretoria home. Her dressing table was adorned with a photograph of her younger self – "I looka like Elizabeth Taylor only with brown eyes" – a statuette of Mary and an etching in an ornate crocheted frame of the three "saints" of Fatima.

Nossa Senhora de Fátima had appeared to three Portuguese peasant children, Lúcia Santos and her cousins Jacinta and Francisco Marto, in 1917. Fatima was about 250 km from the village of Aljustrel, where my mother was born. The children had also lived in my mother's village and were probably the first celebrities ever in the region.

Barbara insisted that all our vehicles be fitted – on the dashboard – with medallions of St Christopher, the patron saint of travellers. Once, when my father went to Rome on business, she requested that he bring back a statue of the Madonna blessed by the Pope, and rosaries for her, my older brother Albert and me (obviously also all blessed by the Pope himself). My father obliged and as an added extra he picked up at the Vatican curio shop a plastic see-through bottle in the shape of the Virgin Mary, the twist-off lid disguised as her crown. The bottle contained liquid, apparently from the healing waters of Lourdes. Floating close to the bottom of the bottle was a small, slimy, indistinguishable black particle. Throughout my childhood (and adulthood in fact) I was convinced it was some sort of scab or sliver of leprosy that had floated off someone bathing in the water while seeking a miracle cure. The bottle thankfully remained full and unopened for years and, despite our move after 20 years from Pretoria to Cape Town, turned up again on my mother's dressing table.

Barbara was highly superstitious. Never walk under ladders, a black cat crossing a road meant certain death, and snapping open an umbrella indoors would most certainly lead to seven years of torrid luck. Don't even think of mentioning the cracked mirror – the bringer of a lifetime of misery.

During Highveld thunderstorms, when dazzling darts of lightning criss-crossed the heavens, Barbara would drape cloth over the mirrors. We were never to swim after eating and I was never to bathe while menstruating because I would drown or make myself vulnerable to some unspoken health threat. When Barbara misplaced something, she would shuffle from room to room chanting "Hasha hasha Santa Antonio". St Anthony is the patron saint of finding lost things or lost people.

After her stroke my mother never recovered her speech.

It was a physical manifestation of the silence she had kept about her life in Portugal, her family, her origins or how she came to find herself working "in service" in England in the 1950s, which was where she met Georg, a German prisoner of war.

Barbara would not reveal much. Perhaps inhabiting these silences felt safer for her. Here she could conceal herself, a self that outwardly never manifested as anything but one-dimensional. It was an impenetrable shield.

When one is younger one does not care too much about these things. It is your own life stretching ahead of you that is important. And so the fact that my mother had four (or was it six?) brothers who all had children (who were/are nameless cousins of mine) was of little concern to me then.

We were here, in South Africa, just the four of us, atomised, unrelated to anyone apart from ourselves.

My mother repeated, for the next fourteen years, only one word in an endless loop: "gethagetha". When she was angry she spat it out – "gethagetha!!" When she needed something she would point at it and say "gethagetha". When she wanted to tell me she loved me she gently cooed "gethagetha" while stroking my cheek.

This new silence, punctuated with pre-verbal gibberish, created even more of an unfathomable distance. Physical tenderness was the last touchpoint inwards.

MY MOTHER died around 7pm on the night of 4 November, two days after All Souls Day. I arrived at her room, which was near the entrance to a long green corridor, to find the pastel blue curtain drawn around her bed. She had one room-mate at the time. Usually three old people were forced to share.

I drew back the curtain to find my father sprinkling the Lourdes water over my mother's lifeless body. No use worrying now about the floating bit of leprosy. She was out of harm's way. It would be great, though, if the Lourdes water actually worked! That would be something worth writing about.

Barbara had died about 20 minutes before my arrival. She had never looked happier or more peaceful. Her right arm, which had withered over the years, was relaxed and had been folded across her chest. Her eyes were partially open. I leaned over and looked at her. She returned my gaze but as if from a great distance. She was still warm to the touch.

"Fly, now you are free," I whispered.

My father was sobbing, clutching the now empty bottle, unable to comfort me. He had lost a spouse. I had lost my mother and here we were, two molecules separate in our grief.

I wanted to spend as much time as possible with my mother before the mortuary van arrived to take her away. The thing about death in the Western world is that we want the corpse gone as soon as possible. My mother had once told me that when her father, a copper miner, had died aged 49 – she was twelve years old – his body had been brought home and the open coffin was placed in the living room where everyone in the village who knew him could come and pay their respects. I quite liked the drama of that. And while it seemed like the decent thing to do, it was a tad impractical here and now, and besides there were rules, strict rules, with regard to removing a body without permits and permission from those who enforce general rules.

Untethered by any religion or prescribed cultural ritual, all I could do was sit with my mother, taking in the familiar shape of her hands, her nails, for the last time. I removed her gold wedding ring and gave it to my father. He told me to keep it. I thought I detected a smile on her face. At least that is how I have chosen to remember the expression that night.

"Bloody hell, man," came a voice from the other side of the curtain. "This has been going on for too long now. It's almost 11 o'clock and I want to get some sleep. Get on with it!" It was my mother's room-mate, grumbling. And rightly so. There is no room for sentiment, no time for social niceties in God's waiting room where the living still need their sleep.

"Coffin?" Mr Tolmie barked, probably not meaning to, but miscalculating the pitch of the question.

He guided us down a dark passage to a gloomy showroom located at the back of the premises. In the centre was Doves' Deluxe model, which must have been one of their premium caskets. It was shiny and black, big and heavy, with ornate brass or fake brass handles. It came in ivory and white as well, Mr Tolmie informed us.

The sales pitch was lost on us, he would have soon realised. My father and I headed straight for the chipboard range (cheaper than pine) towards the rear of the room. The coffins were a standard size. They could fit a tallish person. My mom was short and squat but it would do.

We finished off the paperwork, with Mr Tolmie vigorously wielding a stamp like a bank clerk. Thump, thump. And there it was. The world "deceased" inked across the back and front pages of Barbara's ID book. Like a fullstop to the conversation.

I left the packet of clothing – my mother's funeral garb – with Mr Tolmie. The right thing to have done would have been to dress her myself. She would have hated a stranger seeing her naked. She had always been modest. But I felt ill equipped to handle her lifeless body alone and so I left it to the experts. Besides, she no longer inhabited the carapace.

A few days later we returned to Doves for a small "service". It took place in the chapel at the funeral home. Apart from my father and myself, there were only one or two nurses from the home present. I took one last look at my mother as she lay in the casket.

She was cold to the touch, as if she had been dredged up from the bottom of an icy ocean, and this time she was ashen. There was nothing left, not a trace of who she had once been, even shortly after her death. A lay Catholic preacher, who hadn't known my mother, had been ferreted out from a nearby congregation and he gave a standard service.

On the way out we had to negotiate a huge swarm of bees that had gathered outside the entrance of the funeral home. They were not angry and seemed to linger there for no particular reason. I searched for a hive in the eaves or a tree with fragrant flowers but there was nothing.

Later a friend who had become a sangoma told me that bees sometimes represent immortality and resurrection.

Free and flying.

My mother's corpse was transported, along with others, to a crematorium in Worcester about 112 km outside Cape Town. It would have been the furthest she had travelled alone in years. There, at an unknown hour, the last remnants of her physical being curled up into the air.

Two weeks later my phone rang. It was my father.

"Your muzzer weighs 4.08 kgs."

"Um?"

"I haf her here on ze kitchen scale."

I DIDN'T WEIGH Georg's ashes. On the drive home with the small, plain wooden box that contained him resting on the passenger seat beside me, I contemplated flinging it out of the car window.

Even in death he had managed to thwart my independence, my feminism. At least those were my original thoughts. After years of taking care of his life, his needs, his finances, his moods, his man flu, his dogs, he had made my brother Albert, who had long since emigrated to Australia, the executor of his Last Will and Testament.

All the males in our family were named Georg Albert or Albert Georg (until my brother broke the tradition and named his son, my nephew, Alex). This way families like to remind the bearers of the Y chromosome of the apparent responsibility (or burden) of carrying the family name. Perhaps it signals symbolically this passing on of the immutable Y to generations of men who beget men. The troublesome XX in girls dilutes the line. It is a thoroughly maternal business this. Women carry within us only the traces of our mothers and their mothers, the mitochondria infinitely mutating, changing, altering.

Girls are off the hook then when it comes to bearing the family name. We just disappear or merge – upon marriage – with the Y in some other family. Not to marry, not to bring forth fruit from your loins, is to carry your father's name, should he have bestowed it upon you, until you no longer are.

Was Georg's decision to make Albert the executor his final stand as a patriarch, calling the shots from beyond the beyond? Undermining me as his little XX, a woman, those who are doomed to sweat the small stuff while the big, important matters – the admin, the estate – were a man's job. A woman's feeble brain would be incapable of it.

Or perhaps not. Perhaps Georg had sought some way of involving my brother in the final details of his life, his paltry estate. Give him the benefit of the doubt, I suggested to myself as I eyed his ashes, still calculating the force required to eject them from the passenger window closest to the verge on the highway. It would have been easier to toss him from the driver's side, but he would have ended up a hazard in the middle of the highway, with cars having to dodge the tiny coffin.

Be that as it may, his decision to leave the winding up of business to Albert was not a wise one. It would require an inordinate amount of bureaucratic schlepp. Certified copies of this and that – originals to be couriered halfway across the globe. Disconnected time zones. Endless phone calls to uninterested officials on either end. Delays.

Fuck you, Georg. Fuck you. As if I didn't have my own life as a freelance hack with two young children who needed me around.

The issue was swiftly resolved, however. When my brother learned that Georg's posthumous gift would result in major administrative inconvenience, including filing the will with the Master of the Supreme Court *in South Africa*, Albert immediately agreed to surrender his role to a local attorney. There was no way I could be of any help, Georg having rendered me a legal nonentity.

Georg and I had spent the last three long and painful months of his life dealing with his declining health and impending death. The year 2011 had been a year of tumultuous ups and downs. Before that, four or five years of regular rushes to the local hospital – the "installing" of a pacemaker ("Marianna, I am not sure I am alive. My pulse is 30," he called to tell me while I was on assignment in Johannesburg).

Georg was curious as to how the tiny device implanted just below the skin and nestling in a hollow under his left collarbone – and which, remarkably, turned his hue from grey to pink almost instantly – would "know" or "understand" that his heart might need to stop pumping when the moment eventually arrived.

"It is very new and vhat if it keeps on going vhen I am supposed to die? And vhat if ze batteries run out before zen?"

We researched it all and came to learn that the intelligent design of the device ("Is it German?" he asked) would register and regulate, when time came, the diminishing contractions of the heart it was assisting.

"Ah, zat iss good," he said, "I vill die in my sleep zen."

While I appreciated, I told him, that he might believe he could control the forces of nature, predict the exact time of his death or even outwit an indifferent universe, I myself would rather prepare for a worst-case scenario, seeing that I would be dealing with it.

It was just as likely, I suggested gently, that he might have a stroke and survive. In that case, depending on the severity, he might need 24-hour care. He could also end up lingering in ICU entangled in susurrating pipes and tubes. His medical aid would soon be depleted and his savings could dry up quicker than you could say 419 internet scam.

"Well zen, zey vill just svitch off ze machines," he said confidently.

That was sort of true. There's nothing like an exhausted medical aid to override any apparent ethical notion of the so-called sanctity of life in a private hospital. You might as well hand over all your banking passwords on admission and calculate with the clerk how long you have left, depending on the balance.

It was unlike Georg, however, not to be more realistic or pragmatic. He had been reportedly dying since about the age of 60. There were countless afternoons during my visits when he would routinely lead me to the black cast-iron safety deposit box hidden in his wardrobe, which contained, he informed me, "everyzing" I would need in the event of his death.

Why the box needed to be locked and hidden only Georg knew. I couldn't imagine gun-toting intruders wanting to make off with an old man's will. People usually keep other valuables in safes.

Georg would slip the slim key into the lock and click it open.

"It iss all taken care of. Here are ze funeral policies and I haf lodged my vill vis ze lawyers," he would say, shuffling through the sealed envelopes. The box also contained several old and yellowing documents in heavy Fraktur script. These were the birth, death and marriage certificates of various Prussian ancestors. Also in there were flight logs from Georg's days as a glider pilot, work references, and certificates of naturalisation. Rather have all the papers and not need them than need them and not have them, as many a refugee has discovered. Especially when you are called on by authorities to prove your Aryan ancestry.

I feigned a keen interest. To reassure him mostly. But I appreciated that he didn't want to leave me with a bureaucratic mess. It's the least we can do for those left to dispose of our remains.

I did try to use these opportunities to probe his preoccupation with death. Was he feeling particularly low? Was he needing something? Was he lonely? But no, there was no specific reason – just life and its inevitable trajectory towards nothingness.

Reaching old age, 85 in his case, leaves one with few options in relation to exactly how much time one realistically has left. It is odd when one is not there, to think one cannot glibly say "in 20 years' time". It is also pointless to suggest that someone is lucky to have made it past threescore and ten when you yourself are nowhere near this age.

However, plans for the future had to be made. And in Georg's case it was not going to be more than five years.

At the same time, the reality of impending death, I came to understand, can be a powerful incentive to disavow the truth. It was easy to sit this side of 50 discussing or thinking about oblivion – or everlasting life, depending on one's convictions – while in perfectly rude health. Many productive hours are whiled away by those of us inclined to idly run through potential endings in our minds. We are those who endlessly compile playlists for our funeral and who keep changing them as one song replaces another as a favourite depending on our mood (Queen's "The Show Must Go On" and Gaga's "Just Dance", because in the end, all you can do, when you can do it, is just dance).

And while one might, at any moment, end up entangled in a car wreck or be blown to bits in a nightclub bombing in Bangkok, the reality and the luxury, for the relatively young, healthy and those who do not live in a war-torn country, are that these are abstract thoughts.

A simple visit to the doctor always reminds me of the random nature of life and death.

"Family's medical history?" the doctor inevitably asks.

"A bullet to the head," I reply, thinking of my Prussian ancestors who were shot by advancing Russian troops as they harvested potatoes in Eastern Europe during WWII.

That's life. Random. If you escape a bullet in a war, you might meet one while waiting at a traffic light in a busy city in broad daylight in peacetime while you're WhatsApping a friend. Either way, it comes. Death. Heart attack, dread disease, a slow degenerative condition. Best to make friends with it, acknowledge its constant presence, offer it a cup of tea. And anyway, it appeared that death, or its scary nihilistic alter ego, had become a South African citizen. It seemed always to be with us, in headlines, in the streets, in our heads (where it still remains to some extent not quite banished).

What you don't want, of course, is the lingering, like my mother. But it is likely that those of us who get to enjoy longer lives will find ourselves, sooner or later, lingering in one way or another, dependent on the kindness of strangers or relatives.

For Georg, however, in 2009, the great-no-more, the void, the hereafter, the-not-hear-after, whatever, was a concrete reality, and no doubt not for the first time in his life he retreated into a comfortable Germanic denial.

Later there were prolonged visits to specialists to determine the cause of an alarming swelling of one of his legs (side-effects of medication), and there would come a time when I would accompany him for a series of tests and scans that enabled us to watch, on a screen, his frail heart struggling to do its work. He held onto my arm as we teetered down various dark hospital corridors, Georg dressed in a hospital gown, his large ears thrown into comic relief, and then submitting to wires and sticky pads that would offer us this glimpse inside himself.

We both watched the patchy white-and-black blur throbbing on a computer screen, sending out a weak Morse code signal that yes, he was still alive. This was the same muscle that had once beat more steadily when as a ten-year-old boy dressed in the Hitler Youth Movement uniform of black shorts and khaki shirt garnished with a red-and-white armband with a black swastika, he had taken the oath, en masse, "In the presence of this blood banner which represents our Führer, I swear to devote all my energies and my strength to the saviour of our country, Adolf Hitler. I am willing and ready to give up my life for him, so help me God."

Tucked into the left shirt pocket of the uniform he wore later as a pilot in the Luftwaffe, Georg had carried a *Schutzbrief* (a letter of protection) handwritten by his mother and imploring God to protect her son whom she unquestioningly offered as a sacrifice after drinking Hitler's Kool-Aid. The *Schutzbrief* had also survived the war. Georg kept the yellowing, torn piece of paper pressed between the pages of his Bible.

This was also the same heart that had quickened on the night I had been conceived. That was an uncomfortably Freudian segue, I realised, so I quickly erased it, conjuring instead a vision of my two gorgeous children who needed to be picked up from school while I was watching an old Nazi heart fibrillate.

But was it? The same heart? We are not who we are when we are born. The cells in our bodies renew themselves constantly. Red blood cells survive only four months, white blood cells about twelve. Our skin cells live for about three weeks, the cells in our colons only four days. It is the cells in the brain, however, that last a lifetime. And what we lose up there is not replaced, apart from two regions – the olfactory bulb, which regulates our ability to smell, and the hippocampus, where our initial memories of faces and places are fixed. Only these are capable of generating new neurons.

The brilliant news is that, like canaries, we can learn to sing new songs. But we need someone either to teach us or to be inspired, prompted or compelled to do so ourselves.

So, it is here, in the mind, where we really exist fully, to ourselves at least, mostly as a fiction. There are flashes of clarity, 20/20 hindsight, but for the most part we remain figments of our own imagination, where the ghosts of those who shaped us – usually our parents – and the currents of history that swirled during our lifetimes and our formative years haunt or direct us. There is no one else who can verify why we become who we are or what we think as we live our lives and make our choices. Or sometimes don't make choices.

Choices were always a central theme of the conversations Georg and I had for over a quarter of a century. Why had he or my German family not defied Hitler? Why had they not made different choices? Why had he brought us to South Africa in the 1960s just as the apartheid government was tightening its violent grip? Surely if you know you are on the wrong side of history, you make the choice to resist? You check out of the perpetrator/collaborator class?

And as long as I had relegated him to this position, I could slough it from myself. But it was not that elementary.

I asked Georg what his response had been to the burning of the Berlin synagogues on Kristallnacht – the dreadful night of the broken glass on 9 and 10 November 1938, when Nazi paramilitary forces, aided by ordinary Germans, embarked on an orgy of violence in the city, murdering German Jews, torching Jewish-owned shops, smashing windows, and ransacking homes.

"I vas just a boy on a bicycle," he replied.

He was fourteen at the time.

This was not the end of the conversation. We returned to it obsessively over the years like a tongue probing a chipped tooth.

This way I had hoped to find a way of "fixing" my father. And if I could mend him, I might repair myself. But fixing could also mean encasing him in immutable stone, as I would learn.

THE SUNDAY before he died Georg and I spent alone together in his small, sparsely furnished room in Robari Lodge, a place the owners called a retirement centre but which was, in all truth, an old-age home that stank permanently of stale piss, with the faint, sweet smell of faeces mixed in with the aroma of canteen food.

Georg had hung a portrait of his mother and father, Martha and Albert Thamm (my grandparents, although it was hard for me to think of them this way as I had never met them), to the right of his single bed where they could watch over him. They were young then, their faces fresh and untroubled, their gazes sharp and confident. Both seemed to me to wear subtle smiles untainted by knowledge of the trauma to follow.

As we recede from this life, do we hear the whispers of our ancestors, those we believe are waiting for us, arms open to show the way? Once, awaking from the deep sleep only the aged know, Georg mistook me for his mother. I have never forgotten the look of startled pleasure on his face as his eyes opened.

Georg was always charming to the nurses and other residents – or inmates, rather – when he felt up to it. The photographs of his grand-children, my daughters, intrigued the staff at the home. Who were they? And how was it that this old, white man could be a grandfather to two black children?

My father's dress sense remained European. He preferred cotton shirts, wool suits, cravats and leather shoes. Never shorts or slip-slops. He also enjoyed smelling good and was always well groomed. I shaved him when he could no longer do this himself. He detested facial hair, and Russians.

He had the quiet confidence of a man who knew he had once been attractive to women, but he was not boorish or swaggering about it. He never used sexist language and rarely commented on anyone's physical appearance – unless they were overweight. This, he felt, signalled ill-discipline, a loss of self-control.

While he enjoyed the company of women, and in fact was a mommy's boy, he was of a generation who sincerely believed that women were not and could never be as intelligent as men, or their equals. He was also German and truly believed in Teutonic superiority in all aspects of life, not only in the manufacture of cars.

At Robari an ancient woman, blind, with a suppurating scab on her scalp which erupted from her thinning white hair like an angry volcano, often sat at the entrance in her wheelchair when weather permitted. When Georg had first arrived, the familiar guttural rasp of his accent had been picked up by her heightened hearing. She called out, "Are you German?", adding that she had been a nurse during the Battle of Britain.

Georg leaned on his walking stick, listening to her talk.

"Vell, it vasn't me," he joked in reply.

Shortly before he died Georg lost his voice and could only speak in a hissing, painful whisper. He was skeletal and pallid and weak. His chest heaved as he struggled for every breath with an oxygen mask clamped over his mouth. He hadn't been able to keep food down for weeks and I would watch helplessly as he spluttered and coughed and convulsed when he did try to swallow a spoonful of soup. His heart, lungs and kidneys were failing. The body knows when it no longer needs sustenance and violently rejects any attempt at keeping it nourished. And while Georg had been seriously ill the year before, we both knew it was time.

But which one of us would call it such? Which of us would finally notice death in the room?

"Dad, you are dying," I dared to offer.

His eyes, which were retreating now into his hollow sockets, swivelled towards me. I feared what I might glimpse there – anger, rage, denial. But there was only understanding, tenderness and fear. I felt hopelessly ill equipped.

More than anything Georg wanted a dignified death.

"I really hope I don't soil myself and make vork for ze nurses," he whispered.

It is a rare gift to say goodbye to a parent this way. And difficult. Would I and my father, in these final moments, be able to really see each other? Would there be a reciprocity of recognition? Would he review his life and find it worthwhile? Would he find me worthwhile or would he find me wanting?

Georg had spent much of his life waiting for happiness as if it were a sacrament, a blessed Eucharist, to be delivered from outside of himself. I sensed that he had been somewhat disappointed that happiness hadn't miraculously arrived, knocked on the door of his heart and said, Let me in, oh unhappy man.

It is too late to fill in the blindspots when our bodies are racked with the real pain of physical separation. Happiness, however we might define it personally, I understood in that moment, was not something received, but a state we are obliged to seek out ourselves.

I did not know how to help Georg undertake this journey. I had no spiritual or religious framework to offer him. All I could tell him was that where he was going was where he had been before he was here. All I could try and do was love him as he was, in that moment, and not require a selfish and childish acknowledgement that he did indeed love me in return.

I thanked him for being the best father he could have been, told him I loved him and that my brother and I could take care of ourselves now. Also, everyone who had ever mattered to him, including my mother (and an array of dogs he had loved over the years), were all where he was now headed.

My brother and father had spoken regularly on the phone but had not been able to do so since he had lost his voice. The day before, a beautiful letter from my brother had arrived from Australia and I took it to Georg and read it out loud to him. As he listened a single tear rolled down his cheek.

Our eyes met for what we both knew might be the last occasion. There was such tenderness, sincerity and vulnerability. There would be no way of "fixing" this for me now. We had gone as far as we could. The only searing truth in that moment was death. This was not death cruel and indiscriminate as I had come to know it, but death gentle and welcome. Death had finally popped in for its cup of tea.

Georg was in pain, he told me, and it was this he feared most now. I asked if he wanted me to arrange morphine to ease it, to allow him to concentrate on the spiritual journey, the separation he would have to endure. He nodded.

I called his doctor, who arranged for a chemist to open up and dispense the liquid. It was 11pm on a Sunday and I appreciated everyone's gentle co-operation, including that of the staff at the home.

He would take his first small dose that night, sipping it from a plastic cup. I asked him if he wanted me to sit with him but he indicated that he would rather be alone. I kissed him, stood at the door and said, "I love you."

Through the open door of the room next door I could see Mr Poopy Pants, as my children had named my father's demented neighbour, who usually stood marching on the spot on the carpet dressed in a sagging adult nappy. That night he was tied tightly into his bed with a sheet.

God's waiting room is filled with misery.

GEORG DIED at 7.15am the following morning, 11 June 2011. This time I was calm when the phone rang and the nurse on duty informed me that my father had just died. I drove to Somerset West with my partner listening to Arvo Pärt. It was over.

Georg was lying on his bed still dressed in his pyjamas, his head wrapped in a linen serviette tied in two bunny ears to keep his mouth closed. It was the first time he looked peaceful in ages and wasn't heaving for every breath. He had not soiled himself, he would have been pleased to learn.

One of the nurses who had looked in on him earlier came quietly into the room. She wanted to tell me, she said, what had happened.

"I came in at seven and asked your father how he was. He was struggling to breathe. Then he asked me how I was. I said I was fine. Then he told me to close the door because 'I am leaving now to be with my wife'."

That was Georg. He had been lucid until the last moment and I was proud to learn that he had, in that profound instant, shown concern for someone else. It was this that I loved about him.

I asked the nurse to help me dress him. I picked out his favourite suit, a white shirt and tie. I placed his Bible in one of the side pockets. I slipped my brother's letter and one from my children into one of the inside pockets. And then I found the *Schutzbrief* and placed it in the left top pocket.

He no longer needed it.

It REALLY IS ALL UP TO a ripe and ready ova and a single Olympic swimmer doing the upstream fallopian-tube sperm relay while competing with between 40 million and 1.2 billion others released in one quick ejaculation.

Life is sexually transmitted.

And if all goes according to plan, we emerge mewling into the world (often carefully scheduled around the obstetrician's weekly golf date if you have medical aid) or otherwise with our mothers screaming and pushing us towards the light. And then we plough and claw our way through it all, blind as moles, until we hit an obstacle or two, or three.

You are, technically, a one-in-a-billion physical manifestation. By the time you are lifted out of the womb, you are already a winner of sorts. Oprah Winfrey knows this.

That's the easy part. Then the schlepp begins. The colour of your skin, your designated gender, social class and the religious, economic and geopolitical circumstances that prevail in the random destination of your arrival, all begin to coalesce, conspire and collude to either thwart or enhance your chances at life.

While we may gradually become conscious of these currents, we are, at first at least, cast adrift. Life happens to us and sometimes, if we are lucky, if we have agency, we can happen to life.

I am a genetic and geographic accident. I made a low-key entrance on 12 March 1961 in the Canadian Red Cross Hospital in Taplow, a girl child with a pink skin who enjoyed sleeping. The beginning of the 1960s was a time that brought with it many exciting human endeavours.

And if we possess, as some claim we do, embedded ancestral memories, if we have past traumas and triumphs lurking within our genes, I might very well be a ticking time bomb. The Latin and Teutonic temperaments blended in me, if these are indeed gifted to us by our parents, could not be further removed from each other. Where one is emotional, the other is remote; one loud, the other restrained. In these currents passion competes with level-headedness, an easygoing nature with one that despises a lack of structure.

In the clash of stereotypes, which would triumph? Would I wake one morning and plot to take over the world? Or would I aspire to running a corner shop selling overpriced one-ply toilet paper, loose sweets and wilted vegetables?

And while these traits might not necessarily be inherited, they resided in the cultural DNA of the two people who created my brother and me.

On 12 April 1961, exactly a month to the day of my birth, Russian cosmonaut Yuri Gagarin became the first human in space. His spaceship, the Vostok 1 (roughly translated from the Russian as "east"), made a single one-hour, 48-minute orbit of the earth. Viewed from the twenty-first century, with its strange appendages the Vostok looks rather like a giant intrauterine contraceptive device. Nonetheless, it ensured Gagarin's place in human history.

For the first time since our hominid ancestors had become bipedal around 1.8 million years ago, a human being was miraculously able to leave the earth's atmosphere without using psychotropic drugs. It was indeed a new frontier.

Not to be outdone, a month later, on 5 May 1961, the Americans shot Alan Bartlett Shepard into space in the Freedom 7. His sub-orbital flight lasted only fifteen minutes.

The Russians, much to the irritation of the West, had become the undisputed world champions of the longest intergalactic orgasm.

In retrospect, I have come to view the cosmonaut's journey as a sort of personal lodestar, a sign that at some point I would live long enough to exit the twentieth century, a time guided by the dim lights of habits and impulse, to find myself in the twenty-first. Here, not only would I be puffing on an electronic cigarette and guffawing at Vines on my mobile device, but exist as a lesbian protected by a remarkable constitution that affords me complete equality and the right to adopt children of my own. Before then, becoming a mother would have had to occur either via an immaculate conception (it has happened before, apparently), IVF (which hadn't yet been invented) or through finding myself a character in a bleak JM Coetzee novel.

Now I could stand in front of a shelf of disposable nappies just like everyone else, marvelling at their cost and speculating how they might end up in the ocean plastered over the blow-hole of a threatened whale species.

But that was all still some way off in the future – having children, that is.

Those of us born in the 1960s were caught in a political shit sandwich between two competing global ideologies, communism and Western liberal capitalist democracy. Both had their charms and their downsides. But these dual forces would shape much of twentieth-century politics (before both imploded), including politics in South Africa, where Georg and Barbara had chosen to relocate their young family in 1963.

The forces of history that had swept Georg and Barbara to England and that had shaped most of their adult lives were similar in many ways. Both had grown up in countries governed by fascist, authoritarian regimes – those of Adolf Hitler and the Portuguese dictator, António de Oliveira Salazar. Both men, coincidentally, were born in April 1889, Salazar on the 28th, eight days after Hitler. There must have been a particularly malevolent planetary alignment that year because both leaders were to inflict prolonged misery and horror on the lives of millions.

It was these two men who had also shaped, to a certain extent, the inner lives of both my parents. For Georg national socialism consolidated and strengthened an identity while Salazar's authority was one that appeared to shatter Barbara, prompting in her a need to disappear, to appear insignificant. To escape or survive it one kept a low profile, one kept one's mouth shut.

Georg's teenage years (he was born in 1924) were dominated by the shabby theatre of Nazi parades with all their kitsch, rigid pomp and pageantry. He hurtled towards adulthood surrounded only by uniforms and buildings garbed in political flags and banners. He joined the Nazi youth group, the Hitlerjugend, which prepared him to be a glider pilot and a good national socialist. All around him was the brewing anti-Semitism of a nation being stoked into madness after a post-WWI humiliation.

Barbara was born in 1925 and grew up one of four or five children in the impoverished hamlet of Aljustrel in the southern Beja province in Portugal. It was a region that had been conquered by the Romans and the Visigoths, had become an independent Muslim-ruled principality, was later captured by the Almohad Caliphate, until it was occupied by Spanish and Portuguese armies in 1640.

I suspect Barbara's warnings to my brother, who seems to have inherited her Latin physical attributes, to stay out of the sun lest he should burn too brown, were inspired by this Moorish heritage.

Barbara's father, Manuel Romão Fernandes, was a copper miner who died underground at 49. Her mother, Maria Joana Da Palma, died when Barbara was six months old and Maria Joana's children were raised by a bevy of relatives and extended family. In the egalitarian Portuguese tradition, Barbara carried the names of both her maternal and paternal ancestors, Barbara Maria Da Palma Fernandes.

In a 1930 census, Portugal's population was classified as "illiterate". For years education, provided by the clergy, had been only for a small elite. In the 1940s the country had the lowest literacy rates in Western Europe. Barbara herself was barely literate and, while her early bank book featured her thumbprint as a signature, she later learned to sign her name in a child-like scribble.

She was born as Portugal teetered on the brink of political authoritarianism. The year 1925 was the last occasion Portugal would have a multi-party democratic election. Five months after her birth, in May 1926, a military coup, led by General Manuel de Oliveira Gomes da Costa, ushered in a national dictatorship. This later evolved into Estada Novo led by Salazar from 1936 until the Carnation Revolution of 1974.

Salazar's special police force for "Social Vigilance and Defence", which later became the feared PIDE, had been modelled on and was trained, at first, by the Gestapo. In 1936 Salazar created the Mocidade Portuguese, a local version of the Hitler Youth and it became compulsory for all Portuguese children aged between eleven and fourteen to join it. And so worlds apart, long before they would meet, Barbara and Georg were carried by political cross-currents that had more in common than they themselves would personally bring to their relationship.

Like all undemocratic regimes, Salazar's relied on the PIDE to "encourage" an extensive network of informers who penetrated the fabric of Portuguese life, turning friends, relatives and neighbours into possible deadly state pimps. It was only later that I understood that my mother's paranoia over my questions about South Africa in the 1970s was related to this memory of the fear and terror of others.

Communism was an obsession for the Catholic Salazar and a special unit of the PIDE was dedicated entirely to zealously capturing, torturing, deporting and imprisoning members of the Partido Comunista Português (PCP).

"Donta talk too loud. They can hear everything you say. Donta say nothing about da government. Iss not our country. They will put you in jail," Barbara warned me.

What she would tell me is that one of her brothers had joined the PCP and had been captured by the PIDE. When she did eventually get to see him, she said she had been shocked at his appearance. He was half the young man he had once been.

"Please, I donta wanta thees to appen to you," she pleaded.

Barbara was an economic migrant to the UK, a semi-literate Portuguese citizen who had arrived in 1955 at the age of 30, with several friends, to work "in service" for one Dr PT Ballantyne of Courtlands in Beaconsfield, Bucks. The permit issued by the Ministry of Labour and National Service read: "This permit is granted in respect of employment as a domestic worker only with the employer named therein."

Three years later, looking like a Latin version of a Hollywood filmstar with her milk-white complexion, almond brown eyes and shock of black, curly hair, Barbara began working as a cook at the King

Edward VII Hospital in Windsor. It was in this village that she would meet Georg at a social club designated for those who were not English – immigrants, refugees and those displaced somehow by WWII, in which a staggering 55 million people had died (more people than are alive in South Africa today).

Georg's journey to England had initially been an unwilling one. On 5 October 1944 he was captured by Allied forces during the historic Operation Market Garden, the largest Allied airborne attempt at liberating the Dutch town of Arnhem, which had been captured by the Germans in the last cataclysmic shudders of WWII.

In fact Georg had been taken prisoner on the Roermondsplein Bridge, which he was later amused to learn had been renamed the Nelson Mandela Bridge in 1994.

"Which bridge?" he liked to ask with a chuckle, adding, "We blew it up!"

A letter headed "In the field, 18 October 1944" and sent by Georg's Kompanieführer to his mother, Martha, back in bombed-out Berlin, read: "I have the sad duty to inform you that your son, subordinate officer Georg Thamm, was taken into captivity on 5 October, 1944 at Arnheim [the German spelling of Arnhem] in Holland. During these days the company found itself in heavy battle. When the company re-grouped, your son was missing. Soldiers in the company reported seeing your son's capture. Otherwise nothing further is known about the process. May it be granted that you will one day greet your son back in his homeland."

And with that Hitler's minions signed off on Georg.

In the meantime, Georg had been interned as a prisoner of war at the Glen Mill camp at Oldham, which was the first to be earmarked by the War Office in 1938 at the start of the war and which housed ordinary prisoners. Nazi officers and those considered dangerous were held separately.

Judging from photographs of the time, this appeared to be a rather welcome respite from the demands of war for Georg. He can be seen rakishly sporting a civilian cap, grinning widely, driving a tractor while performing forced labour on local farms. It was either that or a

Russian gulag and as far as he was concerned, Georg had struck it lucky. The *Schutzbrief* was still loaded with some divine airtime.

The prisoners were given lessons in English. I still have my father's POW dictionary preserved in a hand-made leather dustcover with the inscription "This is the legal property of 651645 Thamm G, who has lawfully acquired this book (PW 176. 30.4.46.)".

Georg's father, Albert, was killed on the night of 27 April 1945 while his son was tilling English soil and as the Allies were liberating Berlin, bombing it to near oblivion. Somewhere near the Kurfürstendamm a piece of shrapnel pierced Albert's heart and my grandmother had to retrieve his corpse from the rubble and transport it back to her wrecked flat in Fabricius Strasse on a wooden cart.

On the same date that Albert exited the world, 27 April, but almost 50 years later, South Africa would experience its first democratic elections when Nelson Mandela was voted President by an overwhelming majority.

Georg would never return to Germany. After he was released and the war ended, he chose instead to make England his home. He left the rebuilding of his shattered *Heimat* to his sister, Gertrud, or Tante Tuta as she was affectionately known, and his mother who, along with thousands of other German women who had survived, became *Trümmelfrauen* (rubble women) sifting through the debris and ruins of their city, painstakingly rebuilding it.

Georg proposed to Barbara using a Portuguese–German dictionary. They were both in their 30s, and like many who had survived that terrible war, were keen to start a family and attempt to live what they believed was a normal life in spite of the collateral damage. They both spoke with thick accents. One could not call it communicating. Georg found he had a great affinity for English life and character. He loved The Goon Show and the apparent British reserve. That this might have been because he was German never crossed his mind.

Georg and Barbara married in 1958 and soon found a home in the tranquil-sounding 8 Fairacre, Bath Road in Maidenhead. Georg worked for several engineering companies as a toolmaker – a rather generic-sounding occupation that I never quite understood until much later.

It essentially means he was a skilled artisan but the job does require, according to one description, a scientific, mathematical and artistic aptitude. To earn extra money he mowed lawns and fixed faulty radios.

Testimonials written by those who knew Georg in England shed some light on how he was viewed.

"I first made the acquaintance of Georg Thamm thirteen years ago. I have always found him to be honest and trustworthy. He is intelligent and has a pleasing personality. It is due to his personality and character that we have become intimate friends. He has sober habits and is a devoted father. I have no hesitation in recommending him for a position where these characteristics are required." KC Kirkup – Profession: Civil Servant, Air Ministry.

Another from the Mayor of Maidenhead and dated 11 October 1960 reads: "I should like to thank you for kindly acting as an interpreter when the delegation from Bad Godesberg visited Maidenhead last week. The members of the Council are indeed most grateful to you and the other interpreters for the part played in helping to make the Twinning programme such a success."

I have never understood the practical ramifications of the post-war idea of "twinning" cities. My home town of Cape Town has been rather polygamous in this regard, having twinned, it appears, with a number of cities, including Aachen, Funchal, Haifa, Hangzhou, Miami-Dade County, Nice, and St Petersburg. As a rate-paying citizen, I have yet to experience these cities with benefits, but there we have it.

Barbara became a housewife and a mother, a state of being she relished and enjoyed. She lavished her love and attention on Albert and me, her two beloved, special children, and busied herself looking after us, cleaning our home and making culturally inappropriate meals for my father. Even when we had relocated to South Africa, where domestic labour for white families was cheap and ubiquitous, Barbara cleaned, washed, scrubbed and polished by herself.

She would often clean the house to the soundtrack of Fado music and would play the only vinyl record she owned by Portugal's Queen of Fado, Amália Rodrigues. Mid-clean, Barbara would switch off the wheezing vacuum cleaner and dramatically sit down on the couch or whichever chair was handy, to sing along soulfully (and sometimes cry) to *Barco Negro, Uma Casa Portuguesa* or *Nem às Paredes Confesso.* This was how I came to learn about *saudade*, a particularly Latin feeling of melancholy, nostalgia or longing that one can't quite place or shake.

When it came to Albert and me, Barbara would find unique cures for the bumps and scrapes of childhood. Knock your head and she would scratch a large, cold coin from her purse, place it on the swelling and wrap a bandage around it to keep it in place. This way a minor injury would look like a disastrous accident. Emotionally it worked like a charm.

The story goes that it was Georg's asthma and a recommendation by his doctor that he relocate to a warmer climate that led to his considering a move to South Africa.

Later Georg was to claim that his bad chest had only manifested "after I married your muzzer", but he was in a vindictive, nasty mood that particular day.

Of all the places to choose in 1963 that were "hot", weather-wise that is, he could have opted for elsewhere. Australia, for example. Or New Zealand. South Africa in 1963 was all over the headlines, one would have thought. Georg insisted that the shootings at Sharpeville in 1960, when police killed 69 unarmed protesters, hardly featured in the newspapers he was reading.

And so it was that we eventually found ourselves marooned in Pretoria, a place so ghastly it was only bearable with the help of pharmaceutical assistance both natural and chemical. The country was led, at the time, by an authoritarian, white, separatist Nationalist regime, and its prime minister, Dr Hendrik Verwoerd, was one of the architects of apartheid – right up my father's ideological dead end, in other words.

You would think, considering Adolf Hitler's humiliation of the German people and the near annihilation of the country he once knew, Georg would have been a little more reticent about racist regimes led by militaristic ideological zealots. But a bad chest, it appeared, overrode any deep reflection or contemplation of the world he was about to call home.

I was two years old when we stepped off the BOAC flight in hot, sunny South Africa on 17 October 1963. The family, and all our suitcases, were delivered to the Hellenic Hotel in the heart of Pretoria. We were to be put up there temporarily by my father's new employer, the Department of Defence. The rest of my parents' belongings, which included the contents of their house, would slowly make their way to South Africa by ship and then by road to Pretoria.

From the Hellenic Hotel the family moved to various sparsely furnished flats in Pretoria until we finally settled, on 12 January 1965, in a small, boxy house situated at 875 Burlington Street, Parktown, Pretoria, bought directly from the owner, a Mr Washkansky, for R4 000. Those were the days before banks and building societies understood there was big money to be made as intermediaries between buyers and sellers.

The three-bedroomed house with its scrappy garden of fruit trees was just this side of the Magaliesberg mountain range, which loomed in the distance over my childhood. It was a neighbourhood filled with new immigrants, mostly European, artisans like my father who had been lured to South Africa by the Nationalist government because they were white and had skills the country needed.

We were surrounded by a hostile laager of working and newly middle-class Afrikaner families who viewed us mostly with suspicion, hostility and contempt. Many a weekend was marred by the smell of flesh charring on braais while the sound of a fevered rugby commentator drifted over the shoulder-high Vibracrete walls that separated us.

These new immigrants were not in for a free ride in their new homeland. One of the conditions was that we agreed to be "Afrikanerised". In 1969 the Broederbond, a clandestine organisation which was instrumental in establishing the Nationalist ideology and hierarchy in the country, encouraged members to "incorporate" families like ours into Afrikaner cultural life.

The explosive book *The Super-Afrikaners: Inside the Afrikaner Broederbond* by journalists Ivor Wilkins and Hans Strydom, originally published to great sensation in 1978, sets out how this was to be accomplished.

"Members of women's organisations are invited to visit immigrant wives, arrange church services in the immigrants' languages, organise youth evenings and ask immigrant families into their homes," Wilkins and Strydom wrote of the Broederbond plan.

The Broederbond had accepted that while it was "not prepared to sacrifice our traditional way of life, language and culture", it was "obliged today to accept large-scale immigration as one of the most important aids in our struggle".[1]

The Broederbond was also determined to keep out Catholic immigrants, preferring their Protestant kin, and the government specifically limited immigration from Portugal, Greece, Italy and "the Mediterranean area as a whole". Barbara had slipped in on the back of her German husband.

"An assurance can therefore be given in all honesty. (1) The religious ratio between Protestants and Catholics will not be disturbed by immigration. (2) 'Unassimilable elements' will be kept out of South Africa, and everything will be done to remove those who enter illegally. (3) Care will be taken to ensure that immigration does not become a threat to the Afrikaner's future. (4) Immigrants will not deprive our people of jobs."[2]

Severed from their families and homelands, the British, Dutch and German families who lived in our neighbourhood formed close bonds, visiting each other for coffee and cheesecake and cream at the weekends, murmuring quietly in the lounge. Some weekends our house would be filled with the zesty rhythm of brassy German marches as Georg pottered about.

My mother, however, never felt quite at home. The Portuguese and Greek immigrants around us – who mostly ran small shops or corner cafés – hung out together, enjoying a shared solidarity. Our house erupted in laughter, loud arguing and the smell of fish when they visited. My father would either retreat then to his "study", which was the converted servants' quarters, or went out for a drive or walk.

Georg made a few attempts at culturally acclimatising his strange

---

1 I. Wilkins and H. Strydom, *The Super-Afrikaners: Inside the Afrikaner Broederbond*. Jonathan Ball Publishers, 1978, p 153.
2 Ibid, p 155.

little family. He took us on a visit to the hallowed granite Voortrekker Monument that perches like a giant fascist wedding cake on a hill just south of Pretoria.

We must have been an odd apparition. My mother with her jet black hair and lurid crimson dress would have been completely out of place among those who were clothed more discreetly (and possibly respectfully) to visit this austere monument to Afrikanerdom. My father posed us in front of a huge bronze statue of a heroic Afrikaner mother protecting her children and took a photograph. We did not look like we were going to integrate successfully.

One of the features of the monument is the benben stone, an encrypted cenotaph with the words "Ons vir jou Suid-Afrika". At noon the sunlight illuminates the stone, an apparent sign that something supernatural had occurred at the Battle of Blood River, which the monument also commemorates. To view the phenomenon one has to climb, as I recall, a winding staircase that leads to the pinnacle of the monument. My brother, on reaching the top, looked down, shrieked and sprinted away. Later I found the architecture – when stripped of its political and cultural significance – disturbingly pleasing to the eye, with its clean lines and slabs of granite. All that was missing was gigantic banners or flags and people in jackboots goose-stepping along the perimeter.

My father also joined the German Club in Pretoria, which was situated in a gloomy building in Church Street. Its interior was heavy and lifeless and I often suspected that some of the German men dining alone at the linen-shod tables were Nazi war criminals. After having watched the television series *The World at War*, I would excuse myself and go to the loo to get a better view of the man who, from a certain angle, I was convinced was the real Rudolf Hess.

The Broederbond respected and liked Germans, particularly those who had escaped post-war denazification, and some prominent members, including General Hendrik van den Bergh (known as Lang Hendrik), who founded the murderous Bureau of State Security (BOSS), were often invited to attend functions. Among my father's papers after he died, I found a menu that had been signed by Lang Hendrik with what seemed to me a confident flourish.

I later learned that my father had come to South Africa after having been recruited by the Department of Defence in Pretoria to work on a "classified" project, adding to the already crap karma this strand of my family has bequeathed me.

Even later, a few years before he died, Georg and I were having one of our usual political discussions/debates/arguments in his sunlit lounge in Somerset West.

"Why did you come here?" I asked him.

That was when I learned that the South African government had obtained the plans or the blueprint for the manufacture of the Belgian FN rifle. Local artisans were unable to assemble it at the department's engineering works in Lyttleton, so the likes of my father were sought to help out.

"I calibrated ze machine zat made ze trigger for ze first R1 rifle zat vas ever made in South Africa," he told me casually.

There could be no atoning, I thought to myself. The karmic trapdoor snapped open and I slipped through, doomed for all eternity.

Recovering from the shock, I yelled, "You survive a war in Europe in which 55 million people die and you come to a country with political shit and make a trigger for a gun and you do not think about the human beings who might find themselves at the other end of the barrel!?"

"No, vhy would I do zat?"

I have never understood how men can speak about war in such abstract terms. Especially men who have seen it close up. Discussions between my brother and father were always about how many troops surrounded whom where and what kind of weapons and tactics had been used or deployed. From Napoleon to Montgomery to the fucking Romans. It is a testament to our stupidity that we learn nothing from history. Like a damaged CD, we repeat humanity's greatest tragic hits.

The human cost, the millions killed, murdered and exterminated, the women raped, the children orphaned, the disappeared, buried by strategy and numbers. We may try to keep the dead alive in our hearts and minds, with our monuments, commemorations, our poems, our songs, our books, but the witnesses and the appetite for it all diminish over time.

"Oh and ja. I personally handed over ze first R1 to Verwoerd on ze factory floor," Georg added for good measure.

Not only six degrees of separation between me and Adolf Hitler. Now Hendrik Verwoerd had entered the orbit. I was in a karmic free fall, no zip-line, no parachute.

Years later my aunt, Tante Tuta, in Berlin dispatched the newly published memoir of Käthe Hübner, *Die Kinder des Reichsministers*, to her brother Georg. Hubner, whom Tante Tuta had known as Hübi during their childhood, had been the governess for the last two years of WWII for the charming Goebbels family. The six Goebbels children had lived with Hübi in the family's rural residence in Waldhof am Bogensee while their unravelling mother spent time in a sanatorium in Dresden recovering from a "nervous condition" otherwise known as WWII.

Days before the collapse of Berlin, the Goebbels parents whisked their children away to Hitler's bunker where they determined to await death along with the Führer rather than face liberation or democracy. There Magda injected all her children with morphine before forcing crushed cyanide tablets between their teeth. When liberating Russian forces later discovered the dead children in the bunker, only the twelve-year-old Magda's corpse displayed signs of resistance. Her face was bruised.

The memoir contained several personal photographs Hübi had taken of the children. Pasted onto the back inside cover, Tante Tuta had included one of herself standing next to Hübi in the sunshine outside a Berlin apartment block.

"YOUR MOTHER is a sea kaffir!" the boy with the close-cropped hair and bare feet yelled in his thick Afrikaans accent as I glided past on my brother's Chopper bicycle.

I had grown accustomed to the insults. Dutch immigrants were *kaaskoppe* (cheese heads), British were *soutpiele* (literally "salt dicks", suggesting they had one foot in England and the other in South Africa, their dongs dangling into the ocean between). We in turn called the Afrikaans kids "rockspiders".

But the special epithet of "kaffir", a vicious South African racial slur routinely and casually used to refer to black South Africans, was meant to cut deep.

Portuguese immigrants were viewed with a special scorn. It was part of the political atmosphere these kids breathed, which in retrospect, considering the Broederbond's attitude towards "Latin" immigrants, was not surprising. Not only because most of these immigrants were working class, but also because many in the Portuguese colonies that surrounded South Africa, Mozambique and Angola, had chosen to "integrate" with regional populations, and their men married local women (I had not heard of a Portuguese woman marrying a black Mozambican, however). When it came to the obsessive notion of racial purity and white supremacy in South Africa, this was a cardinal sin and unforgivable.

Most of the time "greasy Porra" was the best diss South African-born English-speaking kids in our neighbourhood could come up with.

They were just ignorant, I thought, concerned more with the fact that I had stolen my brother's awesome bicycle and was now showing it off. The Raleigh Chopper was the must-have cool accessory in the 1970s. Modelled on dragsters, it had a small front wheel and a larger one at the back, with tyres thicker than those of average bikes.

It was Easy Rider for beginners.

The Chopper had raised Y-shaped handlebars, three gears you could shift with a small T-lever and an elongated, L-shaped, padded saddle that could seat two. While it may have looked cool, I have to say it was shit to ride. It was unstable and difficult to steer, which is how, on one such illicit twilight jaunt, I chipped two front teeth when I swerved to avoid a car reversing out of a driveway.

Arriving home with a thick lip, the taste of blood in my mouth, and running my tongue across the unfamiliar rough edges of my jagged teeth, my mother greeted me at the gate and immediately burst into tears.

"What appened? Your smile . . . what appened to your smile?" she wailed.

Barbara liked to wail. A lot. Well, she probably had good reason. Her perfect little girl was a tomboy, often passing for her brother, and routinely disappearing with a local gang of immigrant kids for hours at a stretch. One of our pastimes was to sit under a low, bushy tree on the corner of our street smoking my mother's cigarette ends I had collected earlier from the dustbin. The butts often reeked of old potato skins, the paper tinted brown by old tea bags, but they had to do. We didn't have money to buy our own. Occasionally we clubbed together and bought a packet of ten Gold Dollar or Lexington (generally believed to be suitable only for black people). I must have been about ten or eleven at the time. It was a rare treat to smoke a fresh cigarette right down to the filter.

Sometimes someone would steal a non-filtered, toasted Lucky Strike or Gunston Plain from a parent, and these we sucked at eagerly like little vacuum cleaners, spitting out specks of the strong tobacco.

Back then, everyone seemed to smoke and every single magazine featured colourful ads for cigarettes. Just a few years earlier an ad for Camel cigarettes in the US had featured the tagline "More Doctors

Smoke Camel Than Any Other Cigarette". "After Action Satisfaction" went the tagline for Lexington. The radio jingle for the particularly cynically named Life cigarettes jauntily offered: "Life . . . is what it's all about. Light up a Life today and say 'Oh, man, Life is great'." Then there were the strapping tanned (white) people in the Peter Stuyvesant ads, romping on beaches or waterskiing in distant playgrounds like Monaco or Bermuda; and the sophisticated, groomed Dunhill smokers seen shopping for elegant lighters and jewellery in London. Some brands were particularly targeted at women and made to sound more "feminine". Cameo was one of these.

That was the dumb-fuck twentieth century. It was a time when parents would smoke in cars with the windows rolled up, their kids playing freely on back seat. Seatbelts? Say what?

Food was laced with carcinogenic colourants and additives. "Mom, my chest is closing," I would announce after drinking tartrazine-laced Oros cordial.

"Oh, you musta hava cold."

White people slathered on suntan oil – *oil* – rather than sunblock, with no SPF factor whatsoever. (Cancer? Never heard of it.)

Barbara embraced the technological advances of the twentieth century. Canned food, particularly, was a heaven-sent blessing, one of the charms of European life. My brother and I had no palate for either Portuguese or German food, so she turned in desperation to Koo, Fray Bentos, and whatever else edible could withstand being marinated in syrup or tomato sauce and shoved into a can, including anaemic fruit salad.

And we smoked, yes, just like everyone around us.

Sometimes, when we didn't have enough money for a packet of tens, we would buy BB tobacco, which came in an orange plastic pouch. We'd roll our own cigarettes, ripping pages out of the thick telephone books that hung from heavy chains inside tubular concrete public call boxes.

I learned to use brown paper to roll my BB from Sophia Molea, a young domestic worker for the Greek Papadopoulos family who lived around the corner from us. I would spend many hours with her in her "quarters" at the back of the house, mesmerised by her neat bed with its bedspread lovingly embroidered with Sotho sayings and perched high on bricks and empty paint tins.

"It's for the tokoloshe," she explained, telling me about the mischievous mythical water sprite many believed wandered around at night causing all sorts of harm.

Sophia decorated the walls of her small room with pictures of soccer teams torn from magazines. She prettified her bare shelves with recycled phone books, their pages painstakingly carved at the edges with intricate patterns and then fanned out like paper lanterns. On weekends, before her handsome boyfriend Given came to visit, Sophia would bathe outside in the sunshine in a large cast-iron tub. I loved visiting her. It was a relationship my mother, when she came to learn of it, discouraged.

"You canta let the people see you sitting with the servants," she would warn me, adding, "Why you keepa doing it?"

My mother suspected I stole her cigarette butts and would do her best to ambush me. She would wait at the front gate of our home until she could spot the glowing coals under the tree. Then she would emerge suddenly and begin to move down the street like a raging bull, swishing a leather dog leash that doubled as a whip and that she constantly threatened to use but never did.

"Marianna!" she would shout. "I see you there. Are you smoking! Come here now."

My friends and I would scurry out and scatter in all directions. Barbara would inevitably find me and, to my great embarrassment, lead me back home by the ear, shouting all the way.

My transition to becoming a tomboy began in Standard Three when a new girl arrived at Capital Park Primary School. The government school was for whites only and I had been enrolled there from Grade One, while my brother initially had been sent off to the more expensive, private Iona Convent a few blocks away. Capital Park was a catchment for white kids from middle-class, working-class and poor families in the area – which was about as diverse as it got back then. One family of "poor whites", the Aspelings, had a child in every grade. Peter Aspeling was in my class. He usually arrived at school hungry and dirty, and his skin was stained with grime and hardened with warts. He wore the same clothes every day. No one befriended him or wanted to sit next to or near him in class. One Monday morning our teacher, Mrs Zietsman, clearly troubled by Peter's dishevelled appearance and the smell that trailed him, whisked him off to be scrubbed clean, have his hair cut and be provided with a clean school uniform.

Peter was returned to class, his hair still damp and smelling of soap, in a clean second-hand uniform of shorts and a khaki shirt. But after first break he was nowhere to be found. Clearly humiliated by the shaming experience at Mrs Zietsman's hands, he had left, for all of us, a defiant little gift on the chair at his desk – a fresh turd, expertly pressed onto the seat. He returned to school about a week later, his usual self, lean, dirty and angry.

The new girl, who would alter my view of the world in Standard Three, was Debbie de Jongh. On her first day she asked whether I preferred dolls or cars – duh. Cars of course – and we soon became fast friends. And I did have an impressive collection of die-cast Lesney Matchbox cars that I would push around the cement edges of the slasto paving my father had laid in our driveway. I was always more fond of my miniature blue Ford Cortina (Matchbox Series no. 25) and my gold BMC 1800 Pininfarina (Matchbox no. 56) than the flashier range of vehicles in the collection.

Matchbox cars were a boy magnet, I soon learned, and me and my homies often gathered at different venues and played for hours, creating imaginary suburbs, roads (with staged accidents and pile-ups) and garages in the sand made from scraps we found here and there.

Debbie was the first girl I met who suggested we could pass as boys and so we changed our names to Peter and Dennis. For two years they were who we purported to be. We had learned somewhere that we could arrest the development of breasts by brushing a grass broom across our torsos. I recall the astonished look on Debbie's mom's face when she came across the two of us furiously and painfully brushing our chests when I was over at Debbie's house in Pretoria North one day. We were standing on a hill behind the house, which was gorgeous, airy and modern and had a swimming pool in the huge wild garden and a foefie slide. They even had a room dedicated entirely to the mounted heads of fish Debbie's father, a keen fisherman, had snagged over the years – a marlin with a huge spike and glassy, indifferent eyes bearing out of the wall alongside a hammerhead shark and various other pelagic trophies.

Whenever we went for a swim at the local public baths, Debbie and I would use the boys' changing rooms and emerge bare-chested in our trunks. Once we were confronted by the father of a boy we knew, who asked, "Aren't you Debbie and Marianne?", to which we emphatically replied, "No."

It dawned on me quite early that boys somehow moved through the world differently. Their qualities were grossly overestimated in my view, but they appeared to have more freedom and opportunity than girls. And while I regarded my princeling older brother Albert as a chess-playing tosser, it was clear that on many levels the world out there was for his taking. I had to work for my pocket money, he didn't. My father would take him for chess lessons, a game I was never taught to play. Albert would be taken for a flip in an airplane while I was told that flying "is not for girls".

While my mother had never expected me (or my brother) to do any household chores (I never made a bed nor was expected to learn to cook), I understood that the world wanted something different from me as a girl. Ours was a support act to the main event.

How else to engage with this situation but to become a boy, or at least pass for one and enjoy these benefits by default. Besides, the girls in our neighbourhood, apart from one or two of them, were an unadventurous lot, choosing mostly to hang around their homes playing with "girl" toys, studying the instruction manual that arrived with their packaging from the factory.

This is a doll. Dress it. One day you will have a baby of your own to play with. This is shocking red lipstick. It mimics the effect of the hindquarters of a female baboon in oestrous and is certain to serve as a powerful attraction to men. These are high heels which, while they will inhibit your movement and cripple your feet, will most certainly assist with your fulfilling your destiny.

For my mother, watching her darling blue-eyed daughter discard the pretty dresses she either bought at the Indian general dealer around the corner or had specially sewn by an old Greek lady, Mrs Armadas, up the street, was confusing. She would attempt to bribe me to wear a dress by promising to buy me an ice-cream from the man who would occasionally navigate his three-wheeled bicycle around our neighbourhood, with its bulky freezer-box packed with cheap lollies attached to the handlebars. The bribe was seductive. Like a prisoner plotting a jail break, I would toss a pair of shorts and a T-shirt out of my bedroom window and sit uncomfortably inside wearing a dress, waiting for the tinkling of the familiar bell. As soon as we heard it, my mother would urge me to come outside and choose an ice-cream, but I refused to be seen out in public in a dress. It would feel like one of those dreams where you find yourself naked on a bus.

Barbara would return with an ice-cream and retire to the kitchen. I would immediately dash outside, change into my shorts and pass by the window triumphantly, ice-cream in hand, my mother's voice yelling "Marianna, Marianna, I donta believe it" trailing after me.

Once, she returned home from the corner café to find me admiring myself in the hall mirror wearing my brother's three-piece olive green suit and a pair of his brown platform shoes that were fashionable at the time. I was a dead ringer for the bisexual 1970s singer David Cassidy. Men's clothes were so much more practical and interesting than women's. I loved the various pockets, buttons and clips.

When Barbara opened the door she let out a predictable shriek. "Marianna, whata you doing? Are you mad? You going to maka your mother mad. What iss wrong with you?"

As predictably, I took off, while she chased me around the house, the words eventually tapering off.

Twice I was mistaken for a boy. Once while swinging in a nearby park I was approached by two older girls who giggled and said they would like to give me ten cents so that I could phone them when I was older.

"Do you have a brother?" they enquired.

"No," I lied, feeling hugely uncomfortable, not about the lie but being mistaken for a boy.

46

The second time it happened was at the Ster Ice Skating Rink after they had dimmed the lights and started rotating the disco ball. This was the signal for the short "partner session", which was when boys and girls were encouraged to get more intimate.

I was and still am a terrible skater – my skills as a tomboy were extremely limited (I learned to hide the fact that not only could I not skate, but I was also terrified of climbing trees). A young girl glided up to the barrier, leaned over and asked if I would skate with her.

"I . . . I can't," I stammered.

She turned away, disappointed, and I just sat there wishing I was invisible.

OUR NEIGHBOURHOOD was a seething cauldron of cultural rivalry that occasionally turned violent. There were two groupings of delinquents – ourselves, the English-speaking kids, and a pack of rough Afrikaners.

There appeared to be absolutely no adult supervision outside of our homes. We were almost feral, our lives spooling like film in a twentieth-century camera, frame by frame. Except no one was holding the camera; no one was looking at us through the viewfinder of life. It was peculiarly liberating in a country where the atmosphere was without joy and lifeless with ignorance.

My own parents had handed both my brother and me to "the system", whatever they thought it might have been. The establishment would take care of us, they no doubt believed, as it had taken care of them. No one supervised my homework and neither of my parents ever attended school plays or sports events.

Georg would leave home early for work and return at 6pm as the domestic demands of life were ebbing towards bedtime. While he dropped my brother and me off at school in the mornings, we were expected to make our own way home on public transport. Parktown 24, a whites-only bus, stopped a block away from our house. My mother suffered from mild agoraphobia, and in retrospect who could blame her? She never learned to drive and so was confined to the domestic sphere and surrounds unless she was in the car as a passenger, Georg assertively in the driver's seat.

Later, Barbara took a full-time job as a nursing assistant at the Eugène Marais Hospital and would work 7pm to 7am shifts, often returning just in time to cook us breakfast.

When it rained I knew I would always find her standing at the bus stop waiting with an umbrella. No matter that she needed to sleep to prepare for her night shift. And there would always be lunch, a pot of soup, or toast and apricot jam, waiting for me and Albert at home.

Home from school I would quickly finish homework and then grab my bike and hit the streets, looking for trouble.

Me and my friends spent most of the time congregated somewhere along the apparently bilharzia-ridden Apies River, which snaked around the edges of the neighbourhood. The risk of bilharzia was a particularly European fear, one of the curses of moving to the "third world" our parents had probably read about in pamphlets or brochures on their new homeland. We can deal with segregation and racism but not, in heaven's name, bilharzia.

The river, however, was a perfect playground, its banks camouflaged with thick forest and reeds. Huge rocks jutted out at various bends. We often fished there for crabs. One section, near a bridge, had been concreted in and we used the thick algae that thrived on the bottom as a sort of water slide.

My mother would consistently warn us not to play at the river, partly because she was afraid we would return home with our bellies extended and riddled with parasites, but also because of the urban legend that it was here that white children would be stalked and their warm little hearts cut out by crazed witch doctors. She would sniff my clothes for the tell-tale sweet smell of the Apies.

One of our most prized possessions was a severed car roof obtained from a nearby scrapyard that we would use as a raft, floating down the river using thick reeds as oars. The rival Afrikaans gang had their own roof raft. As the sun set, part of the fun was to seek it out and damage it in some way so as to render it unusable. It was imperative that we conceal our own roof so well that it could never be found and sabotaged. Another pastime was to spy on the Afrikaans kids swimming in the river and to steal their discarded clothes and hide them, requiring them to emerge later, naked, in full view of everyone.

I mastered Afrikaans as a language not only because I was taught it at school but because I found I had an aptitude for languages. Besides, my dirty secret was that I actually quite liked it as a language. At that point I just didn't like the people who claimed it as uniquely their own.

There was a fair amount of sexual exploration, if one could even call it that. It was more like fumbling, really. One afternoon while we sat fishing with a bent pin attached to fish gut tied to a stick, my friend Eugene Grey popped out his little penis and, stroking it furiously, remarked casually, "Look here. If I do this long enough then white stuff comes out." I watched as he ejaculated. I was mildly impressed (I think I said "Wow") but soon turned back to my fishing. I had no such tricks to offer in turn. There was nothing threatening or uncomfortable about the moment. It felt like we were bros, just hanging out.

A girl in the neighbourhood, who shall have to remain nameless, appeared to be more obliging when it came to participating in this adolescent exploration. One evening my next-door neighbour, the son of British immigrants, pitched a tent in his backyard. Hearing muffled guffaws and seeing shards of flashlight piercing our hedge, I peered through to witness a row of boys queuing outside the tent's opening. Curious, I clambered over the fence and joined them. When I reached the entrance I spotted the girl inside, on her back, her legs wide open, showing off her vagina. The last guy out passed me the torch and I entered but she recognised me and angrily shooed me out.

When we weren't floating our roofs, or bicycling around the park or neighbourhood, we played hours of pinball at the Greek café. I was good, very good, a Pinball Wizard in fact, and often spent hours playing with only one coin, enjoying the satisfying clack the machine made with each new free game I was able to rack up.

The most scandalous thing to hit the neighbourhood was when the daughter of the local Italian cobbler, Mr Raffanti, who rented the shop next to the dairy, was arrested for having plotted, along with her lover, Frans Vontsteen, to murder her husband, Cois Swanepoel, a policeman and a Springbok athlete. Sonjia Raffanti and Vontsteen had conspired to slay Cois, concocting an elaborate alibi and blaming "a Bantu man" for the killing.

The trial at the Pretoria Supreme Court in 1972 dominated head-lines for weeks. This was one of the ways the white population could have their attention diverted from the real horror of the world around them, by allowing them to focus on some tawdry "sensational" white murder. Sonjia was sentenced to fifteen years in jail while Vontsteen was hanged for the crime. Afterwards Mr Raffanti wore the air of a defeated man. He seldom smiled and the interior of his shop was dark and grim and reeked of leather and glue.

At that point my only encounter with Afrikaans children or families had been hostile. A particularly nasty man, a violent alcoholic who worked at the local abattoir, lived with his wife and extremely large family in a crumbling council house behind ours. The children had names like Stompie, Anna, Anton, Kleintjie and Francois, and they often lobbed missiles over the concrete wall hoping to disrupt our play and spark a physical fight.

We would climb the huge mulberry tree in our back garden and peer into their dusty domain. The family was dirt poor and almost every night we could hear the wife pleading and screaming or the children wailing as their father beat them mercilessly. They had a dog that was permanently tethered to a long chain in the yard. Its kennel was located next to a corrugated-iron structure in which the family's long-suffering domestic worker lived. They were poor but they were white and could not be expected to clean their own mess.

One Christmas Day we heard the father roaring off in his Zodiac – a car that particularly appealed to those who were regarded as "zef" (or white working class) – after beating his wife badly. She poked her bruised and bleeding face over the wall and told my father that her husband had left them without food.

"Ve can't eat a Christmas lunch ven ve know zey don't have any thing," Georg said, heading off for the corner café which, inevitably, was open.

Later, when the father returned he tossed all the food back over the wall in a rage and threatened to beat up my father.

"Fok julle, fok julle!" he shouted as he flung a packet of mielie meal, raw pieces of chicken, and tins of food and vegetables into our yard.

My induction into the intimate life of an Afrikaans family came via

Riaan van der Westhuizen, who lived a block from our home and whose house I passed on my daily round to pick up the newspaper and bread from the shops. I would occasionally spot Riaan in his front yard, smartly dressed, his hair slicked back with Vitalis hair oil, mumbling to himself. He was a stocky child, not part of the scruffy neighbourhood gang of rockspiders. On one trip I stopped and struck up a conversation. He appeared to be quite lonely and we soon developed a gentle friendship. I was intrigued by this strange boy. Riaan's father, Uncle Danie, who worked at Iscor, a parastatal steel company, was a forbidding and brutal man who smoked Lucky Strike plain and clearly disapproved of his son. Their dog Soekie, a fawn Labrador cross, was always shackled to a tree with a chain and Uncle Danie was not averse to beating it with a metal pipe when he believed the dog was making a *geraas*.

Everyone in the household was clearly terrified of Uncle Danie and the gentle atmosphere in the home changed immediately he walked through the door at the end of the day. The threat was palpable.

Riaan's mother, the mild-mannered Auntie Rienie, lavished affection on her only son. At the time their ancient grandmother, who had actually survived the Boer War, also lived with them in their double-storey house, one of only two on the block. Ouma would usually be found seated at the formica kitchen table murmuring over a large Dutch Bible.

Riaan was different. He played the piano, loved to cook and could make the best coffee and Horlicks garnished with marshmallows. The interior of the Van der Westhuizen home was pristine. It reeked of furniture and floor polish. Heavy ball-and-claw couches and chairs, favoured by Afrikaans families at the time, crouched in the lounge. A light-wood piano dominated their small, cool dining room and it was here that I spent many a scorching summer's day perched on a chair, sipping coffee, listening to Riaan play *Rustle of Spring*, a cheerful piece of music by the Norwegian composer Christian Sinding. I would marvel as Riaan's chubby fingers darted across the keys.

While Riaan's family were quintessential Afrikaners, they were not like the other families that lived around us. The family were members of the local Dutch Reformed Church, which was a few blocks away, and Riaan, and later his sister Anri, regularly attended folk-dancing sessions, called *volkspele*. Generally, though, they seemed to exist outside of these narrow definitions of who they should be. Auntie Rienie was delighted that her son had made a friend in the neighbourhood – a girl at that – and welcomed me always as a child of her own.

Riaan was not immune to the propaganda that surrounded him at school and in the church and he and I would have discussions about our differences. Once he pulled out a world map, smoothed it out on the dining-room table and pointed at England up north.

"Look, see. That is England. And this here," he said jabbing at South Africa at the end of the African continent, "is where we live. Look how small England is. You immigrants must go back there."

"But I'm not from there," I would protest.

My route home from high school would entail catching a bus that would begin its journey at Church Square and make its way north along Paul Kruger Street. The back of the bus was routinely annexed by the English-speaking kids and part of the daily jostle was to see who could secure the rear seat, reserved usually for the most disruptive among us. There we could smoke in secret, start fights or use foul language, much to the audible disapproval of the Afrikaner aunties on their way home from their half-day jobs at Munitoria, a huge building that housed the local municipality.

The bus would make its way up a hill towards the Pretoria Zoo where, shortly afterwards, it would stop and pick up the Afrikaans kids who attended Langenhoven Hoërskool, named after a revered Afrikaans poet and composer of the country's national anthem, *Die Stem*.

This was a moment we eagerly anticipated each day and it would provide further opportunity to argue and fight. Often, as the bus neared the stop, I would watch as a group of burly boys in their navy blue blazers would kick Riaan's school satchel around the dust. Accustomed to the ritual humiliation, he would stand helplessly on the sidelines surveying it all. When we stopped he would hurriedly try to retrieve the bag and sprint towards the bus. I would watch him find a seat near the front. At these times our eyes would meet but we never spoke.

Over the hill the bus approached a stop outside the OK Bazaars where my mother would shop, once a month, for groceries. I dreaded seeing her standing there with her portable canvas bag perched on a frame on two small wheels. Barbara's routine was to walk the six or so blocks to the supermarket, do her shopping and then catch the bus home.

I would duck down behind the back seat when she boarded. She would always opt to sit on the front seat that was secured vertically facing sideways. This provided more space at the entrance for passengers to pass through as well as a sweeping view of the interior. I could hear the air hiss out of the padded cushion as Barbara flopped into her seat.

And then it would begin . . . the humiliating monologue that everyone in the bus could hear.

"Marianna . . . I see you sitting there. Whatsamatter? You ashamed of your mother? You willa see one day iss only your mother love you. Your friends is just nonsense . . .Whatsamatter ha? Why you no come sit with me?"

The kids would all burst out laughing. I would ignore my mother completely. Until we alighted at our bus stop, when she would walk on ahead of me, smarting from my public rejection.

"I'm sorry, Mom . . . but you mustn't do that. It embarrasses me."

Barbara always forgave me. As I knew she would.

WHILE GEORG had grown up in Nazi Germany with the visible signs of fascism all around, the nature of South Africa's fascism in the 1970s was not quite as evident from the vantage point of a white suburb or the city centre. Ours was like so many suburbs and cities across the country – claustrophobic and hermetic, cut off intentionally from the rest of the world.

What we read, the music we listened to, what we knew about global events or our own country, for that matter, was either heavily regulated or censored. This profoundly affected how we viewed ourselves and our place in the world.

Senator Robert Kennedy's visit to South Africa in 1966 was completely ignored by the media. If you didn't listen to the BBC, you wouldn't have known it had occurred.

In 1969, when the first human landed on the moon, all we could do in South Africa was listen to the historic event on the radio. South Africa had no television until 1976, way behind the rest of the world. I stood outside with my binoculars that night, hoping to see the first human on the moon spearing the American flag into its dusty surface.

In communist Yugoslavia kids my age were watching it all on TV. They were aware of the 1968 Paris uprisings. They were living in the real fucking world.

Radio stations in South Africa were all racially segregated and, because of the cultural boycott that was in place when it came to apartheid South Africa, our choice locally was limited. The Nationalists did not like rock and roll, perceiving it as the devil's music, dangerous and "liberal", but allowed it on the local airwaves nonetheless, albeit with stark warnings to Afrikaans children about its potentially degenerative effect on their minds.

Hoping to convince the white minority that it was part of the "civilised Western world", the government allowed the illegal recording of cover versions of all the hits of the time, in so doing defying the boycott that international artists supported by not permitting their music to be played here. These were packaged in a series of LP records called *Springbok Hits* and were available cheaply at a local supermarket chain. Cover versions of songs were performed by local musicians who were instructed to make them sound as close to the original as possible. I had one friend who, when she heard the real Bee Gees for the first time, was certain they were fake. For all we knew back then, Janis Joplin and Jimi Hendrix were still alive.

Springbok Radio, a bilingual commercial station aimed at both white Afrikaans- and English-speaking audiences, had a Top 20 programme, however, where we could listen to the music being made in the US or UK.

The best bet for listening to what was happening musically in the rest of the world was to try to tune in to the independent LM Radio station. This was located in Mozambique and could only be heard on a shortwave frequency, full of static crackling and often difficult to pick up. Nevertheless we spent many Saturdays pointing the radio's steel aerial in different directions and trying to pick up the signal, with varying degrees of success. In 1975, when Mozambique gained independence, the station was bought by the SABC and turned into the tepid Radio 5, under South Africa's control.

But no matter how much the media or the government tried to reassure the white population that all was as it should be in the world, there was a constant feeling of foreboding, that something was dreadfully amiss, that something cataclysmic might happen at any moment.

Advertisements for a 1970s vitamin supplement called Salusa 45, which was aimed at those dealing with the burdens of middle age, featured a range of personal testimonies from a cross-section of ordinary white South Africans who all reported inexplicable bouts of "anxiety" or a constant state of being "ill at ease" that had been assuaged by the miracle Salusa.

To the children, the exact nature of this threat was never verbalised or fully articulated, but we knew it had something to do with the country's black citizens. Something out there was brewing. Something beyond our suburbs. Here black people were only sojourners, passing through with their pass books, en route to "their own places" after cleaning white homes or working in white employers' gardens.

But if they were happy with this arrangement, what was the problem?

Yellow police vans would frequently conduct dusk raids in our suburb, accosting any black person out on the street and asking for a permit or pass book which allowed them to be in the area. As children we would witness these humiliating interrogations. We would stop playing on our front lawns or cycling in the streets. I remember distinctly the palpable tension in the air as police guided those who were without papers into the back of the vans.

But like Georg in Berlin on Kristallnacht, I was just a kid in Pretoria on a bicycle, watching it all.

And when I returned home to ask my mother why it had to be this way, she would put her index finger to her lips and say, "Sshhh . . . they canna hear you."

How DO WE LOCATE our political or moral compass, those of us who find ourselves beneficiaries of an unjust system? I am talking about the perpetrators and the bystanders. If our parents resist, do they inspire the same in us? And from whom did they learn in turn? Do we even have a moral compass?

And what of the pathogenic historical currents that bubble and fester below the sheen of apparent order or order restored. Rwanda, Bosnia, Syria, Ukraine. Spin the globe then stop it and place your finger on any continent, and there you will find the traces of history untamed.

Aristotle thought we learn by doing. Men become builders, he said, by building; harp players by playing the harp. Ill-mannered children learn politeness and to appreciate things by being ordered by adults to thank others. Do we learn to be racist from racists, from a system that reassured, aided and abetted our sense of superior self?

Sometimes oppressors learn from once having been oppressed.

Revolutionaries, however, are forged through baptisms of fire. In South Africa in the 1970s fire burned all around us but, back then, it was nowhere visibly near us, apart, that was, from weekend braais in white suburban backyards.

So, how to learn to become decent, fair and just? To do the right thing? How could we, when most of us thought we had reached the top of the pyramid through our own unique and singular mediocre talents? If life was a race to the finish line by the strongest, the most intelligent, the bravest, then we white children were at a starting line way ahead of everyone else – swept along wearing the running spikes of white affirmative action.

As a child surrounded by adults who seemed to be oblivious of, conspiring with, afraid of, or in complete support of a system, piercing the scrim between fantasy and reality could only be accomplished incrementally, as each dead penny dropped or through the consumption of substances that would induce an altered state. It is, in the end, a lifelong endeavour, the unpicking of the constructed fraud.

Our whites-only bus with its red exterior, bright lights and comfortable blue vinyl padded seats pulled up next to the drab beige bus that was reserved for black people. That bus had hard wooden benches and they were always packed to capacity. Peering in before the buses pulled off, you might wonder why, but that would be all. From a distance you notice it. The absence of black children at the public pool, the library, your school. The long lines of black mothers and fathers queuing at the bus stop located kilometres outside the city centre. The poverty, the misery – they become a backdrop to your life. You stop noticing it. Or you don't stop noticing it, but it becomes habitual, just the way things are.

After attending Capital Park Primary School I moved, until my final two years of high school, to Iona Convent. This was a Catholic school in the same neighbourhood, run by the Sisters of Mercy, an order formed in Ireland in 1831.

It was there that we were able to pick up our first but vague sense of the injustice that surrounded us. Any interventions there were, however, mostly paternalistic. We had to bring extra lunch for "the poor" and were also trained to give literacy classes to adults who worked in the area or who were fed to the school through various charitable organisations. Hiding arms caches was obviously a bridge too far, too empowering of the disempowered. And as long as the majority remained disempowered, a minority of the minority could seek to assuage this, to become better selves, through helping out.

But that was about it, really.

At the convent there was, of course, the now-common malfunctioning parish priest they appeared to forge in the assembly line in a Vatican basement. Our one was Father Bernard, who would insist on wearing a tight Speedo – known universally to those who don't wear it in public as a budgie smuggler. He would splash around with the girls in the school swimming pool during our physical education class while the virginal brides of Christ, the Sisters of Mercy, looked on with benign, vacant smiles. And why not? Father Bernard was, according to the spell, a man like Adam, created in God's image, while they, as women, were forever condemned to shuffle in the pews doing lowly church work because of that cheapest of all cuts, the spare rib, from which we of the cloven crotch were somehow miraculously fashioned.

Sometimes Father would request that the girls form a line in the water and part their legs as if they were in a juvenile Olympic synchronised swimming team. He would then attempt to swim through the tunnel of young, sturdy legs underwater. Years later I read in a newspaper that Father Bernard had been accused of sexually assaulting several girls. He was not burned at the stake or left out in the wild to be torn apart by wolves, but transferred instead to new canned hunting grounds in the Western Cape.

The Irish nuns were generally stern and cheerless – perhaps a life of chastity does that to one – but at least the environment felt contained. Above the blackboard in each classroom was a colourful print of an Aryan Jesus, rather handsome, white of course, with long hippy hair like a rock star and penetrating blue eyes that seemed to follow every move. You couldn't crib during a test because you'd look up and there he'd be . . . watching you, always.

Jesus on the cross did have an impressive six-pack and a modest loincloth, but one knew one was not to wonder whether he was wearing underpants. It was a reasonable question, I thought. Anyone standing below the cross would have to look up.

Those of us who were Catholic had to say prayers three times a day (those who were not were asked not to recite them). One of these prayers was for the dead, which was pointless, I thought, because the dead don't need our prayers. But the nuns had to find something for us to talk to God about, so a bell would ring and, like little Pavlovian puppies, we would recite.

Sometimes we would attend mass and sing in the choir, which was mostly an opportunity to snatch an unseemly panama hat off someone's head and place it on the bench for them to pucker with the weight of their arse. There were also regular turns in the dark confessional at the back of the church where Father Bernard would sit, hopefully fully robed, behind the curtain. Sometimes I would pull my panama hat down low, turn up my dress collar and attempt to disguise my voice.

"The name's Bond, James Bond. It's been twelve months since my last confession."

Not that I had anything to confess.

Bless me, Father, for I have sinned. Last week we got blind drunk at Kathy's house, smoked loads of weed, laughed for about six hours, stole plants off other people's front stoeps and lied to our parents.

I gave him the censored version: "Bless me, Father, for I have sinned. I stole an apple from the shop because I was hungry. I was cheeky to my father because he was being unreasonable. I haven't been to church on a Sunday for three years because I have better things to do . . ." Or words to that effect.

Father Bernard always seemed to instil in one a sense that there had to be more. Something badass one might not be confessing. Surely a young girl in such excellent health must be indulging in a little self-exploration that the Lord would want to know about?

"Anything else?" he always insisted.

In my case there was nothing to report on that front. My genitals were strictly functional at this point, used for eliminating fluids.

Father Bernard would murmur from behind the curtain that missing mass on Sundays was a "cardinal sin" (worse even than abusing girls) and would give me 39 Hail Marys and a few How's Your Fathers.

On my release, I would kneel in a nearby pew and immediately think of what my best friends Kathy and Marijke and I had planned for later in the day. If it were a Friday, maybe we would steal her mother's car that evening. Or perhaps we'd hang out at our Italian friend Talia's house (another self-raising adolescent), where we'd loll about on a carpet of mattresses that lined the floor of an outside room, which had been painted entirely black and was fitted with subtle lighting and a kick-ass music system. There we would bust dagga pipes in bottlenecks and get paralytically stoned while listening to Jefferson Airplane, the Rolling Stones, the Greatest Show on Earth, Neil Young and Rodriguez. We thought Rodriguez was huge in the world.

Later, the three of us, who were at the beginning of our budding flirtation with juvenile delinquency, transferred to the massive government school, Clapham High, in Colbyn, which was in the east of the city, while we all lived way out north. It would require four daily bus rides to and from school. All this did was to provide more opportunity for unfettered exploration.

I didn't make the move because my parents couldn't afford my precious private education. We had heard a rumour that Clapham High was particularly wild. The legend was that a pupil had slipped LSD into a teacher's coffee and this was, Kathy, Marijke and I collectively agreed, the perfect institution for us to continue our education.

Without our parents' knowledge we conspired to swing a transfer to Clapham. We lied about why we wanted to leave the convent – knowing that the only way the nuns would let us go without question was if we made ourselves utterly morally reprehensible. Shamefully, we used apartheid. We told them that our parents had said we couldn't remain at the school because they had learned that black children would soon be admitted there. The Sisters of Mercy immediately signed off our transfer forms with pursed, disapproving lips. You can't get worse than that. Did I feel uncomfortable doing it? Not really. A world of adventure was waiting and we were determined to get there by any means necessary.

We used a fake address that belonged to a friend who lived in an area "zoned" for Clapham. We convinced her rather gullible mother to lie on our behalf. We bought second-hand grey uniforms. And then one day I came home and simply informed my stunned parents that I was, from then onwards, going to a new school. And that was it.

And so it was that we found ourselves, after spending three years in small, contained classes at the convent, in a huge rambling brick school with about six classes for each grade. And better still, it was a co-ed school, which meant boys. Boys and drugs. But for me, sex was still a long way off.

It was the beginning of two exhilarating years of dangerous freedom that our parents could not begin to imagine. We were adept at lying and covering up. We spent little time on homework or schoolwork and most days after school would hang out at Kathy's house in Capital Park chasing adolescent oblivion to various soundtracks. Kathy's mother was a single parent and worked long hours as a bookkeeper for a scrap metal dealer, so this house was the perfect hangout. Zilch supervision. My mother, of course, believed her darling was conscientiously studying with her classmates.

Around 6pm, Marijke and I would attempt to straighten up by drinking cups of powdery chicory. This was the time when my father or her parents would usually pull up outside to collect us.

To claim that we received an education at Clapham would be an exaggeration. I recall nothing from my lessons apart from learning that cells have mitochondria. We were never encouraged to think or question. Nothing in, nothing out.

White Christian nationalist schooling might have been passed off as an education but it was designed rather to keep us ignorant enough to turn us into good white South African citizens. We could read, write, some of us could "do" maths, and we could tie our own shoelaces. Later some of us would learn to use a gun.

None of this would matter, however. We would all find jobs. We were white and the world was ours for the taking. No one advised us on the possibility of a university education. Neither my parents nor my teachers ever suggested this for me. There were no enthusiastic explanations of bursaries that might be applied for. No one seemed to care what any of us might one day choose to do, career-wise.

This was not a school churning out children destined to become intellectuals or make any impression as managing directors or business leaders. The boys would all be conscripted into the army. Ultimately, we would work in banks or become indifferent municipal clerks or postal officials, draughtsmen, bookkeepers. We'd be teachers, maybe, or hairdressers or sales reps, or else we'd work in retail – not the tills, but some low-key management position. Drones, small cogs in the machine.

In a "career guidance" class I had specified that I would like to become an ice-cream seller. This way I felt I would have direct access to the product just like a drug pusher. The teacher just nodded.

Years later, when one of my daughters asked me if the sun revolved around the earth, I really had to think hard. It felt as if I had never been to school at all.

I had vaguely thought of becoming a journalist. My father religiously bought the *Pretoria News*, the *Sunday Times* and *Sunday Express*. There one could read about the "trouble" or look at photographs of young white women with voluptuous breasts in bikinis, but the news was always tailored for white readers.

Years earlier, in 1966, when Verwoerd was stabbed to death in the House of Assembly by Dimitri Tsafendas, an enigmatic immigrant messenger egged on by a tapeworm, headlines alongside the main one on the front page were "Axe Threat to Girls in Bedroom" and "2 Masked Whites in Hold Up" and then, below a large black-and-white photograph of Verwoerd, a small item titled "Dealer Ejected from Shop".

This story ran: "A 75-year old Indian general dealer, his wife and 30-year-old son with R10 000 worth of groceries and furniture were ejected today from their shop and living quarters in Club Street, Turffontein. The ejectment in terms of the Group Areas Act was made as a result of a court order obtained by the Minster of the Interior on September 1, last year.

"Mounds of tinned foodstuffs and other groceries were piled up alongside mattresses and wooden furniture on the pavement. The ejectment is being carried out at state expense. Mr Kara, white-bearded and looking bewildered, said: 'I have held a general dealer's licence in Turffontein for over 37 years. This action will force me out of business. Because of my age I cannot start again even if I could obtain a new shop licence.'"

Later I would find the print equivalent of a little axe between the pages of the tabloid *Sunday Express*. This was satirist Pieter-Dirk Uys's early columns, written as his alter ego, Evita Bezuidenhout. Hers was a voice that immediately resonated with me. Mocking, funny, cutting and dangerous. It was my weekly electro-shock therapy. There was nothing like it anywhere and Pieter-Dirk would fearlessly make visible in his writing that which the government was desperate to hide. I felt less alone. Pieter-Dirk Uys – with these early columns and then his later his stage plays and one-person shows – became the moral compass for white South Africans.

Once a week the boys at Clapham High turned up dressed in dark brown uniforms for cadets. Cadets was a milder version of the Hitler Youth movement and was intended to prepare the boys for conscription into the Defence Force, which all of them would be forced to enter after matric (my brother Albert included). The boys would be drilled on the playing fields. I have no recollection of what the girls were expected to do during this time or what me and my friends actually did. We were probably bunking, smoking in the toilets.

Some mornings there were emergency drills. A bell would sound shrilly and we would all have to file out hurriedly and quietly onto the playing fields. This was no doubt in preparation for the angry black hordes that were bound to arrive sooner or later, brandishing pangas, come to chop off our heads and boil us in pots.

A cartoon on page 261 of our matric history book (the book was written by CJ Joubert and it was prescribed in all government schools) attempted to illustrate the country's "racial problem" to white children. The cartoon depicts a white man as a befuddled tailor holding a measuring tape. Lined up facing him are a large black man, a smaller coloured man and a tiny Indian man (their individual sizes were meant to indicate the size of these populations). Each man is wearing ill-fitting clothes and the tailor is scratching his head in puzzlement. Oh, the burdens of God's chosen people.

The questions in a box titled "South Africa's non-white population" below read:

Name the four population groups represented in the cartoon.

Explain the difference in the size of the three figures.

What, in your opinion, is expected by the 3 persons from the outfitter?

Why is the White population represented by an outfitter?

What does the pose of the outfitter suggest?

In another chapter, headed "Separate Development and the Creation of Self-governing Bantu Homelands", Joubert writes: "Separate development is probably a more realistic approach to the racial situation in South Africa than was attempted before 1948. The White man has come to realise that he cannot close his eyes to the aspirations of the Bantu: during 1959 Dr Verwoerd told Parliament that South Africa could no longer avoid the realities of the political and nationalist development among Non-Whites of Africa."

Of the black majority, he explains: "The Bantu of South Africa is now displaying the same aspirations; he too is striving for a situation which can best further his interests. This is only possible where he governs himself. Separate development takes full cognisance of this aspect of the African situation. The final result has therefore to be general emancipation. The success or otherwise of this process of emancipation depends on two cardinal principles – the recognition of *ethnic differences* and *orderly emancipation* [Joubert's italics]."

Orderly emancipation meaning forced removals, bannings, mass detentions, state-sanctioned assassinations and beginning, of course, with locking Nelson Mandela (and others) away for 27 years.

Of Nazis there was this nugget by Mr Joubert: "With the help of these organisations, Hitler conducted a political *reign of terror* [Joubert's italics]. Yet it should be borne in mind that the Hitler regime remained not only acceptable but popular among the vast majority of Germans because it had brought unprecedented prosperity. The reign of terror affected only political opponents of Nazi Germany."

And in one sentence over six million German Jews, gypsies, homosexuals and other "undesirables" were turned into "political opponents", all laundered for the nice white South African children.

My father was exactly one of those ordinary Germans, so where, in all of this, did Georg and his family fit in? And how did we fit into South Africa?

It was only when the SABC screened the Thames TV 26-part series *The World at War*, narrated by Laurence Olivier, that I began to understand and grapple with the enormity of the horrors of WWII, the Nazis and the Holocaust.

Television broadcasts only began in 1976 in South Africa. The

Broederbond-controlled SABC board was hugely cognisant that television could potentially open up the world to South Africa and as a result was extremely cautious about what would be screened. Also, the cultural boycott at the time provided slim pickings for the minority pariah regime but, ironically, the SABC did consider *The World at War* as suitable and educational.

We couldn't afford a colour set, so Georg brought home a bulky black-and-white Blaupunkt which he attempted to disguise as a colour TV. At the time one could purchase a detachable, framed plastic film that hung from two clasps and covered the screen. It was tinted blue and green at the top and bottom and yellow in the centre.

I became obsessed with watching *The World at War* and never missed an episode. It opened with the ominous and melancholic soundtrack composed by Carl Davis and performed by the Prague Philharmonic Orchestra, playing beneath a shot of flames licking at the visuals. Barbara had no appetite for "reality" TV. Georg thought the series was "American propaganda", so it was my brother and I who sat in the lounge mesmerised by the appalling footage, although I suspect for different reasons.

For me the Second World War was not something that happened in a far-off place. It was in my home. In one of our albums there was a photograph of my father, a soft smile tugging at the corners of his mouth, dressed in his Luftwaffe uniform with its characteristic visor cap with a silver badge of an eagle clutching a swastika. On our bookshelf in the lounge I discovered, between the Bible, books on Napoleon and some Dickens novels, a copy of Hitler's *Mein Kampf* covered in brown paper. I had been looking for an encyclopaedia when I came across it. It was an English translation, but I was too afraid to read past the title lest some virus leap from the pages, shoot through my eyes and bore into my brain, turning me into a fascist. I asked Georg why he had the book. He mumbled something about how one should read it because Hitler "had some important things to say about the economy".

Yeah right, and much more than that. Passing the bookshelf, I was always aware that something malevolent lurked there.

I now looked at the tall man shaving in the bathroom mirror and wondered who he was. Did my father goose-step when no one was watching?

Georg would turn, look at me, smile, wipe shaving cream from his lips and pout them at me, expecting a kiss.

It became increasingly difficult for me to view him outside of the context of WWII. He had been an integral part of it and had survived. What if he was Adolf Hitler, who had escaped the bunker and had had a face transplant in Argentina?

I became convinced that there would come a night when I would be watching an episode of *The World at War* and I would see my father on the screen, brutally herding frightened German Jews in a captured village, standing outside a train bound for Auschwitz, or proudly marching in one of the parades carrying a flag with a swastika on it. Would I see him shake hands with Hitler? Would I catch a glimpse of the Führer himself lovingly pinching my father's ear in a line-up of Hitler Youth boys standing to attention?

I never did spot him, but until today I cannot look at a photograph or piece of archival film about the war or the Holocaust and not search for Georg among the crowds.

It began to haunt me. Suddenly, the man who was my father, the man I loved, morphed into a collective. He was one of them. He was German. The people who were on the wrong side of history. Who had done these terrible things. And he was inside of me. I was, and am, of and from him.

It was a horrifying realisation and it marked the beginning of my need to pull away from my father emotionally, to challenge his authority, to do everything not to be like him in any way. My father had expected me to be a "good daughter". He had wanted me to wear my hair long and in a plait. He probably would have liked it if I could yodel. He had wanted me to learn to cook. Instead I cut my hair short, wore boys' clothes and refused to be domesticated in any way.

Later on his work travels overseas, he would always bring home a gift that I considered inappropriate – a weaving loom (for girls) or jewellery (which I never wore), while my brother got something like a fabulous windbreaker.

To provoke him during an argument I would charge that I had been swapped at birth, that there must have been some grotesque mistake. The fact that I was the only one in the family with blue eyes was proof of this, I spat out. Barbara would become extremely agitated during these arguments. She did not like to upset the equilibrium when it came to Georg, whom she affectionately called Georgie. She generally accepted his benign authority and encouraged us to follow suit.

"I am not yours!" I would hurl at him, making a swift exit as the words left my mouth.

Barbara would slip into my bedroom afterwards and gently admonish me. "You must notta talk like thees. You hurt your father when you say thees. You are ours. I know that. You are mine."

Much later I would come to understand that my father's natural patriarchal dismissal of women had also prompted my need to erase my femininity. I was already a tomboy, but now I was going hardcore. If femininity was what he despised in some way, then I would not be it – a girl. It was a complex, confusing and conflicted state of needing to repel and attract at the same time.

The day after Georg died, I began growing my hair for the first time in my life. I was able to wear low-cut tops. It was an immediate response to being liberated from his gaze. I found myself gradually restored to myself, on my own terms.

Apart from *The World at War*, I increasingly found escape in music in my private, alone time. Music formed an essential backdrop to my life. It was where I could connect emotionally and it was through music that I was able to explore my confused teenage feelings.

Here I bow to the sage wisdom of Plato. Music, Plato said, was "a moral law. It gives soul to the universe, wings to the mind, flight to the imagination, a charm to sadness, gaiety and life to everything. It is the essence of order and lends to all that is good, just, and beautiful."

Two years after I had ruthlessly used apartheid as a convenient excuse to transfer schools, I discovered Bob Marley. Marley did not make music for white kids, but somehow his music resonated with many like me across the globe. It was white kids, to Marley's own astonishment, who packed out his concerts when he toured the UK.

I came to Marley through marijuana. Bob and dagga went together like gin and tonic, like brandy and Coke, like apartheid and casual violence.

In the song "War" he mentioned South Africa. He knew we existed. He explained to this child what that feeling had been. He put music and words to it and I soaked it in. My discovery of Marley and the world he slowly opened up led to a longing to be separate from it all. To get out of the matrix.

But where to go? I was a child with no income or means of escape. Here we were, just the four of us, marooned at the tip of Africa. No extended family, no relatives close by. I lived in a home where my mother kept special crockery and teacups in the sideboard with the hope that, just on the off-chance, "important" visitors – hopefully a priest – might pop by, but no one ever did. This was a generation unmarked by global consumerism and consumption, a generation which preserved everyday things to hand to the next generation. Cutlery sets, gravy boats and the cups and saucers that, in the end, never did get used.

One afternoon while driving with my father down Paul Kruger Street I spotted a hardware store that sold pressed-wood Wendy houses. They looked like those gingerbread houses Germans eat at Christmas, the ones with two small windows and a door. If I couldn't leave the country, then the least I could do was move out of the house into a place of my own.

I kept up a steady and relentless campaign. Georg could have simply ignored me, but I suppose I must have been very persuasive, and before long a truck delivered the prefabricated structure to our house. It was erected at the far end of the garden close to the mulberry tree and the sad family in the council house who hadn't been allowed to enjoy my father's largesse that Christmas Day.

No one asked why I wanted to live apart from the rest of the family. Perhaps Georg understood my need; he too had his own room. Whatever it was, he appeared to accept with silent resignation my transition from his *kleine Süsselein* ("little darling" as I found he had scribbled on the back of one baby snap) to a Justin Bieber 0.1. Perhaps he thought, like so many parents with children who do not conform, that it was merely a phase, a hormonal blip, and it would pass in due course.

Whenever he could, however, still offer nuggets on critical questions of life and existence, he didn't hold back.

Washing the car together once, he asked me to stop and put my hand in the bucket of soapy water. "Now, take your hand out. Zat," he said, "is how much you mean to ze world out zere."

This was not his opinion of me he was trying to demonstrate, but rather the greater indifference of the universe and the capitalist military-industrial complex. At least that was how I chose to interpret it. In life nothing is personal. It just is. And the trick to it all is solving a problem, whatever it may be, and moving on to the next one and the next.

My immediate problem back then was the extreme cold of the Wendy house in the garden where I had chosen to sit out my self-imposed exile. Before I thought to run an extension cord across the yard, I warmed the space with a paraffin heater and I studied for tests with a lamp that gave off thick black fumes which might, in retrospect, have impaired my academic abilities. The structure was solid and small but roomy enough to fit in a bed, with its legs removed of course, a desk, a portable record player and a packet of cigarettes.

No one was allowed into my room. I had a key and locked it when I left for excitement and adventure.

My mother would often tap on the window with a cup of tea or hot Milo late at night, and when I played Bob Marley on repeat, as I tended to do during this period, she would shout from the kitchen door: "Marianna, you stopa that doofa doofa dooofa. Iss playing all day long driva me mad."

The only place for me, for now, to act out this rebellion was through music. There were no revolutionary cells one could seek out in the neighbourhood. No one was tuning in to Radio Freedom in my neck of the hood.

The only way to distinguish oneself was to reject the rules and, in so doing, believe one was showing some kind of solidarity with the black majority. Comfortably opting out, if only in our minds.

IN THE MIND MAP of our parents and teachers, race and sex were final frontiers, strange worlds they would not dare to boldly go, to quote the famous Star Trek split infinitive.

But if they were not going to talk to us about sex, there were, I soon discovered, more than enough predatory wankers (literally and metaphorically) around who would zealously and happily oblige.

As a girl, albeit a rather boyish-looking one, freely roaming the streets, it is astounding in retrospect just how many men or boys I encountered in my neighbourhood, in parks, outside school. They cruised the streets in cars or hung around in public toilets in an apparent state of perpetual arousal looking for women and girls to harass.

Well, we did walk upright and have vaginas. Being alive, it seemed, was reason enough to be considered a seductress or a legitimate target for unwanted sexual attention.

These men had an air either of enviable entitlement or unhinged madness about them. And while disguising oneself as a boy might certainly have served as a decoy when it came to fooling strangers, there were always those men who lived close by who knew you were a girl.

Gary Puckett and the Union Gap's 1968 hit song *Young Girl* sums up perfectly the general prevailing attitude and ethos of the era when it came to sexual politics. Men, I began to think, were generally quite sad. They appeared to be completely helpless, utterly under the spell of and in thrall to their sexual impulses and hormones. And Gary Puckett's song epitomised it all. The song is about a man who is in love with a girl, it is a love that is "way out of line". Puckett suggests that the subject of the song better "run, girl".

I did run. But not away. I usually sprinted straight home to my mother. I knew she would always believe and protect me. And, besides, there really was nothing quite like watching her tear up the road in a rage ready to confront some old perv while I stood behind her watching, wearing a smug and satisfied grin.

When it came to sex I was clueless. Didn't think about it, frankly. I suspect my parents secretly hoped I would learn from watching our dogs and other suburban wildlife. We had had several dogs over the years. We were one of those families who never thought to neuter them.

Toffee, a ragged roving beau of a dog with one eye, a sort of Johnny Depp of dogs in the neighbourhood, covered our bitch, Meisie, at least twice. She gave birth on both occasions to a single puppy, which we kept, and didn't neuter either. One was called Rover and I forget the name of the other, possibly also Rover. Sometimes the dogs would "get stuck" and we'd watch with fascination and horror as they yelped in pain, a strange two-backed beast, until some adult would rush out with a hosepipe or a bucket of water to "cool them down".

The first time I heard the word "menstruation" was in Standard Four (Grade Six) when one morning our teacher at Capital Park primary hurriedly shooed the boys out of the classroom and methodically covered every single window with newspaper and masking tape. The atmosphere grew tense. Next a neatly dressed woman arrived with a laminated chart which she placed on an easel in front of the class. The teacher told us this lady was going to talk to us about something that was very important and that we should keep quiet and pay attention.

"Who here has started to menstruate?" the stranger quizzed the class.

Debbie's (Peter, in my world) hand shot up. I stared at her with surprise. What was she doing?

"You can't mend straight," I said indignantly. "You lie, man."

"Marianne! Quiet please!" the teacher barked.

Sewing class for girls was compulsory. I had been attempting to make a doll's dress, from scratch, for what felt like a lifetime. It was a disaster. I just couldn't wrap my mind or my fingers around the finicky needlework required. Mending, as far as I was concerned, referred to sewing. And I knew for a fact that Debbie could also *not* mend straight, that she was just as bad at it as I was.

When we had our domestic classes Debbie and I would always watch with envy as the boys got up and headed for an outdoor shed where they would do woodwork. There they would saw and hammer away making wall hangings – pieces of wood painted black with nails knocked into them in various geometric patterns. Colourful threads of cotton would then be twirled around the nails, resulting in very psychedelic-looking art. How I longed to join them. But no, we were destined to mend straight and bake cookies.

Debbie shot me a surprised look of her own, her eyebrows raised, as if I had just asked her whether cherry-red lipstick was "in" this season.

The lady with the chart then flipped the first page to reveal a diagram of what I thought was an elaborate Belgian water fountain. Two shower-heads hovered over two small egg-shaped appendages below them. This all ran off what appeared to be the central water feature attached to a long pipe that trailed off into, well, nothing really.

"Now these," she said, pointing at the showerheads, "are your fallo-pian tubes."

Our fallopian tubes? But where was all of this stuff located in our bodies? Our heads? Our stomachs?

"And these are the ovaries. Once a month you release an egg . . ."

Release an egg!

" . . . which settles in the tube. If the egg is fertilised by sperm then it begins to divide and make a baby . . ."

Sperm? Now hang on. That word I knew, although it was commonly known as spunk in our world. Sperm, mmm. Isn't that what comes out of a boy's penis, like when Eugene showed off his little trick that day we were fishing? My brother had a penis, so it was no big deal. But if sperm comes out of the penis, then how does it get into the fallopian tube?

No, it can't be!

Meanwhile the visitor was busy wrapping up. "And that is why you should not have sex before you are an adult. It is very dangerous and you can fall pregnant which you don't want to do," she said.

I stumbled into the sunlight afterwards, stunned and bewildered. That afternoon, back home, I told my mom about the woman and the lesson.

"Mom, what really happens?" I asked.

"When it appen, cuma tella me. Because you willa be a 'ooman then and 'ave to stop playing with da boys," she replied casually.

I left praying that "it" would not happen soon. I did not want to be a woman dropping eggs once a month. Also the manner of this telling, this imparting of biological information unique to me as a girl, made it sound like some affliction, something to be hidden, something to be ashamed of, to be spoken about in a darkened classroom, away from the boys.

This was an era obsessed with "feminine hygiene", when supermarket shelves offered "feminine sprays" and wipes and when sanitary towels were slipped discreetly into brown paper packets as if one needed to shield men from this most natural of occurrences. Supermarkets never offered men special products to keep themselves "clean and odour free".

The only blood I encountered, however, was during one or two legendary street fights where I learned to defend myself. While I hated the violence, the pain of a punch or a slap, I seemed to thrive on the surge of rage that enabled me to retaliate.

In one fight I beat up a guy called Ralph, who had knocked me off my bicycle behind a clump of bushes that grew along the edges of two fields in the nearby park. As he pressed me to the ground, I socked him hard in the face.

Only once did I suffer a public humiliation in front of my gang, when my brother, realising I had once again stolen his Chopper, marched into the park and delivered a short powerful uppercut, from behind, almost knocking me out. It was to be his one and only finest moment in the neighbourhood. Albert seldom ventured out of his bedroom, where he ate tons of toast with apricot jam, read *War and Peace* and played with his toy soldiers and model airplanes in preparation for his cannon fodder period. This was a rare public appearance.

When Albert and I were about ten or eleven, I remember that Georg would take my brother to a specialist toyshop in town, where he would buy him model planes and tanks. Sometimes he allowed me to tag along. It was from this toyshop that I purchased a set of Action Men, with realistic "flock" hair and beards and "eagle" blue eyes. You could dress them in a variety of authentic miniature military uniforms – including the uniform of a Nazi SS officer. I fell in love with one of my Action Men, the one with brown hair, and wished he would come to life. Of course where his penis should have been was a harmless plastic mound. Perfect.

My Action Man was my closest intimate male companion. He lived in a suitcase in my bedroom, tossed in with his uniforms, his helmets, his rifles and guns. That I might have been using him to work through some Oedipal tangle, rendering my father a small man whom I could dominate, have power over and even make die, did not occur to me then. Such are the miracles of the unconscious.

I hung onto my Action Man for years until Barbara threw him out when we moved to Cape Town. I still imagine my little true love buried or smothered under a mound of decaying debris in a dump. A bit like one's childhood memories before we dare to don a mental hazmat suit and make the trek back to retrieve and understand them.

Today, of course, the uniforms and my Action Man would fetch a tidy sum on eBay, where he is much sought after as a collector's item.

As far as physical action went for me, the brawl with Charmaine Daniels has to stand out. Charmaine attended Hillview High School and she would catch the same bus home as me. One afternoon she began taunting me almost immediately after we had settled into the back seat, telling everyone who cared to listen (which was everyone) that she had spotted me walking to the shops wearing hair curlers. This was the ultimate insult and she knew it. I threatened her verbally.

"You talk shit, Charmaine. I'm warning you, I'm going to hit you."

A bit later, when we were a few metres from her stop, she started taunting me again. "Well, come on then," she goaded. I watched as she grabbed her satchel and moved towards the exit, still jeering and mocking, and made an impulsive decision to get off with her and beat her right outside on the grass verge where everyone could see and I would salvage my reputation. I lunged at Charmaine and smacked her on the head. She hadn't been expecting this but instinctively she hit back. The bus and our audience moved off, their eager, cheering faces peering through the rear window.

"I'll meet you in the park at three and we'll do this properly," I challenged her.

"Right," she said, stomping off angrily.

Close to the appointed hour I began rounding up supporters. I knew Charmaine would be doing the same in her neck of the hood. At exactly 3pm we stood facing each other on a small grassy mound in the park surrounded by a group of noisy boys and girls enthusiastically egging us on.

"Hit her! Hit her!" chanted each group of supporters.

We circled each other cautiously. I threw a left punch. She ducked. She threw a punch, I stepped back. Then suddenly, the children scattered. As if at an unheard signal they were running away from us, like antelope at a watering hole after spotting a lion.

I looked up to see my mother striding towards us brandishing the dog-leash-cum-whip and emitting her familiar bellow.

"Marianna! Marianna! . . . I donta believe it! . . . Stop it! My God this issa terrible. You come home right now . . . All of you, get away . . . go . . . go."

She was serious and, frankly, I was relieved to be interrupted. I allowed my mother to drag me home by my ear, while she kept up a steady stream of admonishments. At least I didn't lose the fight. That would have been much worse.

"I donta know what to do wit you anymore. You wait until your fadder come 'ome. I going to tell him. You going to get a hiding . . . I tell you, a hiding."

He didn't. Give me a hiding. I don't from this distance recall any specific punishment my father might have meted out. Georg had resigned himself, it appeared, to his "difficult" daughter.

Being difficult, though, provided me with a sense of agency. This dissident attitude towards everything and everyone offered a shield with which I felt I could encounter the world and be less vulnerable.

And so it was that when arbitrary men crossed my path when I was out on my own, I felt emboldened by my own power. One of my most memorable encounters with guys out on the prowl was when a car with what appeared to be four young conscripts on AWOL inside cruised up to the pavement. The driver hailed me over, apparently needing directions.

"Ag man, excuse me. Do you know where we can find Proes Street?" he asked with a knowing smile.

Proes Street was a well-known street in the city. Its charm is that it sounded, when one left out the "r", like *poes*, the Afrikaans equivalent of the word "cunt".

"Ja, I think I can help you out. You turn left when you get to Piel [dick] Street, take a quick right at Hol [arsehole] Road and then immediately left again into Bal [scrotum] Street," I replied.

They drove off, disappointed.

There was the wanker who waited at the entrance to the girls' toilet in the park and who would whip out his dick as soon as he spotted us and begin to masturbate. We would stare at him, repulsed but curious. It looked so elemental, primal and pathetic as his face reddened while he stroked himself furiously. He let out little sighs and squeals before ejaculating onto the concrete floor. Afterwards, when he had slunk off, we examined the streak of ejaculate on the concrete floor with a stick.

And then there were the men who knew me.

One afternoon, finding himself alone with me as the only customer, the old Portuguese owner of the local café invited me behind the counter to choose a selection of sweets. Hell yes. As I leaned in, he shuffled closer, breathing loudly, and pressed himself against me. I felt the weight of him and his hard-on prodding through his trousers. In an instant I pushed him away and scampered out of the dark shop with its reek of wilted vegetables and fermenting fruit.

The surge of adrenalin from the flight response propelled me home, and as I ran I grew angry and indignant. Arriving out of breath at the front gate, I shouted for my mother.

"Mom! In the shop just now Mr S came up behind me and pressed himself against me," I told her.

I had hardly finished spitting the words out when Barbara was already out of the door, out of the front gate and beginning to stride in that familiar determined gait I had come to know so well. She seemed propelled by a superhuman fury. I could hardly keep up with her. She kept up the pace for the entire block of about seven houses until she reached the last stretch leading up to the shop.

Then she began shouting, in Portuguese, and gesticulating, working herself up into full rage. It was deeply gratifying watching my lioness mother protect me. It was courageous and brave and role-modelled for me how to deal with anyone who chose to violate my personal space.

The shop owner must have heard Barbara's spectacular approach and by then was attempting to scuttle out of the back of the shop. My mother stood at the darkened door and yelled at his retreating back, still in Portuguese. As she turned to leave she switched to English. "I tell you today, I willa killa you. I tell you. Touch her again and I willa kill you."

Then she put her arm around me and we walked home. I was not to go back to the shop, she told me, ever again. From now on we would give all our custom to the Papadopouloses, our Greek friends.

Riaan's father, Uncle Danie, was an occasional visitor to our home at the weekends. He was a creature of rigid routine and would usually hang around his own house doing chores and generally terrorising his family, or forcing everyone to keep quiet while he watched TV, smoking his Lucky Strike plains with his feet up on the wooden coffee table.

Sometimes he would instruct Riaan to wash his pristine beige Austin 1800, which he seldom drove and kept locked in the garage during the week. Every weekend, either Uncle Danie or Riaan would reverse it a few metres into the driveway, where they would soap it down before buffing it and parking it back in the cool garage.

One weekend I was lolling in a chair in our lounge, flipping through a comic book. It was early afternoon. The house was quiet. My mother was out visiting her Portuguese friends across the river and my father was in his "study" at the back of the house, probably taking a nap. Uncle Danie let himself in.

I looked up to find him suddenly looming.

"Ja, hello, Mariaantjie. Waar's jou pa?"

"Ek dink hy's in sy kantoor," I said, looking up briefly from my comic.

And then he lunged at me, one hand aimed for between my legs. I shot up off the chair and began to yell. "Get out! Get out of this house! Get out!"

Roused by the noise, my father appeared in time to encounter Uncle Danie, who pushed right past him and stomped out of the house in a rage, slamming the iron gate behind him.

"Vat iss going on?" asked Georg.

"He tried to touch me! Dad, he tried to touch me!" I spluttered, expecting him to respond as my mother had done and to chase after and confront Uncle Danie as he made his way down Burlington Avenue.

But he didn't.

"Are you sure, Marianna? No, man, he wouldn't do that," said my father, and he was already turning away, diminishing it, heading back to his study.

Contempt washed over me, contempt and anger. You coward. You weak, weak man, I thought to myself. I understood that Georg did not like confrontation but in this instance confrontation was what had been required.

"You have no fucking balls," I muttered.

Later, when she had returned, I told my mother about the incident. She advised me not to visit Riaan's house again. I told her I couldn't do that. How would Auntie Rienie, whom I loved, as well as Ouma, Anri and Riaan interpret or understand my sudden withdrawal when they had made me feel so welcome? I would miss the nourishment of their company and chose to keep the matter away from them. I had challenged Danie and was not afraid of him. If he did arrive home while I was visiting, he and I would know and hopefully he would not dare cross me. I continued to visit but would try to ensure that I left before 5pm, the time Uncle Danie came home from work.

Later on Danie bought a plot several hours outside Pretoria and he took to spending weekends there in a self-imposed exile, returning only late on Sunday evenings, thus liberating his home from his morbid grip.

During my visits I would either listen to Riaan playing the piano or sit around the kitchen table, talking, eating and drinking Riaan's marshmallow coffee, finding with the family the little joys that existed. While Auntie Rienie might have hoped that something would blossom between Riaan and me, he and I understood the safety of our asexual friendship.

All my friendships were asexual, come to think of it. I loved hanging out with boys but there was no physical attraction or curiosity about them. I found girls generally tedious, apart from Kathy and Marijke, so no major hormonal rustlings on that front either, for now.

Boys were fun to be with, but the girls I liked brought to the friendship something different, something illusory, difficult to define or pinpoint for me. Not quite sexual but definitely some flicker of desire, more emotional than physical.

It was only a matter of time before my male friends would begin to fall under the apparently irresistible spell of their raging hormones and that the ease and comfort between us would begin to alter incrementally until I lost the safe space I had once enjoyed being one of them. The boys around me were morphing into men, their chins sprouting a fine layer of hair, pimples popping out on their necks. And by now they had also learned that their penises were not just for showing off.

With most girls in the neighbourhood safely indoors, they turned to the only girl they knew who they believed could oblige their budding sexual arousal. Me.

One friend, Ronald, like me, lived outside in the backyard of his home. His room was a rondavel, while I still had my Wendy house. I would spend time with him, his younger brother, Richard, and their sister Bonita, playing Scalextric and swimming in their pea-green kidney-shaped pool. This particular afternoon I arrived to find no one inside the rondavel. I called out and, as I turned to go, a cupboard door suddenly crashed open and out spilled Ronald, with a porn mag in his hand and an impressive erection. As his boner reared towards me, he casually said, "Hey, Marianne, won't you lick this?"

It seemed, to my mind, deeply unnatural, counter-instinctual. And while his dick was certainly quite spectacular, it did nothing for me. He might as well have shown me the hosepipe.

"Ag, no man, Ronald, man, that's gross, man," I said.

I went back outside and not long afterwards he came outside too (I think he might have returned to the cupboard to deal with the task at hand), wiping his hands on a towel, and then plunging into the pool. Nothing like a post-wank swim.

I did ponder why I wasn't interested in sex, and wondered whether everything was in working order. But I stopped short of thinking about actually finding out. If you said masturbation to me I would have thought you were referring to the working of a combustion engine. Practically speaking, I might as well have been given some sort of long-acting epidural that had numbed my groin.

On Friday afternoons Georg usually took me and my brother to the central library in Pretoria. Here we would disappear among the shelves in the sections containing the genres we preferred. I routinely found myself in the reference and non-fiction sections and one Friday I looked up a term that had recently drifted into my lexicon – "homosexual". It might have been in reference to a Bible text at school because, thinking back now, I cannot pinpoint any other way it might have found its way into my consciousness, lodging there like a whisper, like something I might have known.

Homosexuality was only removed from the American Psychiatric Association's Diagnostic and Statistical Manual of Mental Disorders (DSM) in 1973 and the thick-spined book I hooked out of the shelves presented me with a definition of the "condition" as a "mental illness" which "can be cured".

Well, that's not me then, I thought to myself. I am not mentally ill.

So if I wasn't a homosexual, what was I?

I was largely untroubled by this lack of certainty, though. I expressed my libidinal energy elsewhere. My life was epic enough to keep me happy and busy, which was why, unlike my brother, I seldom left the library with a pile of books.

I read the Hardy Boys series but soon grew bored with the suave teenage amateur detective brothers, solving the mysteries long before they did. My literary tastes were confined mostly to pulp photo-comic books with titles like *Tessa, Sister Louise, Ruiter in Swart, Luiperd,* and

Mark Condor. These *poesboekies* – as they were known – the equivalent of TV in print, consisted of still photographs in black and white and bubbles of dialogue. They were available at any corner store and were hugely popular in South Africa. *Chunky Charlie* was another one, and this was one of few photo-comics tailored for black readers: the hero of the title was a hefty, loveable thief whose coat was lined with loot.

I came to books much later in my life and only in my 30s turned into a bibliophile. As an adult I continue to hoard books and often look at my burgeoning shelves wondering whether my predilection might have something to do with my mother's illiteracy and her desire that we, unlike her, should benefit from an education and what books could teach us.

Apart from primary school, my reports were generally lacklustre but this did not deter Barbara from proudly showing them off to our neighbours. She couldn't read, so was not to know that my marks were not exactly worth bragging about.

"Mom, I got an E for typing," I would point out.

"I donta care. I know you clever," she would smile.

Barbara loved us no matter what, this I knew.

MY CRUSH ON Kathy was more of a slow burn. She was the most adventurous of our little delinquent trio, and the brightest. She was funny and wild and, like me, enjoyed pushing boundaries, not that we knew what these were exactly. At Clapham we were exposed to boys but they were all too young for us, we reckoned.

Outsiders everywhere find each other, and Kathy and I soon attracted those who lurked at Clapham. This served to extend the number of homes or venues we could use to experiment with new substances – cough mixture and diet pills, which we stole from pharmacies and took by the fistful. One of our new friends, Rensky, seemed to know an astounding number of older boys who had already left school and who seemed, for now, to be drifting aimlessly, either dodging going to the army or on a day pass from a mental institution.

One such boy was Mad John, who owned a dangerously unroad-worthy bakkie. John was schizophrenic, someone had told us, but this didn't stop him from further testing the bounds of sanity by imbibing vast quantities of whatever illicit chemicals we managed to procure. Mad John would often arrive to pick us up from school blind-drunk. He would have already bought a five-litre canister – it could not be described as a bottle – of cheap wine and an armful of dagga. Often we would have to shout at John from the rear of the bakkie as he veered suddenly into oncoming traffic.

Of the three of us girls, Marijke was most likely to be the first to have sex, and also to score the most handsome of the older boys who clustered around us.

If my daughters are reading this now, I would like them to understand that this is why, when it comes to the secular Rumspringa they will no doubt experience on their passage to glorious adulthood (inshallah), I know it all. I have a PhD in everyday teenage rebellion. With our brains still building bridges between the various regions – particularly the frontal lobes and the executive functions these control – and while waiting for these links to become fully myelinated, it is not surprising that we behaved like early primates. And ours was, make no mistake, a very conventional rebellion. Riaan, in many ways, was a braver rebel than I. He loved classical music, studied to become a teacher, never took drugs, and only smoked and sprayed shaving cream in postboxes because I encouraged him.

Psychoanalyst Adam Phillips writes lucidly about the "difficult" child in a *London Review of Books* essay published in 2009. Phillips notes that in adolescence we become aware that there are "many kinds of a good time to be had, and that they are often in conflict with each other. When you betray yourself, when you let yourself down, you have misrecognised what your idea of a good time is; or, by implication, more fully realised what your idea of a good time might really be. You thought that doing this – taking drugs, lying to your best friend – would give you the life you wanted; and then it doesn't. You have, in other words, discovered something essential about yourself; something you couldn't discover without having betrayed yourself."[3]

---

3 http://www.lrb.co.uk/v31/n03/adam-phillips/in-praise-of-difficult-children.

Phillips also speaks of the "truant mind". The act of truanting, he says, "has something utopian about it, and not truanting something unduly stoical or defeated. The truant mind matters because it is the part of ourselves that always wants something better; and it also needs to come up against resistance to ensure that the something better is real, not merely a fantasy."

Surviving in South Africa in the 1970s, one was compelled to cultivate a truant mind.

My limits back then were that I would never inject anything. That was it. And while I do realise my frontal lobes had not yet fully developed, I nevertheless had a keen sense of self-preservation. I think it came from being loved unconditionally. It was this, I am sure, that saved me. Barbara's unconditional love.

When Marijke, Kathy and Rensky plotted to "run away from home" and spent a week hitch-hiking around the country on their own, I opted out. I could not subject Barbara to the anxiety. While I longed to join them, on that occasion good sense outweighed the risk of adventure. And although I had been sworn to secrecy, when Kathy's distraught mother called to ask me if I knew where Kathy was, I ratted on them immediately.

WHEN I FINALLY discovered my homosexual self, it was while I was drunk and bunking school.

My brother Albert, who was eighteen months older than me, had, like every other white South African boy, been conscripted into the army. There was no resistance to this in our home; in fact it was a rather proud tradition among the men in the family, it appeared.

I accompanied Georg to say farewell to my brother, who was boarding a troop train at the Pretoria station. On the platform were hundreds of young men, some with their hair already shorn in preparation, others rebelliously hanging onto their last vestiges as citizens and individuals. They stood around with their teary-eyed parents, tending to last-minute forgotten *padkos* or simply lingering for a last hug from a mother or a stiff handshake from a father.

As the train pulled out of the station, I watched from a distance. Georg stood close to the rails, too close, it turned out. As the last carriage trundled past him, someone stuck an open hand out through the window and smacked him hard on the head. Georg dropped to his knees, clutching his ear in pain. The scene, while shocking, was also comical, and I burst out laughing. Georg looked up at me, his expression horrified, as if I were an alien. I understand now, in adulthood, that I tend to laugh at mishaps; it is a nervous response, one that comics like Charles Chaplin understood. My father, however, rightfully, did not forgive me for a long time. Perhaps part of my cruelty was because he seemed so sad at saying goodbye to his son and I felt left out of the triangle. I was the spare part, bearing witness.

In fact I hardly noticed my brother's absence. He had spent most of his time in his room anyway, and now my competitor for affection and resources was safely out of the way. This was, after all, what men did. They left home as boys and were, everyone said, soon to return home as men. The process that would result in this was unquestioned.

A few months later my parents left me in charge of our home one weekend while they drove to the military base in Potchefstroom, about two hours outside Pretoria, for my brother's passing-out parade after his basic training.

In their absence I did what all delinquents do. I had a party.

At our house that weekend an entirely different passing-out parade took place as we helped ourselves to my father's drinks cabinet and emptied, into one container, varieties of alcohol that should never be blended. We managed to milk about a litre of a cocktail of gin, whisky, brandy, vodka, various liqueurs, and Coco Rico out of the assortment and downed it like street winos.

We were joined intermittently by various other neighbourhood thugs. We danced, played music loudly and then passed out. The details of what followed remain sketchy but I regained some consciousness to find Kathy and me kissing on my brother's single bed. What I do know is that 'twas not I who made the first move. I would not have dared. But it felt right and in that delicious instant I knew it. I liked girls. Not all girls. This one particular girl.

Afterwards we never spoke of it. We remained close friends and I was careful not to remind Kathy of it. I had had my one moment of bliss.

Years later, when she visited me in Cape Town, we talked about it for the first time. By then Kathy was married and a mother of two. Lost to me entirely. But not as a friend, which we remain to this day.

That I loved Kathy was to remain my secret, though, for quite some time. If the rest of the world believed that what I was was "mentally ill", I was certainly not going to be flaunting it and risk being dragged off in a straitjacket. The twentieth-century understanding of mental health was no different from the nineteenth-, I reckoned, so best to glide through life detached from an essential part of my being.

I LONGED TO BE Janet Weiss. I wanted to slip out of the seat in the cinema and disappear through the screen.

In the mid-seventies a thin sliver of light entered the gloom of my strangely gendered world when the film *The Rocky Horror Picture Show* was screened, for a few weeks only, before it was banned by the censors and disappeared from view. That it had slipped through in the first place was, to my mind, a small miracle. The censors must have either dropped off to sleep or failed to watch the entire film when they had first passed it for general public viewing.

I sat in the darkened Pretoria cinema in my school uniform, marvelling at the exotic images that lit up the large screen. There were also the unusual and unfamiliar stirrings elsewhere in my body, from my loins to my still-growing frontal lobes. I had no idea what the film was about, but it was Tim Curry as the sweet transvestite Dr Frank-N-Furter who tripped a switch. What *is* this? And why do I find him attractive? And Janet Weiss. Although, hang on, don't I want to be her? I'm not a full-blown homosexual after all! I like one girl. But do I now fancy men in women's underwear? What the hell is going on here? And where in South Africa will I find a man like Frank-N-Furter?

Later, as Susan Sarandon, playing Janet, sat in her underwear post-coitally stroking Rocky's hand while Magenta and Columbia lolled around watching them lasciviously on a screen, singing "touch-a touch-a touch-a touch me", the neurons in my tiny brain tripped, triggering a delicious electrical storm. I had never seen or heard anything like it. And it was thrilling. For a brief moment the film offered a vague notion that somewhere out in the world there were others who were like me; other people who were different. Men who wore dresses, women who wore suits. People who fucked each other up the bum.

For now I would have to carefully wrap and conceal this nugget of liberating knowledge in a secret drawer in my mind for those emergencies when I might escape to Transsexual Transylvania. When the film was banned, this knowledge was sealed for me. I *knew* it had to hold great truth and wisdom.

I soon learned that resisting a stereotype comes with risks, reward and some losses. If I was going to insist on dressing like a boy, I would be deprived (my parents reasoned at first) of communing with the rest of the troupe.

"If you don'ta weara dress, youa not coming out with us," my mother would attempt to threaten as the family prepared to leave for yet another fraught and forced Sunday lunch at the ghastly Boehmerwald German restaurant in Pretoria.

Not going to the Boehmerwald was not a punishment. This they didn't seem to understand. I would rather poke my eyes out with hot fondue forks than sit through a heavy three-course à la carte meal that included Avocado Ritz served in a small aluminium bowl, followed by a meat dish, which was usually chunks of pork in a sea of sauerkraut.

But what to do with me while they were out? The solution they settled on was to lock me safely indoors, away from the pleasures and temptations of the streets, river and neighbourhood. I would meekly agree. This, I told them, seemed like a fair exchange.

Within minutes of their departure I would escape through the only set of unbarred windows in the house, those of the enclosed front porch.

My parents had obviously decided that they would play no part in enabling my life as a tomboy renegade. Dresses were still bought and hung in my cupboard. Repeated requests for a pair of Lee jeans were ignored. (The prize would have been a pair of Levis, but because of economic sanctions these were unavailable.) The American dream would have to be lived out in the next-best, cheaper option of Lee or Wrangler (which sounded vaguely obscene, I always thought).

I had a few sets of shorts and T-shirts I could rotate, as well as a tracksuit I could wear when it was colder. I still had to wear a dress to school during the week, which was bad enough, but in winter our uniform included a tie, which I quite fancied.

Possessing a pair of jeans became a singular obsession, however. In time I realised this could only be done through bartering with someone who had access to this prized item. I fixed on Charmaine Daniels's brother Eddie, who appeared to have several pairs. In the end I managed to convince him to pass on to me an old pair he no longer wore. These I decorated and personalised with a butterfly, poorly embroidered in wool on the back pocket. The butterfly, we had been told, was a symbol of rebellion drawn from the 1969 bestselling memoir *Papillon*, by Henri Charrière, a convicted felon and fugitive.

You could not move through the world in the 1970s as a woman without being objectified or somehow reminded that your role was one of subservience, that you were created to be used in some manner – for sex, child-rearing, cleaning or part-time secretarial work (in that order).

Consumer markets seemed to be aimed generally at men with the thinking that advertisers simply needed to drape a woman over the bonnet of a car, have her fondling a packet of cigarettes or swinging alluringly in a hammock in front of a glass of beer for men to lose control of their faculties and immediately rush out and buy the product.

Even an ad for the "Beer is Best" campaign, which was run in the local, unambiguously titled women's magazine *Fairlady*, spoke to women through men. The text read thus: "Everything a man wants. Five feet three. Looks good in slacks. Great in sweaters! Never late for a date. Laughs politely at old jokes. Real doll. *And she likes beer!* Thinks two beers is the friendliest call. And she's right. Beer is the companionable drink – the traditional, warm-hearted inspirer of cosy conversation. The only drink that successfully combines cool refreshment and warm good cheer. No wonder more and more women are joining men for a beer or two. And what more could a man want?"

The tone of the small print at the bottom was serious: "Issued in the interests of better understanding between the sexes by the brewers of Lion beers."

Of course the tacit understanding is that it was perfectly reasonable to try to get a woman drunk and that this would lead to "cosy conversation", whatever that might be.

Being black in South Africa must have felt tantamount to having been sucked into a world of complete and violent psychosis. While you were absent entirely from media images, your physical presence in real life was most certainly seen. Not only seen, but immediately acted on. You were confronted, barked at or physically removed against your will.

There were no black people in any of the advertisements aimed at white consumers in the 1970s, apart from one.

The *Fairlady* of January 1976 (five months before the Soweto uprisings) featured a black woman, heavily made up, wearing a feather boa, provocatively blowing smoke from an elegant cigarette holder while perched on a new Frigidaire washing machine. (That the brand contained the word "frigid", used to describe "sexually unresponsive women" back then – why not ply them with beer? – is remarkably Freudian.)

"When I bought my wife the Frigidaire it did something to our maid," trumpets the main tagline, followed by smaller text: "Now she insists on only wearing Yves St Laurant [*sic*] fashions when working with our new Frigidaire twin-tub washing machine. She says it is because the Frigidaire has been quality tested to the exacting standards of General Motors Corporation America and backed by the best after-sales service throughout South Africa. Wonder where she got that from? It's true though."

The entire freak show was end-noted with "Good Taste starts with Frigidaire".

Fuck political rights. Give maids a new washing machine.

To point out this insanity was to risk being labelled insane oneself. If only I had, at this moment, been able to hold onto Yuri Gagarin and his space flight and what it represented about a better future, it might have made living through this era slightly less torturous and scarring.

With an outer life pollarded and constrained, one could only travel inwards, away from it all. And thus I separated my mind from my body and the physical space in which it found itself. That brief moment of connection with Kathy became a distant and much cherished memory

that would lead to a lifetime of tending towards blissful limerence –
"a state of mind which results from a romantic attraction to another
person typically including compulsive thoughts and fantasies", according to Wikipedia, that is.

My imagination would become my safe space, my internal panic
room. Here I could conduct a silent monologue while life and the world
unspooled itself in front of me. I was in it, but not really. I was playing
a bit part. I would keep placing one foot in front of the other and see
where it took me.

And so it was that I found myself pinned to a chair in front of a
dressing table, my short hair being rolled into curlers. This was proving
to be an out-of-body experience. I thought of Frank-N-Furter and how,
in this light, I was beginning to look like him.

The occasion was my matric dance. This was an opportunity Barbara and Auntie Irene, her dear friend and wife of Uncle Perry, who
owned the shop, were *not* going to miss. They were going to savour
every moment. And savour it they did, with little triumphant whoops,
as if they had caught a mottled, dirty street dog and were now cleaning
it up and taking before-and-after photographs.

We were not allowed to wear "slacks" to the dance, and buying a
dress for the occasion was a comedy of errors in itself. My mother
jumped at the opportunity to spend "girl time" with her tomboy,
hoping that perhaps mid-shop I would discover my feminine self, if
only we found the right, flattering dress.

Truworths, a retail chain clothing store, was where we headed to
buy an "evening dress". My lack of enthusiasm did not dampen my
mother's as she fingered and pulled out an array of shiny dresses from
the rail. Finally, mutely, I pointed at a black one, which I reluctantly
tried on. Inside the change-room I felt like Quasimodo. My mother
parted the curtain and clasped both her hands to her mouth.

"Marianna my darling, you looka so beautiful."

"Mmm."

We headed for the checkout where Barbara set about shopping the
only way she knew. By attempting to bargain down the price.

"Now, thisa dress issa R80 [around R800 today]. But you looka at it. If I buy thisa material myself from da shop iss about R15. So I tell you I give you for thees dress R50," she explained to the young shop assistant, who stared at her nonplussed.

"Mom –" I tried to interrupt.

"Marianna, you keepa quiet. I do da talk here," she snapped back.

"But, Mom, this isn't Portugal. The price you see is the price you pay here. You can't bargain."

"Pah! You cana always bargain. Whata nonsense." She turned back to the assistant. "Hokay . . . I give you R60. Issa my last offer."

I wanted to run out of the shop screaming, "Beam me up, Scotty", only I didn't because we hadn't seen *Star Trek* on TV yet and didn't know it even existed.

"I'm sorry, ma'am, but you have to pay R80," the young woman insisted.

My mother glared at her as if she had just spat in her face. "Wella then I pay, but I tell you, theesa dress issa not worth more than R60," she said, handing over notes from her purse one at a time. She had never learned to use a credit card and quite frankly did not understand how a piece of plastic could be money, for God's sake.

We left with the dress folded neatly in a plastic packet. If I had possessed a tail, it would have been between my legs.

Now seated in front of the mirror, I surveyed the stranger looking back at me. My hair looked poofy and ridiculous. My lips were inanimate as Auntie Irene and my mother attempted to apply lipstick. My eyes, despite the blue eyeshadow, were lifeless.

Dennis Bruwer, a young Afrikaans boy who lived at the other end of the neighbourhood, was going to be my date for the evening. He arrived in a ridiculously small car wearing a beige suit and brown shirt. By then I had mastered the act of threatening to kill any boy or man who thought that our friendship was anything but platonic.

The only reason I had agreed to go to the dance at all was for the after party, where I would be able to discard my drag outfit and wear my jeans and a T-shirt and get blind drunk with Kathy and Marijke. Praying all the while that Kathy and I might kiss once again. Dennis discreetly left the dance as soon as it ended and I was free at last, back in my own world. I still have a photograph taken of us as we arrived at the school hall. I keep it hidden and seldom look at it.

Kathy, Marijke and I passed matric, with university exemption, which meant that should we want to further our education, we could be considered. Furthering my education, however, was the last thing on my mind in December 1978. Like thousands of other matriculants in the Transvaal (as Gauteng was then), we made our pilgrimage to Margate on the Natal north coast where we planned to spend at least a month smoking the best weed in the country, having sex (well, some of us) and partying from dusk till dawn.

There appeared to be no sense of urgency on my parents' part with regard to guiding me further in this new chapter of my life. Perhaps they had given up, realising I was not a child who could be guided in any way. And I don't blame them.

"I'm going to Margate on holiday with Carol and Andy," I informed my mother and father, and off we went.

Andy's identical twin brother, Eugene, joined us, no doubt hoping we would make a hot foursome, and we drove down to the coast in a battered old powder-blue Fiat. The month-long fun-fest in Margate stretched into two months and then three. And then I ran out of funds. I phoned my long-suffering father from a call box and asked him to send me money poste restante. He sent R70, enough to hang out for a few more days, pay the rent at the holiday cottages we had taken occupation of, with some left over for petrol for the journey home.

Kathy, in the meantime, had fallen pregnant. The father of her child was the first man she had ever slept with. She was nineteen. The last vestiges of hope that I had clung to were shattered. She could never be. Then straight out of school Marijke began working behind the counter of her mother's pancake parlour, which was in an arcade in the city centre.

With no real plans on the horizon, which left me stranded, I looked forward to doing nothing but plot the epic, exciting life I was going to make certain I would lead in a country that was, by now, regarded by the rest of the world as a pariah state.

THE BRANCH of Barclays Bank, 123 Esselen Street, Sunnyside, Pretoria, was not exactly an illustrious departure point for this epic life. But I was eighteen, it was work and I needed money. My monthly salary was R234 a month. It was a job I had wangled through a friend's mother who was a receptionist at the bank's head office. The white network. Apart from the tea lady, there was not a single black employee in the place.

There was nothing redeeming about the job. Certainly not the pale blue uniforms the women were forced to wear and that were designed, I suspected, to show off our cleavages; not the "air hostess" shoes or the Saturday mornings when we were required to work until 1pm; or every other day when I was confined to the cool interior of the bank with its cubicles and the constant soporific hum of machines spinning through wads of banknotes. Employees shuffled around wordlessly, carefully closing doors so as not to disturb the serious business of taking care of other people's money.

There were piles of it, so much so that banknotes eventually lost their strange magic and allure and were rendered ordinary, like sweet wrappers. If cash doesn't belong to you, it immediately loses its value. Some trusted senior staff member who had been anointed to look after the cash jangled a clump of keys and was trailed by a bevy of minions who would make sure that a wad might not accidentally find its way into someone's underwear or a secret pocket in your hem while unpacking and stocking the tellers' trays for the day.

Apart from depositing the odd coin in a money box shaped like a squirrel and handed out by the Allied Building Society in order to lure children back as clients when they were adults, I knew absolutely nothing about banking. This apparently didn't matter. My first department as a trainee would be Enquiries, which the accountant, Mr Lees, explained was where everyone quickly learned the ropes.

"But, Mr Lees, I don't know anything."

"That is why we put you on Enquiries."

This of course explains the early origins of bank rage which grew exponentially in the 1990s as these high priests of capitalism began to understand that it was they, and not the clients, who owned and shaped the world. The minute everyone had access to finance – not real money, in fact less than money: credit and massive debt – the playing fields were finally levelled, setting us up for the crash that washed cataclysmically ashore in 2008. In an instant, as governments bailed out banks "too big to fail" with taxpayers' dues, it was socialism for the rich and sado-capitalism for the poor and the middle and working woman and man.

If banks had existed in biblical times they would have featured in the apocalyptic Revelation. But here I was, an innocent in the belly of the beast.

About a week after I had started work, a man in a suit burst in. He was pink, sweating and out of breath. Someone had cut through the sunroof of his car and stolen his briefcase. Inside was his chequebook and other banking paraphernalia. He came straight across to Enquiries.

"How awful for you," I commiserated. "Have you called the police?"

"No, no. I need you to stop all those cheques," he said impatiently, frowning at me.

"Of course you do. Yes, one should do that," I replied.

How did one stop cheques? I didn't even know where to begin. And how on earth did cheques get from A to B anyway, from his chequebook back to our branch? There was no drawer or file in my mind that could be referred to. I peered at the piles of forms that wilted out of a perspex holder on the counter in front of me.

"Mmm. Let me see," I said, fanning through them. "No, this is a deposit slip. No, this one is a transfer slip and that's a withdrawal . . . mmm."

The man, understandably, became increasingly agitated, realising that he had obviously ended up with a lower-order primate. I sensed a rising aggression and, not wanting to exacerbate matters, I backed off towards Mr Lees's desk, in my fucking court shoes, conscious of my plunging neckline, to discreetly ask for help.

The job at Barclays lasted a year, in which time I was transferred to several departments. My favourite was the time I spent as a glorified receptionist because I got to operate the switchboard. Mrs Cornell, a fierce woman with piercing blue eyes and close-cropped grey hair, headed up the Ledgers Department just yonder of the shoulder-high navy blue partition that separated us.

It was a mind-blowingly boring job and so to liven it up a bit I would answer the phone in different accents all day long.

"Barclays goeiemôre, good morning" (Portuguese).

"Barclays goeiemôre, good morning" (German).

"Barclays goeiemôre, good morning" (high pitched).

"Barclays goeiemôre, good morning" (deep bass).

Another pastime would be to press several numbers on the internal intercom at the same time and listen in as confused voices on the other end tried to make sense of it all.

"Ja, you called?" someone in Savings would announce as I leaned in. If I had popcorn I would have popped a kernel in my mouth right then.

"No, *you* called me," the manager's secretary would reply, irritation rising in her voice.

"What *now*?" another discombobulated voice, this one from Waste Department, would chime in.

Folding bits of sticky tape and placing them on the earpieces of telephones was another way to while away the time. These were epic hours I knew I would never be able to reclaim.

Not surprisingly, Mrs Cornell had me moved. I was sent upstairs to Waste, the Siberia of the banking world. This was long before banking had been computerised and my job was to sort out all the cheques that had been deposited from other banks as well as write up all the debits and credits, and stuff all our own cheques into big plastic boxes that someone would come and collect later (at least I think that was what I was doing). At last I sort of began to understand how a cheque made its way through the world.

Once a day drones like me from other banks would all meet at the Bank of Athens up the road and physically swap cheques. I would give Trust Bank all their cheques, they would give us ours and so on. A trained hamster on Valium could have done it for half the price.

On the way back I would stop off at the corner café and play a few rounds of pinball, the cheques safely weighted with a bank stamp resting on the top glass panel.

"What took you so long, Marianne?" Mr Lees would ask sarcastically.

"So many cheques, you won't believe it."

"I don't," he would shoot back.

I made a few friends at the bank, the most memorable being the brother of a frighteningly efficient Greek woman who worked in the glamorous-sounding Foreign Exchange department. Her brother (who shall remain nameless to protect his adult integrity) was a gunsmith who drove a red Sunbeam Alpine sports car. He was a wiry, tense man, who wore a beard and carried a gun, cocked at all times.

What the two of us had in common was that we both loved Bob Marley and marijuana. We spent hours smoking, listening to music, and thinking about the oppressed while ploughing through bowls of delicious ProNutro with warm milk. We lovingly painted an enormous mural of Bob Marley in an outside room where we listened to "Exodus", "Babylon by Bus", "Kaya", "Uprising" and "Positive Vibration" with giant NAD speakers positioned so that we could lie on a mattress between them and "feel" the bass. I felt safe with the brother and knew he understood this was just a friendship.

During my Bob period Georg seemed to feature on the perimeter of my life. There were few exchanges between us. He seemed remote and preoccupied with his own world of work or the odd chores he would perform around the house, such as laying out his shoes in the sun on a Sunday and polishing them silently, or positioning yet another Persian carpet he had bought as an investment, only for it to be shat on later by one of our dogs.

It was Barbara, of course, who had to clean up the mess. This she did while keeping up a running monologue with Tiny, the dachshund carpet crapper, who would occasionally growl at her.

"You . . . you want to bita me now! But who iss cooking your food? Who iss cleaning up da mess. Iss me . . . You naughty dog. Go outside."

Our dogs were fed sheep lungs which Barbara would buy at the supermarket butchery. Once a week she would boil these in a huge steaming pot on the stove and the house would be permeated by the unpleasant reek of innards. It was a job she hated but someone had to do it.

With Barclays Bank proving a rather depressing dead end, I looked elsewhere for a new fork in the road and my mind began vaguely to settle on journalism. I thought it would suit perfectly my temperament as an observer. I could participate, only one cool remove from it all. I could not only witness what I saw but write about it and, hopefully, this way make a difference – although in what way exactly wasn't clear.

The Technikon in Pretoria offered a three-year course, two of them at the institution, and the third in a newsroom later on gaining practical experience.

Georg had suggested that I perhaps learn how to become a hairdresser or a secretary as these were jobs women could always fall back on if they needed to work. ("People vill alvays vant or need zere hair done," he told me.) He also seemed to place a high value on these types of jobs – grave-digging, hairdressing, typing documents. Someone would always have to do these things. Death was a constant; hair grew and would always need to be cut; bosses would always need women to do their typing. Maybe this was why I believed that Georg was opposed to the idea of me being a journalist, although later on I would come to understand that this wasn't true, that he didn't try to talk me out of it.

ENROLLING at the Technikon would come at a time when Georg had found a new, better job in Cape Town at Atlantis Diesel Engines. This required the family to relocate to Durbanville in the Cape. I insisted that I wanted to study and so I remained in Pretoria, staying with friends as the family migrated southward.

The new firm offered Georg a university bursary for one child only and my brother Albert, Georg reckoned, was the priority. Albert enrolled at UCT to complete a BSc and later an MSc in Geology. Because he was a man, my brother would, Georg believed, someday have to become a "breadwinner" while I, as a woman, would probably end up married and dependent on a man, a substitute father. No point wasting too much on an education for Marianne then. Of course, now that I am a parent I have come to understand that he might not have been able to afford it. It did not cross my mind then, so entitled was I to the idea, even though it had never been encouraged.

Barbara supported my push to study journalism and undertook to save money and send it as I needed it.

The high value and status attached to university education and my lack of this perched for many years like a large and intrusive chip on my shoulder. Later, when it was too late, when the juggernaut of life had swept me too far along, I undertook to educate myself. The reading that could not be done while I had been too busy living would come later as a young adult, when there was more time.

The journalism course at the Technikon was little more than an additional two years of high school, requiring rote learning and no questioning or rigorous debate. I was only one of two students in the class who spoke English. All our lectures were in Afrikaans, but I would take notes in English. Our political science lecturer urged us to ignore the "unfair" ranking of South Africa as an undemocratic country at the back of our textbook. No debates would be entered into on this matter.

For many years I clung to the notion that Georg had not supported my decision to gain a tertiary qualification. It is only now, in retrospect, and as I read through the letters he wrote me from Cape Town during this period, that I have realised, to my shame, that this was not necessarily the case.

A letter in his then still firm handwriting, dated Durbanville 25.05.81, begins: "Hello, my little darling!

"Mummy just told me that you, my darling, feel that we have already forgotten you, that we never write to you and so forth. Now I can only tell you how much we miss you and how much it hurts me not having you around! I have nobody to fight with as you can imagine. Anyway, may this be as it is. We, and especially I, miss you very much and if you would only obey my feelings, you would come home! But I know that you want to finish at the Technikon and it won't be too long anymore."

And later: "Now my baby, I will come to a close. I miss you very much and hope to have you here soon! I enclose R20 pocket money for you! Now lots of love, my Baby. Be good and write me also sometimes. Your loving dad who misses you tremendously. Come soon!!"

How then to recalibrate a fiction, a useful adolescent untruth that conveniently served to redirect my own confusion about my identity, my sexual orientation, the country I lived in, safely back onto Georg? In so doing, I of course got to play the untainted heroine of my own tale. How to backtrack and undo an essential component, a bedrock of an established personal world view and a relationship of over 50 years?

We truly do not see things as they are; we see them as we are (as observed in the Talmud).

And so it is too late now for me to tell Georg this, unless he's a ghost and is reading over my shoulder. We were, as our relationship evolved, both trapped in the other, which, while it bent and flexed over the years, never quite broke.

FOR MY FINAL YEAR in the journalism diploma I had to secure work at a newspaper. There was no network of media houses linked to the Technikon so in this you were on your own. I moved to Cape Town where there were a few options: the *Paarl Post* (Georg's suggestion), the *Cape Times* or *The Argus*.

Becoming a journalist in South Africa in the 1980s was about to shatter my assumptions that listening to Bob Marley and noticing a disjuncture between my life and what was out there somehow absolved me from being part of it all, having a part in it all.

If I had found a measure of safety and security in my own mind, occasionally leavened and anaesthetised by quantities of THC, I was about to encounter and bear witness to a ghastly reality others could not escape that easily.

TRUTH IS, I was like a village idiot with a messianic complex. I knew nothing. But even worse, I didn't know what I didn't know.

And so it was that I found employment at the *Cape Times*. I came to the job via a strangely circuitous route involving, literally, my ovaries. Since returning to Cape Town I had stopped menstruating, which was an utter relief in my mind, so I thought nothing of it.

My mother and I had long since had the talk, the one she promised to have with me after the lady in primary school had popped in with her Belgian ovary fountain chart. And a few years later, when I did begin to menstruate, I shouted for my mother from the bathroom.

She asked me to wait while she shot off. I could hear the creak of the brass hinges of the wooden kist in her bedroom. Inside the kist she kept all the "best" linen (the linen we never slept on) and a few private treasures, or so I thought. I heard her rummaging.

She came back to the bathroom a short while later carrying what appeared to be a hammock for a small marsupial. A long gauze hammock with a pink underside and two loops at the end you no doubt tied to the tree.

What do you mean it's not a hammock?

She dangled the maternity pad in front of me. It had been left over from when she had had to undergo a hysterectomy. Not one to waste anything, Barbara had stored the package, with its leftover pads, in her kist for a moment just like this. Fishing in her pocket, she pulled out a slack elastic belt with two plastic clips attached to two smaller strips of elastic that dangled off the main belt. Barbara secured the pad to the clips. The construction was now beginning to look more like David's slingshot.

Watch out, Goliath, I have my maternity pad!

She lowered the slingshot onto the tiles.

"You see, you putta thees on," she said, indicating for me to step in with my feet on either side of the pad so that she could secure the elastic around my hips. Only it reached my shoulders.

She stood back and shook her head. "Maybe ifa I cut it and sew it . . ."

This could not be happening. I would not be walking around trussed up in elastic with a canoe between my legs. There had to be another way.

"Tampons, Mom?" I suggested.

She glared at me.

"You never gonna wear dissa things. Issa not natural. It breaka your virgin."

And so, until I insisted that I buy my own feminine fucking hygiene products, a packet of Dr Whites would find its way into Barbara's shopping trolley every month.

But in 1982 I found myself mysteriously freed of tampons and being in synch with the moon and the tides. I was running on my own biological clock. Barbara found out because I had moved back home, was unemployed and I had not asked for pads or tampons for several months. I imagine her first thoughts . . . although she would have had to puzzle through who the father might be.

She asked, I explained, she listened and then made an appointment at the doctor. In the consulting room I was sternly warned that if I had not begun to menstruate three days after taking a course of pills I would have to be admitted to hospital for further tests.

Exactly how journalism entered the discussion I cannot recall. Ah, said the doctor, he knew someone at the *Cape Times*. This turned out to be Bob Malloy, the columnist who I later discovered was the ghost-writer for a weekly column purporting to be penned by the famous heart surgeon Chris Barnard. Give him a ring, he said, which I did, two days later when my body had re-synched with the universe. The threat of hospital had clearly jolted my ovaries.

The editor of the *Cape Times* was Tony Heard who, I noticed some time later, kept a surfboard behind his office door. I would take this as a good sign.

My interview, though, was with Chris Greyvenstein, the paper's congenial managing editor who, disturbingly, was a dead ringer for Jan Smuts. When asked, I naively replied that I wanted to become a journalist to "tell the truth".

"Ah well," he must have said, although I don't actually remember this, "that's good enough for me" . . . Maybe that wasn't how it happened but anyway . . . shortly afterwards I found myself working as a junior reporter on the city's most influential English-language morning paper.

I had just turned 21, hadn't had sex with anyone yet, and now I was in a new city where I didn't know a soul. But none of this mattered. I was about to embark on the career of my choice and had escaped the dreadful confines of "snor city", Pretoria, and it's over-abundance of white male civil servants who favoured this peculiar facial decoration.

As an investment, Georg had purchased a small bachelor flat in Senator Park, a newly renovated block in the city which squatted on the corner of Keerom and Green streets. It was a short walk from the four-storey offices of the *Cape Times* in Burg Street. The rear of Senator Park looked onto Long Street, which in the 1980s had not yet been gentrified and which featured a series of cheap residential hotels, their clientèle mostly poor and working-class whites who had drifted to the city.

It was a Rodriguez song in the making.

Playwright and satirist Pieter-Dirk Uys's play "Carnival Court" was inspired by the eponymous establishment with its Victorian broekie-lace balcony that offered a clear view, from across the road where Uys lived, into the tiny rooms with their handbasins which opened out onto it. The Blue Lodge buttressed Carnival Court and served as an anchor for local alcoholics who would congregate in its dingy bar while someone played some maudlin old tune like *Danny Boy* on a battered piano.

I couldn't wait to move in. From my window I would smell the faint odours of alcohol and urine and watch the passing parade in Green Street below. I was enchanted by these new urban sounds and sights. By day Cape Town was a jewel; by night it was down and dirty. My kind of city. And while Cape Town is regarded by many as possessing, in abundance, some of the world's most spectacular examples of natural beauty – sea, forests, mountains – these were not what beguiled me.

Give me sirens and asphalt, give me people and life, lights, litter and urban decay. And while the city was surrounded by both the cold Atlantic and warmer Indian oceans, these held no charm for me. The sea is nice to look at, that's all. Its constant, demanding and relentless motion, its routine excavation of rotting, stinking kelp, the sharp edges of crushed black mussel shells on its shore, or its overcrowded beaches with hot sand, hold no appeal. Its only attractive qualities are the insistent screeching of seagulls and the occasional banks of briny, clammy fog that roll in, enveloping the angular blocks of flats that still hunch over Sea Point's promenade.

In my new little flat I had everything I needed: my music, a hotplate, a kettle, a small bar fridge (Barbara sold a gold bracelet she had treasured and bought this for me with the proceeds), a mattress on the floor and a panoramic view of Table Mountain from curtain-less windows. What more could a girl want?

It was from my third-floor window that I heard my first snippet of an insult in shrill Afrikaans. It drifted up from the street and it was so deliciously disgusting that I wished I had thought of it myself.

"Jy's uit jou ma se hol gebore want haar poes was besig" (You were born out of your mother's arse because her cunt was busy).

At the time Senator Park also served as a home base for French engineers and construction workers who were in South Africa to complete the country's first nuclear power station at Koeberg on the west coast. These men, all separated from their families, regularly made use of the services of sex workers, and weekends were punctuated by much screaming, laughter and loud music. Using the lifts, one would inevitably encounter an inebriated Frenchman with a woman nuzzling his neck.

Georg set a rental that was about a quarter of my salary, which was about R500 a month. He believed this way I would learn the value of money, quoting, ad nauseam, from Charles Dickens's *David Copperfield*: "Annual income twenty pounds, annual expenditure nineteen [pounds] nineteen [shillings] and six [pence], result happiness. Annual income twenty pounds, annual expenditure twenty pounds ought and six, result misery."

THE *CAPE TIMES* newsroom was situated on the second floor of the building. It was an airless, green-carpeted, open-plan office. On each desk there was a typewriter and a telephone. A small globe on the telephone would light up when it rang.

I was one of the youngest cub reporters along with my colleague, Ronald Morris, one of only a handful of black journalists in the newsroom.

As I think back, the entire scene plays itself out in black and white, like a grainy silent movie from another age. How could there have been a time before cell phones and computers? How the fuck did we manage to work or get anything done? We typed out our stories on recycled blank pages using carbon paper to make copies. The news editor would correct mistakes with a red china marker before sending the story off to be subedited. Then it would be set in hot lead type by the setting department before being sent down to the printers in the basement of the building.

Just writing about the process now is exhausting enough.

It was a laborious and time-consuming endeavour that could only be borne, it appeared, through long boozy breaks at the press club, the Café Royal, around the corner. There journalists could be found drinking and chainsmoking almost 24/7 depending on which shift they worked.

With this technological disadvantage all we could manage was one or two stories a day. To get these stories, journalists had to actually step out of the office to cover their respective beats. There were three daily shifts at the paper – 10am to 6pm, 2pm to 10pm, and 10pm to 2am – and these would rotate depending on your beat. When we were out on a significant story we would stay in touch with the office through a two-way radio in one of two *Cape Times* vehicles with drivers and we'd often file copy from call boxes, dictating it to someone at the other end. For minor stories, such as a drowning or a fire, journalists had to request a "self-drive" – these were VW Beetles.

A few months after I started at the *Cape Times* the technological age dawned and all of the typewriters in the newsroom were replaced with a computerised Atex system. Clunky terminals and keyboards took up most of the space on our desks, with a few communal pods dotted around the open-plan office.

We were all given a crash course in log-ons, DOS, sending messages and how to save on floppy disks. Now we could type our stories on clunky keyboards and see them appear in front of us on bulky computer screens in lurid green print. And we could send them directly to the news desk. Even more miraculous was that we could send someone who was sitting right next to us a private message. While the news editor might look up and think you were working, you might actually be writing to a colleague, telling him what a huge self-important prick he was. You could also spend hours playing Snake or a slow-motion ball-and-bat game and appear to be writing the lead for the day at the same time.

Newsrooms were run like little military units – well, at least when it came to juniors. We were routinely shouted at and humiliated, mostly for some spelling mistake or for delivering tawdry copy. This, we understood, was apparently good for us. We had to be tough fuckers.

I had two sets of work clothes: two pairs of pants, two shirts and one pair of shoes, which I wore – in rotation, obviously – for about three years. My socks, however, could make it through a week between washes. Ain't nobody got time.

As a junior journalist I was immediately assigned, along with Ronnie, to the lower magistrate's courts, where it was believed our skills in patience and accuracy would be perfected and honed. And it was here, in the dark warren of corridors and wood-panelled courtrooms, that the full weight of the administrative havoc wreaked by apartheid would become horrifyingly evident to me. Here I would witness at first hand a daily parade of citizens in the dock who had fallen foul of a myriad of absurd laws. Apart from the usual tide of petty criminals, thieves and murderers making their first appearance, there were those who had been caught in the country's not inconsiderable political legal net.

These were not high-profile cases featuring well-known activists. They were nearly always poor women, with babies on their backs, who had travelled from the Eastern Cape to join husbands who had found work in Cape Town. Influx control laws rendered them illegal in the city, and the tired and bewildered women, who had been arrested as they stepped off buses, trains or taxis, would be herded into the dock, charged with contravening the Act, fined an amount they could not afford, and ordered by the magistrate to return to "your homeland" immediately or face a jail sentence.

The law was applied in a mechanical, industrial fashion, relentlessly and without mercy, the magistrate often offering a parting "I'm sorry, but you knew you were breaking the law" before the women would be ushered by a court orderly back down the stairs to the holding cells below the court. Those who could pay the fines would be placed on a bus then and there, which dispatched them back to the Transkei. Those who could not pay languished with their babies in the cells.

One morning a friend I had met through another court reporter suddenly popped up in the dock from the cells below. He looked hung-over, dishevelled and startled. He had been arrested for "soliciting" on the Sea Point beachfront the night before. Police would regularly entrap and gleefully arrest homosexual men who used the promenade as a cruising spot. My friend was relieved to see me in the press bench and mouthed that I should please pay his bail.

In the lower courts there was no escaping or denying the utter misery. All we could do was witness and record what we saw, and expose our white readers to this reality in the hope that it would serve to inspire outrage – locally and internationally – and at least some show of resistance.

Apart from the courts, we would also gain access to those places where the state ruthlessly applied the law, forcibly removing entire communities, firing tear gas into crowds, beating protesters with quirts. White journalists were prohibited from entering townships without a permit, which needed to be carried at all times. Being caught without one resulted in immediate arrest with calls to the newsroom and the paper's lawyers to have us released.

Vehicles marked with the newspaper's logo and cruising the townships would inevitably be visible, exposed, and journalists were routinely pulled over by armed police or soldiers enquiring what exactly it was they were doing there.

"You know it's dangerous here," they would inevitably offer in white solidarity. "And where's your permit?"

It was best not to engage but to rummage in a bag or pocket and produce the stamped and signed official document as well as your press card.

"Ja, okay. But you can't come in today. We're conducting an operation," someone would offer in another attempt to officially get rid of the crew.

You had to think fast, through and around what you understood was an attempt to get rid of the press from the area.

"Well, we're not reporting on that," we would lie. "We're going to the SHAWCO clinic to interview a doctor."

They knew it was untrue but there was nothing they could do.

"Well, be it on your own head if you get hurt. Just don't call us." This was usually their parting shot before handing back our documents.

But at the end of it all we were always able to extract ourselves, to leave and return to the safety of the newsroom or our homes, flats or communal houses, far away from the brute force of it all.

As juniors it was usually on weekends that we would find ourselves exposed to stories – crime, fires, accidents, enormous pumpkins grown in a suburban garden – outside of our regular beats. You never knew what would come your way.

One Sunday I was assigned to cover a story about a huge pile-up on the N2 highway. I rushed out with a photographer and we managed to push our way past the traffic and the fire and rescue vehicles. As I moved through the smoke I saw the first of two cars at the front of the pile-up. It was an open-topped sports car and inside were the charred remains of the driver and passenger, still smouldering, who had both horrifically burned to death. It was the first of many encounters

I would have with dead, mangled bodies. The scene didn't seem real, even though I could smell the burning flesh and feel the heat. The man's hands were still stuck to the steering wheel.

These transient encounters with death and corpses must have had an impact on my young mind, though I might not have been conscious of it at the time. I came to understand that human beings, particularly when it comes to crime and violence, including political violence, are capable of unspeakable horror. Just outside of what passed for ordinary life was a more brutal reality. It has always been there, sort of since we've been able to walk upright and wield a club or sharpened object.

The institutional culture of journalists working in stressed circumstances, including war zones – or police or medical personnel, who also witness and deal with unnatural death – serves to mitigate and contain the "real" emotions such as despair, rage, and confusion. You get back and talk about it as if it were happening somewhere else, as if you had not seen it.

Away from it all for me there was always music. Music and marijuana, or some alcohol. And then the camaraderie of fellow journalists and photographers. There was no sense that anyone might have required counselling or psychological intervention back then, and why should they, when the entire country needed therapy? For children, young adults or anyone in the townships there were no such existential luxuries. No containment apart from the love of family or comrades. While activism and politics and the solidarity it brought certainly held a collective rage and channelled it, the routine witnessing of corpses in streets or existing in a constant state of opposition to armed police and soldiers could not be escaped. Here there was little respite.

But the resolve and the energy of the fight-back, of the disruption of power, the determination to undermine it, was thrilling and inspiring.

For other work, one wore an invisible shield. In time I would come to cultivate the defence of professional detachment, particularly when it came to covering gruesome events. Murders, stumbling across the corpse of a raped elderly woman with her throat slit in her backyard, accidents where the casualties might be a busload of children whose small bodies lie strewn across a field or embankment – for these some

form of detachment was essential. Needing to take notes and ‚
tions was a distraction, a cover, from thinking about the loss o.
real people who lay beneath the newspapers or blankets that
their corpses. My notebook became my shield.

Outside of the routine application of apartheid to daily life, the
country itself was simmering. In fact it was enveloped in a low-grade
civil war. Not that you would have noticed it in cities and suburbs
until a bomb went off in a restaurant or a lift shaft. There was no
gunfire in the city's streets, newspapers and milk were delivered, people
went to work, children went to school – or not, when they were pro-
testing. But out there in the townships, out there was a different story,

That year, 1982, the country's townships were in a state of lock-down,
teeming with armed forces and police. Hundreds of black journalists
and activists were detained, banned and routinely tortured. The juggernaut of state transgressions seemed unstoppable. And because we were
young and stupid, we focused on what was happening in front of us, in
the moment. Our more senior colleagues, our editors and political
reporters, were those who were at the front line and engaging with the
wider currents of repression and resistance.

That year, while I had not been aware of it at the time, the news editor
of the *Sowetan*, Thami Mazwai, was sentenced to eighteen months for
refusing to testify in the trial of Khotso Seatlholo, a 1976 student leader
who had fled into exile in Botswana but who had re-entered the country
and been arrested and charged with terrorism.

Keith Coleman and Clive van Heerden of the Wits student magazine were released after five months in detention and then immediately
banned for two years. Police raided the offices of the *Rand Daily Mail*,
the *Sunday Times* and *Rapport*, and seized documents relating to a
coup in the Seychelles. That same year *Cape Times* and *Rand Daily Mail*
political reporter Anthony Holiday was released after serving a six-
year jail sentence on charges of terrorism. These were the journalists
who were really at the forefront of the battle lines. Not us. We were
preoccupied with the immediate minutiae of it all, but when we knocked
off, we went off to party and set about forgetting it all until the next
shift, and the next.

In March 1982 Nelson Mandela became prisoner 466/64 after his transfer to Pollsmoor Prison on the mainland and after serving eighteen years of his life sentence on Robben Island. Walter Sisulu, Raymond Mhlaba and Andrew Mlangeni were also moved with Mandela. No one inside the country, apart from his wife and family, had seen Mandela's face since 1964. His name, as well as that of Oliver Tambo, was mentioned only in the struggle songs we journalists could hear in the streets or at the meetings we covered at the weekends.

The political climate was toxic. It spilled over to neighbouring countries. At 4.30pm on the afternoon of 17 August 1982, exiled academic and activist Ruth First was blown to bits in her office at the Universidade Eduardo Mondlane in Maputo, Mozambique, by a letter bomb sent by Craig Williamson, a South African security policeman and one of the state's most notorious assassins.

In the same year trade unionist Neil Aggett died in police custody after being beaten and assaulted while in detention without trial for 70 days. Aggett was the first white activist to die in police custody. Also in the same year, ANC member Ernest Dipale became the 47th detainee to die behind bars. Dipale had, the state claimed, hanged himself in a cell at the notorious Security Branch headquarters at John Vorster Square. In 1982, 85 people were restricted under the Internal Security Act, 264 were detained and 87 had their passports withdrawn or refused.[4]

It was also the year that COSAS activist Siphiwo Mtimkhulu "disappeared", the year that Albertina Sisulu was banned for the fifth time, the year that three black journalists from MWASA were detained, and the year that bills restricting the media and refining definitions of sabotage, terrorism, subversion and communism, and "intimidation" were drafted. Newspapers that reported on detentions faced heavy penalties if the state believed these reports "endangered the state security". All white men between the ages of 14 and 65 were called up to the military, doubling its size.

---

4 https://www.nelsonmandela.org/omalley/index.php/site/q/03lv01538/04lv01539/05lv01573/06lv01576.htm.

In the *Cape Times* newsroom there was a small cabinet with four jam-packed drawers cataloguing the names of all the people who were either banned or listed and whom we were not allowed to mention or quote in our stories.

In other words, serious shit was going down, but for us this was how it was. This was life. And at the time it did not feel as if it would ever end. Each day would bring its own new horrors punctuated by strange delights away from it all. We lived in a fractured world.

WHILE OUT THERE revolution began to bubble and boil, I lost the precious virginity Barbara had feared would be claimed by Tampax. I was already 21 – halfway to being a proper adult, I reckoned – and if I didn't find someone to have sex with soon, I thought I might die unloved and unfucked.

Meeting someone, however, was proving a challenge. I knew no one in Cape Town and had slipped back into my childhood habit of cultivating extraordinarily close male friends. Most of the other court reporters, including Ronnie, became part of my entourage and we would spend our time outside work drinking, eating and cavorting about the city. When I was not hanging out with these reprobates, I was spending time with my less wayward new friend, the Natal Farm Boy, B. Deep down he was as much of a dweeb as I was. While B was slightly older than me (we shared a birthday) and had studied journalism at Stellenbosch University, we were both country hicks when it came to navigating and savouring the delights Cape Town had to offer. We were both sexual naïfs.

By some extraordinary fluke B had managed to secure a room in a cottage nudging the white sands of Clifton's Fourth Beach, regarded by those who were in the know as the Cape Town equivalent of St-Tropez. He shared the cottage with seriously trendy housemates, one of whom was a photographer who wore heavy black-rimmed glasses; another was a clothing designer. Being out-of-town innocents, neither B nor I had any idea what a desirable address this was in Cape Town.

Once, when B's housemate had been invited to a dress-up party, he left a note on his bed that read "Going to a Nerd party, borrowed some of your clothes".

111

B, like me, had a limited, practical wardrobe. Two tweed jackets, two pairs of smart pants and a few white shirts, and he wore the same shoes every day. He had a neatly trimmed beard and a polite exterior that masked a quick and wicked sense of humour. We both drove unreliable VW Beetles. Mine was yellow and his was lime green.

We stumbled through it all like two Forrest Gumps. B was as much of a voyeur as I was, and we found we were both capable of spending hours enthralled by even the most banal or uncomfortable of situations, including lengthy, obscure court cases we had sniffed out on the court roll. We would hang around theatre or gallery openings, watching and scanning the crowds, reading body language, looking at the art, learning things. We would attend social occasions and hang back. We shared a sense of humour. In fact there are few people today who are able to make me laugh as much as B could and still can.

He saw through it all.

Eventually B said he had had enough of journalism. He found it "humiliating", he said. Having to ask the family of a murder victim to point at the spot where their relative's body was found so that a photographer could capture it was undignified, intrusive and trashy. As was chasing ambulances rushing to the scene of accidents. After several years he bravely abandoned journalism and returned to farm sugar cane on his mother's farm. This he later gave up to pursue his true passions – he has many – of growing indigenous trees, designing websites and gardens, collecting art, serving on various historical bodies and becoming an expert on the history and the ecology of KwaZulu-Natal. Today he is the godfather to both my children.

Gay clubs in Cape Town were some of the few spaces that were not racially segregated. These clubs, while homosexuality was not yet enshrined in any bill of rights, appeared to operate relatively openly. Occasionally police would raid them, more because of drugs, and rustle up the homos and dykes into the street, but they seldom arrested patrons. They saved their hunts for the Sea Point promenade instead; specific units were dedicated to this most threatening of behaviour. When they did raid the clubs, the cops could always be seen laughing among each other at the sight of the "moffies".

At that time the Wine Barrel was *the* premier gay nightspot in Cape Town. It was in a seedier part of the city towards the harbour end. The ground-floor entrance led to a tatty bar, which was usually tightly packed with gay men marinated in the latest fragrances. A short flight of stairs led to a huge dance-floor area that permanently smelled like an old sock drawer thanks to the quantities of amyl nitrate, or poppers, everyone sniffed from small brown vials. The walls of the club were bedecked with giant mirrors in front of which gorgeously toned men would dance with themselves for most of the night. It was a distinctly male space and lesbians were begrudgingly tolerated because, well, we were all sort of family and we will *moer* you if you get in our way – or so at least we wanted the men to understand.

Once a month, around the back of the club, a sort of a pop-up lesbian "women only" bar would appear. Lives were planned around these events, but the clientèle would soon begin to thin out a few months later as women paired off and immediately seemed to move in with each other and cocoon, as lesbians across the world are wont to do.

On one of my after-work prowls of the city I came across a lesbian club, unmarked and located near the docks. This was before the docks became the Waterfront and a tourist attraction in democratic South Africa. Back then, lesbians were firmly divided into two distinct groups, butches and femmes. Inside the club, which was actually an empty room on the first floor of a building above a fast-food restaurant, women in suits sat clustered around tables at one end while women in dresses congregated at the other. I was, at that stage, part of a new androgynous breed of lesbian emerging out of the '70s, although I had no idea that this was what I represented. While I had enjoyed wearing my brother's clothes in the privacy of our home (and had not worn a dress since my matric dance), I felt uncomfortable dressed as a man. So I adopted a style that suited me. It was the '80s – please don't make me tell you.

The acting out of a heteronormative stereotype among the women didn't work for me. I found it stifling and difficult to navigate. I wasn't attracted to women because they might be butch or femme. I knew I would only be attracted to someone I liked. If I had a type, I was not aware of it.

That evening a woman wearing the universal alternative butch uniform, a checked shirt and a pair of velskoens, had put her back out while dancing. She lay on the dance floor writhing in agony while the owner summoned an ambulance. Before it arrived the owner took the mic in the DJ's booth and instructed patrons to please sit quietly and not dance when the medics arrived. "We don't want them to notice this is a lesbian club," she said.

The music was turned off and we all sat in silence sipping our drinks, waiting for the ambulance. When it arrived, two medics rushed up the stairs with a stretcher. They took one look around the club before scampering back down to call their colleagues. The men guffawed as they loaded the lumberjack onto the stretcher and carried her out.

After they had left, the DJ cranked up the music again and everyone drifted back to the dance floor, the butches politely asking the femmes for a dance. I left, certain I was doomed to never, ever, ever have sex. To be a dyke nun without even the comfort of a wimple.

Later, while visiting the home of another male colleague, Bester, a gorgeous, blond, blue-eyed apparition of loveliness, who worked for the Afrikaans newspaper *Die Burger*, I was introduced to a mysterious older woman. In a certain light she looked like Patti Smith with mousey curly hair which she wore like a rock star, casually unkempt and long. That night she behaved like Greta Garbo. While the rest of us danced and smoked it up, she lolled uninterestedly on a couch fingering a book. At some point in the evening a striking young woman arrived. She was tall and lithe, with short dark hair. And she was clearly angry. Angry and sexy.

The older woman shot up and the two of them disappeared into another room where they could be heard arguing loudly. I prayed that she would emerge and hang around, the younger woman that was, clueless as to the fact that they were mid-fight and that this would probably not end well. Shortly afterwards the young woman stormed out of the room and the house and crunched up the driveway. Another one bites the dust. I would, of course, not have known how to approach her. I was under the impression that those struck by an instant attraction would just sort of know it and want to immediately jump each other's bones.

She had not even seen me.

Shortly afterwards, the older woman began what I can only describe as a "wooing" of sorts. If she had been a male peacock, she would have been outside my flat door lekking. I would return home to find enigmatic poems in gorgeous Afrikaans pinned to my front door. My very own Ingrid Jonker. Flowers and gifts would arrive and, while I was flattered, I did at the time think she was ancient. She was 30. And I wasn't feeling it.

The harder I was to get, the harder Garbo played, which was all beginning to feel rather interesting, rather pleasant. This was it. If I was not going to die a virgin, then it was time to go with the flow. That I was an emotional halfwit at this point, Garbo was not to know.

The collateral damage of being raised, on the one hand, by a mother who loves one unconditionally, while dealing with a remote father, on the other, is immense. I had expected those within my orbit naturally to continue my mother's tradition of believing that I was indeed the most unique and amazing creature in the universe. Worthy completely of love and affection without doing much in return. Entitled and stupid.

The notion of reciprocity was not a state with which I was familiar (is it in anyone who is 21? I wonder) and when it came to romance I had the emotional range of a carp. *Weltschmerz* I could do. *Saudade* was my default. But allowing vulnerability to sully any relationship was, in my one-dimensional book, a weakness. My defences made the Berlin Wall look like a picket fence. My guns were all pointed outwards.

Besides, being exposed through my job to carnage, danger, blood, gore and violence rendered the personal needs and emotions of others, to my mind, somewhat obsolete or trite. Sort of "For fuck's sake get over it, out there people are dying".

While the poems and mysterious unattainable quality Garbo seemed to exude were intriguing, I had no idea how to actually relate. My male friends, no problem – we all had the same razor wire guarding our hearts.

But what really terrified me was, actually, you know, doing it – having sex.

The first and only description of lesbian sex that I had ever read and that was burned into my brain was in the Judith Krantz 1980 pulp romance *Princess Daisy* (pages 242 to 245 in the hardback, if you must know). It is a steamy scene between the character Vanessa Valerian and Topsy, and I have no recollection of their relevance to the storyline whatsoever.

Some of it reads: "'Fuck me, for God's sake – fuck me!' Topsy muttered, unable to endure anymore. Vanessa knit the three middle fingers of her right hand together, and worked them several inches up between those eager lips. Topsy strained upward frantically, and Vanessa, kneeling, bent again and took the girl's vulva entirely into her hot, avid, wide mouth, sucking rhythmically on the clitoris at the same time that she slid her three fingers firmly in and out of Topsy's vagina, sometimes only an inch or two up, sometimes as far as they could go."

Now that was something to look forward to. Avid mouths, eager lips, sucking on the clitoris.

The time was now or never. Hit me, baby.

On the Judith Krantz lesbosexmeter, the experience probably clocked a two and a half – for both of us. Fumbling, awkward, embarrassing – apart from the kissing, which was amazing. For me it was, to date, the single most disappointing and underwhelming experience, right up there with that lucky packet I ripped open as a ten-year-old only to find a slim harvest of pink sweets rather than the hefty handful I'd been anticipating.

Now if this was what sex was, I thought to myself, if this was the thing everyone in the world was gagging for, writing about in magazines, then it was all lost in translation.

The relationship with Garbo, which was turbulent to say the least, lasted about two years. The sex got better, and more intimate, but we were not a well-suited pair. I kept thinking about the Striking Young Woman I had seen the night I had first met the elusive Garbo. If I had not had a type then, now I knew what it was.

Garbo and I had a beautifully doomed and dramatic couple of years. It ended, not too well, when fantasy finally became a reality, and Striking Young Woman and I moved in with each other. This relationship lasted about a year.

Although I was now a fully fledged, well and truly fucked young lesbian, for the immediate future my one true and only love would be my work – the blood, the gore, the fear, the danger. It was here that I felt alive and connected. It was here that I didn't need to get close to anyone and yet I could still do my bit, as we all believed we were doing, for others, for the struggle.

It was through Garbo, however, that I was to encounter someone who would later come to play a significant part in my growth, my trajectory towards becoming a human, my adulthood of sorts. It was while Garbo and I were enmeshed in our turbulent silent movie that I met the enigmatic and peripatetic Afrikaans Philosopher, V.

V was the fiercely intelligent daughter of a diplomat. She had grown up in Europe and this rendered her exotic in this arse-end of the world where few managed to escape and breathe the exhilarating air of freedom elsewhere. With her piercing blue eyes, intelligent hawk-like gaze and rudimentary wardrobe, V moved through our circles like a revered sage. Like an expensive label, she had lived in Greece, Germany, Paris, New York, London and Belgium, relying mostly on the kindness and generosity of others. In a photograph of V taken at the Acropolis in 1979 she can be seen wearing a pair of checked blue chef pants, sneakers and a hippy blouse. In 1985 she posed there again, still wearing the same outfit. She seemed to have no fixed employment, although I suppose there were hardly permanent positions available anywhere for someone with her skills. Her diet, too, was cheap and simple. Lentils, rice, vegetables.

She travelled often, and it was while she lingered in Paris rolling her own cigarettes and hanging around health shops that she had encountered the Canadian Writer, C, who at the time earned a living as a magazine and fashion ramp model. Drawn to the city by the writings of Henry Miller and Anaïs Nin, C was determined to escape her small-town upbringing and travel the world while on the way to becoming a literary star. V, who was difficult to resist, had convinced her that South Africa was an ideal and fertile destination for just such a budding scribe, and we eagerly anticipated C's arrival.

Being beautiful could be viewed as a curse, a disadvantage, in the world of cut-throat and rudimentary feminism that began to blossom and grow in Cape Town in the early 1980s. I was an organic feminist. I found my eyes glazing over while reading tomes like *Sleeping with the Enemy* by feminist separatist Robin Morgan or the works of Andrea Dworkin.

Feminist theory I could not do. It was its practice that mattered most to me.

C duly arrived, regal, elegant and eccentric, but with a mind not fashioned, shaped or impaired by near-sighted racial separatists. In truth she was a breath of fresh air in a country racked by sorrow, fear and danger and punctuated with occasional bursts of what appeared to be ordinary life. To us, she sounded like an American. We didn't have many visitors from across the shores around these parts, apart from the odd journalist or an Eminent Persons Group. They all came and then left. South Africa certainly was not a preferred global holiday or relocation destination back then.

But here was this strange, interesting and interested new person. And she regarded us with the sharp gaze of a writer who found herself suddenly in a landscape as complex as it was simple, as brutal as it was gentle. And besides this, she thought "second-wave" feminist Erica Jong's *Fear of Flying*, with its notion of the "zipless fuck", defined a brave new form of autobiographical writing. And because she thought we were interesting, we believed that we just might be interesting too.

It was C who brought to our small patch of earth a new way of regarding ourselves. She had had a colourful past in her home country as a model and a topless dancer in a bar, hardly the kind of feminist pedigree we were accustomed to.

"A topless dancer, you have got to be joking."

"It was a vac job," she would explain.

"And the modelling? Please, pray tell. Allowing yourself to be objectified?"

"It's taken me all over the world. It's really hard, horrible work but I can earn enough to free me to write wherever I want."

C used words like "cunt" not as an insult but as a confident and matter-of-fact description of a vagina. It was she who introduced us to the uses of sexual fantasy at feminist meetings in crumbling Victorian houses in the "grey area" of Observatory.

"Write your fantasy on a piece of paper. We'll drop it in the box, pull it out and discuss it," she gently urged a group of us once.

Later, extracting a folded slip of paper from a box she read out, "I would like a motorbike" or some such interpretation of the word "fantasy".

What she had been hoping for, of course, was more along the lines of "I'm in a lift with a sexy older woman. It gets stuck between floors. She only speaks Mandarin . . . and wears a monocle."

It was all terribly exciting.

Unfortunately, she was also V's girlfriend.

But not for long.

The lesbian pond in Cape Town, in South Africa, was a shallow and murky one. If we could have procreated we would have all ended up being related one way or another. It was an alarmingly incestuous community. Everyone seemed, at one time or another, to have fucked everyone else. And they all remained good friends afterwards, playing topless darts and Scrabble at each other's homes while plotting a way to slot into the struggle. This was not a pool into which to dive headlong if a girl wanted to remain anonymous and unknown. I vowed not to swim too deep in its tempting waters.

Georg and Barbara remained blissfully unaware, or so I believed, that their daughter was a newly initiated lesbian. Albert was moving between res at UCT and home in Durbanville while he studied. Georg was finding his way in a new job and Barbara was left stranded, friendless, in a suburban home in the middle of nowhere as far as she was concerned. I visited them on alternate weekends when I was not on a Sunday shift at the newspaper. Home always felt safe, safe but disconnected. I spoke to Barbara regularly on the phone but told her nothing of my life.

So HERE'S THE THING. You're a woman, you're gay, you're an immigrant. Pretty far out on the margin but not as far out as being black, or a lesbian and black. Or transgendered. And if being gay and black placed you in the outer tundra, being transgendered rendered you invisible.

But I was white, which in the '80s was all that mattered. This fact overrode all the others that might have rendered me marginal or oppressed. I could walk into a bank, apply for a home loan, show someone a salary slip and the money was mine (well, technically, the bastard bank still owned what I thought was mine). I finished school, I got a job, I studied. The road I trudged along – albeit believing myself to be an outsider – contained all the comforting middle-class markers. I could move freely between many worlds – straight, gay, professional, private, immigrant and versions of white South Africa – always with a sense of agency.

The black world was a parallel universe in which I was an occasional sojourner. There people had to keep fighting, finding ways, struggling, pushing back, staying alive. Reminded always. Resolved always.

Pieter-Dirk Uys once asked what the difference was between being black and being gay in apartheid South Africa. The riposte was that if you were black, you didn't need to come out to your parents. But it is, of course, far more complicated than this.

For me there was no need to come out. Georg and Barbara were accustomed to me, their ungovernable daughter. This was who I had always been. There was no need to tell them anything. I had never agonised about this. It was of no consequence for me. My colleagues and friends didn't seem to care one way or another, and if they did, I was too self-absorbed to notice.

Generally I lived openly, without fear, but there were always, in a deeply conservative, patriarchal and homophobic country, occasions when one needed to cultivate caution.

Years later, on a stroll on Sea Point's promenade, a girlfriend gently tried to take my hand. Up ahead I had spotted a group of men clustered around several bottles. They were animated, loud, clearly drunk and looking for trouble. And it came soon after one of the men had seen me withdraw my hand from my partner's. He broke away from the group and sauntered up alongside us, gesturing, talking at me. "Is jy 'n manvrou?"

I had plotted quickly how this conversation would play out. I would take it there and he would come along. The social coding contained in the encounter gave me the upper hand. I might have been a vulnerable gay woman but the trump card here was whiteness.

I stopped mid-stride and turned to face him. "Listen, if you want attention, then this routine isn't working," I said. "Besides" – and I gestured to my partner – "look at my girlfriend."

She shot me side-eyes.

"She's gorgeous, you have to agree. Now. Look at you. You're drunk, you're fucking toothless and you are aggressive. And you want me to be interested in you rather than in her?"

I could hear the little wires in his head fizzling and, as I watched, I could almost believe smoke might actually puff out from his ears. But it made sense to him. As I knew it would.

"Ja, now that's true," he agreed.

"Besides, you would not want to be married to me. Really. No hanging about with your friends here, drinking, causing kak. You'd be at home, mowing the lawn, fixing the roof."

Silence. Then, "Listen, my name's David. Come on, have a drink with us."

"You must be out of your fucking mind. But thanks."

He walked off, laughing.

"Where do you get the energy to do that?" my girlfriend asked.

"Self-preservation, the streets . . . I don't know."

POLITICALLY, during the 1980s Georg and I were at a low point. To my mind it was quite simple. The Nationalist government was illegitimate, violent and racist. Apartheid was the crime, not the struggle for political rights.

"Ah, you are just a hothead," he would charge on weekend visits home, when I would recount what I had witnessed in the courts or townships the week before.

Exposure to the reality of life for the black majority in the country set white journalists somewhat apart from many other white South Africans, those who were not politically engaged and who continued to live as if the civil war was an inconvenient obstacle, a rumble that could be contained and dealt with. Unlike these citizens, as journalists we could never say we didn't know. Generally the attitude among many whites was that the government, whom they seemed to believe and trust, knew what it was doing. The government understood who the real enemy was and would ensure that life, as we knew it, would safely continue.

Meanwhile, out of sight the Nationalist government was already attempting to arrange secret meetings with a still-incarcerated Nelson Mandela. In February 1985 Mandela had rejected outright an offer by President PW Botha that he be released under ridiculous conditions, including that he relocate to the Transkei bantustan. But in November the Minister of Justice, Kobie Coetsee, quietly met with Mandela after he had undergone prostate surgery at a clinic in Cape Town. This was the first meeting the Nationalist government had sought with Mandela and it would set the course for tentative further meetings for "future negotiations".

But the state was clearly feeling the heat, not only inside the country, which in the 1980s was in a permanent state of revolt, but also externally as anti-apartheid movements, trade unions, activists, artists and churches stepped up pressure. The country was economically isolated as sanctions began to bite. In August that year, three months before

Coetsee had approached Mandela on his sickbed, Chase Manhattan Bank had announced it would be making no new loans to South Africa. Other US banks began to reduce their lending to South African companies. Federal Reserve data indicated that between December 1984 and March 1985 there had been a 12 per cent reduction – from about $4.7 billion to $4.2 – in loans from US banks to South Africa.[5]

In reality it was money that was doing the talking, not some Damascene conversion on the part of the Nationalist government.

However, most white South Africans firmly held onto the fiction that black South Africans were somehow being used, that they were ciphers, mindless zombies or puppets of evil communists intent on infecting civilised, Western, Christian South Africa with their atheist, anti-capitalist propaganda. The ANC was the Soviet Union's "fifth column" in South Africa. Blah, blah, blah . . .

This was a view tacitly and openly shared by many in Western governments, including the UK, the US and France, particularly in the 1960s when these countries had used their veto in the UN Security Council to override decisions by the General Assembly to boycott or isolate South Africa. This support, as well as healthy economic relations with some of these countries, emboldened the Nationalist government and provided it with a sense of legitimacy, in its own eyes and in that of the white electorate.

I had never heard Georg say anything racist, and in fact his interaction with black South Africans, when these encounters occurred in his workplace or out and about, was always cordial, polite and decent. Later, going through his papers, I came across a letter to him written in 1980 from Phineas Kgwadi of 1688, Zone 1, Ga-Rankuwa. The occasion was my father's resigning from his job to move to Cape Town.

It reads: "Dear Mr Tham, you were very nice to me, you were like a father and a father is the one who loves and looks after his kids, one that always encourages and cheers them. You too were like that. I will not forget you and I will always think of you when I kneel down to

---

5 http://articles.latimes.com/1985-08-02/news/mn-5598_1_south-africa.

pray . . . I thank you for everything you have done for me until this time of parting."

I was not surprised by the letter. Black people, like women, Georg believed, while they deserved to be treated well and decently, needed the paternalistic protection and guidance of men like him. And while the system itself – of rendering anyone who was not white or male as Other or less equal – was firmly in place, one could, according to Georg, at least still be decent and kind. Ultimately, though, the white dudes in charge knew what they were doing. The government must surely be in control.

Georg believed this. I didn't.

"This is all very childish, Marianna. Ze government can't change ze country overnight. Zees people are not ready to govern. Look how zey burn zeir schools."

It was inevitable that at some point in these discussions I would accuse Georg of being a Nazi. Godwin's law. And that would signal the end of the conversation.

Barbara would remain in the kitchen and sit out these uncomfortable and awkward conflicts. I reduced Georg to a single political dimension positioned between two very concrete poles – wrong and right, black and white, good and bad. There was no grey, no subtlety. He was the enemy x 2. And if he and other white South Africans were on one end, I would be on the other.

It was easy to conceal my life from my parents – the three arrests for either being in an area illegally or for attending "an illegal gathering" during the State of Emergency, my girlfriends, my social life. Barbara would have been beside herself about the arrests, so it was best not to worry her, although there was no danger that I would come to any harm. Unlike some of my colleagues, I was small fry.

On 8 November 1985 our editor, Tony Heard, was escorted out of the building by Security Police to face charges of contravening the Internal Security Act after publishing a full-page interview with ANC leader-in-exile, Oliver Tambo. Like Mandela, Tambo was banned in South Africa and was prohibited from being quoted. That year there was almost a blanket blackout on reporting anything to do with "unrest". Of course the little hospital visit to Mandela was kept entirely secret.

124

That day *Cape Times* journalists took turns picketing outside the offices in Burg Street. We knew the Security Police were coming and clutched posters which read "We Demand a Free Press", "Who's Afraid to Face the Facts?" and "Hands Off Our Editor". I happened to be standing at the entrance when Heard was escorted out by Lieutenant Frans Mostert. Mostert was a ruthless sociopath who took particular pleasure in hunting down and assaulting local activists. One of these was former *Cape Times* journalist Zubeida Jaffer, who was pregnant when she had been detained a few years earlier. Mostert had threatened to force her to drink a concoction that would prompt a miscarriage.

The Saturday edition of the *Cape Times*, which carried the news of Heard's appearance in court, serves as a time capsule, a mutant insect wing trapped in amber. Alongside the story on Heard (and featuring a photograph of me holding up a poster) is the lead headline "Police Ban Conference on UDF".

"Hard on the heels of the banning of a meeting organised by 23 organisations to protest against the State of Emergency, police have banned an academic conference on the United Democratic Front and its role in South African politics. And in another development, a meeting scheduled for this afternoon in Atlantis has been banned by the magistrate of Malmesbury, Mr WA de Klerk."

The conference on the UDF, which was an affiliation of over 300 anti-apartheid organisations, was titled "The Future Is Ours. The UDF – Building a Non-racial and Democratic South Africa".

Below this story, another titled "Teargas Fired at School, 4 Held" and another, "Police 'Bring In' Van Eck, 7 Newsmen".

"Seven members of the local and foreign press and Progressive Federal Party MPC for Groote Schuur, Mr Jan van Eck, were yesterday stopped by police in Primrose Park before being escorted to Manenberg police cells. The journalists who were travelling in convoy from Manenberg Senior Secondary School, where there was reported to have been police action, were cut off by an armoured car at the corner of Ebrahim Way and Orion Street about 12pm."

The nuance of language was to avoid prosecution: " . . . stopped by police and escorted to police cells", when in fact they were arrested and detained. And we all knew what the term "police action" meant.

A story on page 11 inside provides clearer insight into the climate of repression and paranoia. Headlined "Alleged 'News Incidents' Listed", it read: "The Deputy Minister of Information, Mr Louis Nel, yesterday presented a list of six unrest incidents he alleged foreign journalists had been involved in . . . Mr Nel said he was satisfied that the government's action in barring television and other audio-visual crews in certain areas was justified."

In November 1985 police figures indicated that 799 people had died in "unrest" in thirteen months between September 1984 and October 1985. The figure was disputed by many – including the Detainees' Parents Support Committee, who argued it was at least 20 per cent higher. From July to November 1985, 3.4 people died in South Africa every day.

SOMETIME in the mid-1980s I graduated from the court beat and was appointed as one of two crime reporters for the *Cape Times*. It was a gruelling job, with long hours, but I felt up to the challenge. There were few women who had made the beat and I was determined to prove I was tough, as tough as the men, perhaps even better. Proving it to myself, of course, because no one else really cared. But I was not to know that then.

In an era before cell phones we all shared a "bleeper", which we needed to keep on during shifts either at night or at the weekend. B, Farm Boy, was promoted at the same time, as a crime reporter for his paper, but he soon asked to be moved.

The heavy bleeper, which clipped onto my belt, felt like a police ankle monitor and reminded me not to have too much fun on those weekends I was on duty. One minute you'd be having dinner with friends and the next you'd be hurtling out of town at high speed with a photographer to the scene of a horror bus smash on some highway.

It rearranged my internal neural architecture. The routine rush of adrenalin and dopamine gradually created a state of permanent hyper-vigilance, an unseen mental cicatrice I have never quite been able to shrug off. I missed it a few years later travelling in Canada where no one locked doors and women could safely walk home in the early hours of the morning.

One of the downsides of the job was the daily press conference at the Thomas Boydell building in Cape Town where the South African Police public relations department occupied a floor. Crime reporters from all the local papers attended a daily 9am conference where details of ordinary crimes, the names of victims and perpetrators, would be routinely read out. There we could ask further questions or follow up. But the pickings were generally slim.

For the real stories we had to cultivate our own sources. These were amateur radio enthusiasts who eavesdropped on police radio frequencies and who would tip us off, for a fee naturally; or an ambulance driver, a tow-truck operator or lower-ranking policeman taken in by the excitement of it all. Some of the male crime reporters would regularly attend social functions at the headquarters of the notorious Murder and Robbery Squad in order to "network".

It was not an environment conducive to my mental health so I broke the tradition. I would find my stories, if I could, without the help of the police. The further the distance, for me, the better.

I had now officially crossed over to the dark side – a space populated by corpses, killers, rapists, arsonists, robbers and outlaws of every variety. I once watched as a young armed intruder who had been shot in the groin and who lay alone in a street surrounded by police and journalists exhaled his last rasping breath while we waited for an ambulance. No one cared. People stood around kicking stones and talking on crackling radios, a step back from the dying suspected criminal. It was sad and depressing.

The job also included covering family murders, which was a unique phenomenon at the time and usually involved Afrikaans men who would wipe out their entire family before violently killing themselves.

Being a good crime reporter would inevitably require ferreting out information that fellow crime reporters on competing publications, particularly *Die Burger* and *The Argus*, could not. The scoop was what it was all about. This way your paper led on the story and you got all the glory.

Arriving one morning at one such family murder in the fishing town of Gansbaai about 170 km from Cape Town, I padded around the eerily quiet home peering into the bedrooms where a father had, only a few hours before, assassinated two of his children and his wife before blowing his brains out in a bathroom. Chunks of grey matter still dangled from the ceiling and clung to the tiles. One of the children, a young boy, had managed to escape and had frantically run to safety in the village nearby. The search was on to locate him and those taking care of him – for an interview, naturally. He had luckily escaped the circling vultures.

The mattresses in the children's rooms were swollen with blood soaked through from the single head wounds.

Police forensics had finished up at the scene and journalists were free to go about picking through the private lives of those caught up in the tragedy, scouring the home for photographs or clues that might explain the carnage.

A bloody handprint on the telephone perched on a low table in the entrance hall pointed to some anguished last-minute attempt at either summoning help or making a connection with the outside world. Whose print was it? It was impossible to imagine the cataclysmic struggle that had taken place inside the now-silent house only a few hours earlier.

Next to the telephone was the family's directory, which had been left open on the details for the family doctor. I scribbled the number down in my notebook before closing it, hoping to hide this nugget from my competitors.

Turning the reality of the tragedy into some sort of game, where clues are collected before you move on to the next level, was a method of creating an emotional distance from it all.

On days away from the crime beat we covered political meetings or hung around the townships, where there was always bound to be some sort of action, tear gas drifting, cops and soldiers itching for a confrontation.

With time, one dead body became much like another. Unreal. The perverse routine at every crime scene was acted and re-enacted in a macabre loop – invade the privacy of the dead, get a photograph (of

Left: My Portuguese Oupa, Manuel Romão Fernandes. He was left to raise five children when his wife, Maria Joana, died shortly after my mother's birth in 1925.

Below: Martha and Albert Thamm before the war, before life. This is the portrait that watched over Georg for most of his life.

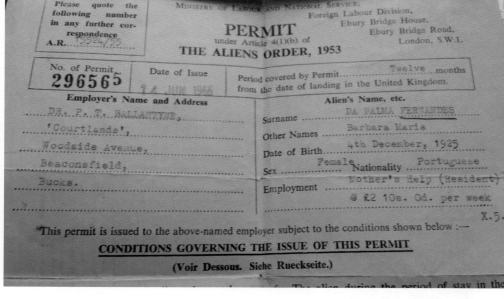

MINISTRY OF LABOUR AND NATIONAL SERVICE.
Foreign Labour Division,
Ebury Bridge House,
Ebury Bridge Road,
London, S.W.1.

Please quote the following number in any further correspondence A.R. 2224/55

PERMIT
under Article 4(1)(b) of
THE ALIENS ORDER, 1953

No. of Permit 296565

Date of Issue 14 JUN 1955

Period covered by Permit....Twelve....months from the date of landing in the United Kingdom.

Employer's Name and Address

DR. P. T. BALLANTYNE,
'Courtlands',
Woodside Avenue,
Beaconsfield,
Bucks.

Alien's Name, etc.

Surname ....DA PALMA FERNANDES

Other Names ....Barbara Maria

Date of Birth....4th December, 1925

Sex....Female Nationality....Portuguese

Employment....Mother's Help (Resident)
@ £2 10s. 0d. per week

X.5.

This permit is issued to the above-named employer subject to the conditions shown below :—
CONDITIONS GOVERNING THE ISSUE OF THIS PERMIT
(Voir Dessous. Siehe Rueckseite.)

Above: Barbara was one of many post-war Portuguese migrants to the UK. This is her work permit as a "mother's helper" and domestic worker.

Top left: Georg in his Luftwaffe service dress uniform circa 1943. The single gull on the collar indicates his rank as a Private.

Top right: Barbara circa 1955 looking like a movie star. She reckoned she looked like Elizabeth Taylor.

Above: Barbara's 1955 registration permit with the Consulate General for Portugal in London.

Left: Barbara in her favourite cerise dress, posing with our first car, an Opel – German make, obviously. Circa 1963.

Above: Georg the war pilot.

Opposite top: Georg in his Hitler Youth uniform.

Opposite bottom: Georg after the war and his release circa 1957 in a carefree moment, visiting his mother and sister in Berlin.

Dienststelle Feldpostnummer 26637 B.   Im Felde, 18. Oktober 1944

                    Sehr geehrte Familie T h a m m !

                    Ich habe die traurige Pflicht, Ihnen mitteilen zu
muessen, dass Ihr Sohn, der Unteroffizier Georg T h a m m , am 5. Oktober 1944 bei
Arnheim in Holland in Gefangenschaft geraten ist.
                    Die Kompanie befand sich an diesem Tage in einem
schweren Gefecht. Als die Kompanie wieder sammelte, fehlte Ihr Sohn. Soldaten, die sich
zu dieser Zeit noch bei der Kompanie befanden, wollen gesehen haben, dass Ihr Sohn in
Gefangenschaft geriet und abgefuehrt wurde. Sonst ist hier bei der Kompanie nichts
naeheres ueber den Vorgang bekannt.
                    Moege es Ihnen vergoennt sein, Ihrem Sohn eines Tages
wieder in der Heimat begruessen zu koennen.
                    Ich gruesse Sie in aufrichtiger Anteilnahme.

                                          Bohmer

                                          Leutnant und Kompanieführer.

Above: Georg and Barbara, gorgeous and happy, before kids and married life.

Opposite top: Tante Tuta in post-war Berlin. Picture circa 1962.

Opposite bottom: The letter informing Georg's mother of his capture at Arnhem in 1945.

Above: Me in 1971 aged 10, cleaned up for a professional portrait.

Opposite: Off to my first day at Capital Park Primary school. Albert being a caring older brother.

Above: Albert and myself in my early Antjie Krog phase.

Top: We've got hats, sandals and leather pants and you have not. This early encounter in our new homeland speaks for itself.

Opposite top: Family portrait with ears.

Opposite bottom: Georg being a proud dad in one of the first bleak blocks of flats we lived in shortly after arriving in Pretoria.

Above: Out on the job somewhere before cell phones and wearing the dreaded bleeper.

Top: Cape Times Crime Reporter with pipe. Circa 1983.

Opposite top: Our house in Burlington Avenue, Pretoria. Its walls contain 20 years of our lives.

Opposite bottom The popular Flying Saucer Road House between Jo'burg and Pretoria. I always like to think of it as the craft that brought us here.

Above: Eat dust, Marilyn Monroe – Kenya on Table Mountain surveying infinity and beyond . . .

Opposite top: With one half of my two soul brothers, Tom Lanoye. His partner René Los is the other.

Opposite bottom: Our gorgeous, talented children, Kenya (left) and Layla (right) with one of their gorgeous, talented mothers.

Me now . . . halfway to 100.

the victim/s or the scene), find potential witnesses, speak to neighbours, look for clues that might have been overlooked, head back to the office and write a kick-ass story before knocking off to have fun with friends and colleagues.

Finding and expressing tenderness inside of this carapace proved difficult for me, and this marred many of my relationships. Letting down the guard would render me vulnerable, without skin, without armour. And the energy and effort required to keep wearing the armour was less than that required to remove it.

IT WAS WHILE I was on the crime beat that my mother suffered a mild heart attack, which would later lead to her debilitating stroke. Georg was abroad on a business trip and my brother was a student at UCT and living at home when Barbara phoned me at work. She had been suffering for some time from terrible nosebleeds. She refused to take "Western medicine" and we would often find containers of un-opened pills for high blood pressure or diabetes.

Barbara was unhappy in Durbanville. She had found herself un-tethered by the move to the verdant and sprawling suburb which back then was decidedly rural. Without a car she was stranded in a new home that she had had no part in choosing. She spent her days alone with the dogs, or with my brother when he was home studying. Suffocating in the routine and out of desperation, one day Barbara uncharacteristi-cally left home on her own and walked to a corner café about six long blocks away to ask the Afrikaans owner whether he might know any-one who was Portuguese.

It so happened that a baker in Kraaifontein, who supplied pies and cakes to the café, was in fact Italian. Portuguese, Schmortuguese. Barbara left her number anyway. A few weeks later the Italian baker called, no doubt curious.

It must have been difficult for Barbara to make contact with strangers, particularly men, and this small interaction points to her frustration and loneliness. But through this reaching out Barbara was able to meet the baker's wife and her neighbour who, it turned out, was Portuguese. These two women became the only intimate friends Barbara made in the Cape. They would often collect her to spend the day with them at the bakery, where they would drink tea, play cards and gossip.

Because she had worked as a nurse Barbara understood that the tightening and sharp pain she had felt in her chest that morning had been a mild heart attack.

She called to tell me.

"Marianna, I think I hava heart attack today. But iss okay now," she said.

"No, Mom, you have to go to the doctor immediately. I'm making an appointment and coming to fetch you."

The local GP did an ECG and immediately advised that Barbara be admitted to ICU at Tygerberg Hospital for close observation. "There could be a clot somewhere," he told her. "We have to make sure you'll be all right."

My mother wasn't keen.

"But Georgie is not home. I musta cook for him and puta food in the freezer. Is coming back today and I not there. And what about Alberto? Who is going to looka after him?" These were her first concerns.

Barbara insisted on stopping off at the grocery store to stock up on food for the men in the house. Then we drove to the hospital. She was afraid and nervous.

"Your father issa not going to believe me," she fretted.

"Stop worrying," I told her when we got to the hospital. "I'll fetch him from the airport and we'll come straight here. You have to rest now and just relax. The doctors will look after you."

"I donta wanta to have a stroke. I would ratha die," she said, prophetically, as it happened.

While she was being admitted to Tygerberg Hospital my fucking bleeper went off. I had to find a payphone, call the office and tell them I was currently indisposed.

Barbara was immediately taken to ICU and hitched up to various machines. I waved goodbye through the glass, telling her I would be back soon with Georg. Later that evening I collected my father from the airport. He grew quiet at the news and when we arrived home immediately called Barbara in the ward to enquire if there was anything she needed.

"Kentucky Fried Cheeken," she replied.

We bought a small meal at the KFC in Voortrekker Road in Bellville en route to the hospital. Barbara looked afraid. She had never not spent a night in the family home. I slid open the drawer of the hospital bedside cabinet and spotted two loose Ransom Select cigarettes rolling about.

"Mom, you can't smoke now. Or here!"

"Just leave it," she ordered.

We left the food. It was getting late and a bell indicated that visiting hour was over. I kissed her, told her I would be back the following day and said that she would probably be home soon.

The following morning my father called in tears.

"Mommy had a massive stroke last night. She's in a coma. Come to ze hospital."

B ARBARA LAY SILENT and unreach-
able. For three weeks she lingered in a coma in a general ward at Tygerberg Hospital. Between shifts I would try to coax her out of it, passing
on news of Georg or Albert or the dogs at home, asking her to squeeze
my hand if she could hear me. Nothing.

There were no prayers at her bedside, although she might have
welcomed them.

I do not believe in a god. I arrived at atheism through religion, specifically Roman Catholicism. It was a route, I was thrilled to learn later,
highlighted by Slovenian philosopher Slavoj Žižek, who pointed out
that on the cross Jesus himself implores: "My God, why have you for-
saken me?", proving that Jesus had clearly been expecting a different
outcome.

As Georg later suffered through the last three months of his life,
shifting half a metre from his bed to a vinyl upright chair, I understood
differently what the crucifix that hung in his room came to mean to
him. Jesus and the Via Dolorosa brought deep comfort to my father.
If Jesus suffered so, then I, too, can bear it.

While friends said prayers for Barbara, I could not. I waited while
she remained suspended and out of conscious reach. The prognosis
was not good. The longer the coma, the greater the possibility of severe neural carnage – brain damage.

For three weeks I shuttled between the office at the newspaper,
Barbara's bedside and Georg's house in Durbanville. Somewhere

in the abnormal bustle of this, my visits and Albert's did not seem to coincide. I have no recollection of him in the tragic hospital tableau.

And then – good news. Barbara had surfaced. She was gradually assembling and restoring what she could consciously locate or recognise in the debris of her mind. While she noted our presence, she still seemed confused. But at least she could tilt her head and suck from a straw and even swallow food when spoon-fed. Her right arm, however, lay motionless on the white bedding.

Soon she was discharged and admitted to a rehabilitation unit, where it was hoped she would gradually regain some semblance of speech and movement.

When I arrived for a visit one day, one of the nurses pulled me aside.

"Look, I think you have to accept that your mother has suffered serious brain damage," she said. "She's sitting up but doesn't seem to respond to anything we say."

I had a notional understanding that often those who have suffered brain trauma, particularly a stroke, or who are in mental distress will find expression or reach for a comforting and familiar mother tongue, that language which whispers through the womb, past a budding ear and lodges somewhere essential.

Barbara smiled when I entered accompanied by the nurse. Searching my own hard drive for fragments of my mother's mother tongue, all I could retrieve was an old song she had once taught me about a sea plane that had run out of fuel and crashed in the desert. Later someone finds a small suitcase buried in the sand.

It went, "*Olha à mala | Olha à mala | Olha à malinha de mão | Não é tua nem é minha | É do nosso hidroavião*" (There! A suitcase. There! A suitcase. There! A small suitcase. It is not mine. It is not yours. It belongs to the aeroplane).

When I sang it, Barbara's eyes danced. Then she burst into tears while we embraced.

The song had made sense. She was not entirely beyond reach.

"*É tudo ok agora. Nós vamos te levar para casa*" (It's all okay. We're going to take you home).

And then she tried to speak.

133

"Gethagetha."

"That's what she's been saying all the time," said the nurse. "What does it mean?"

"It's not a word."

"Gethagetha, gethagetha."

And that was it. From then on, this was just about all my mother could manage, along with a few "ai, yai, yai's". For the rest of her life this came to mean nothing and everything.

Georg and I prepared to move her back to the house in Durbanville, still hopeful then that in time she would recover. Albert had returned to res to complete his studies away from the upset and new routines of the household. Barbara seemed relieved to be going home but was clearly frustrated and confused that she could not walk or use her right hand. She was brought home in an ambulance and carried on a stretcher to her bedroom.

Georg took early retirement to look after her. He was certain he could manage this, he informed me. Georg had bought all the medical supplies and equipment required, a bedpan, a semi-circular plastic food guard you could attach to a plate so that you could eat with one hand, a brace to support her rigid right leg and another for her wrist, to stretch the now-withering muscle.

The first few weeks were hellish as Barbara gradually began to understand and grasp what had happened. She was furious and frustrated at not being able to move or do anything for herself and needing to rely on Georg for everything.

Inevitably, she slumped into a deep depression and spent much of her time sobbing or sleeping, refusing to eat or get up. I recalled her comment to me as we had driven to the hospital after her heart attack that she would rather die than survive a stroke. Watching her suffer was heartbreaking.

It was taking its toll, too, on Georg. He had underestimated how much care she would require and also how difficult it would be for her to adjust. And, for the first time in her life, she took her frustration out on him. Thirty years of frustration and misunderstanding, of talking at cultural cross-purposes. Thirty years of sublimated self came bubbling forth.

134

Georg would set a plate of food in front of her, only for Barbara to hit it angrily away, sending the plate crashing.

Mostly he was patient, but being trapped in the house with an angry wife who did not seem to be willing or able to make any progress could not have been pleasant for my father. I watched as he helplessly tried to make up for all the times he had been remote, cruel or undermining. Their marriage, from my perspective, had over the years seemed clinical, sterile, practical. I seldom saw any affection between my parents. They slept in separate rooms (my mother shared a bedroom with my brother during his childhood). Barbara was a housewife; she fed us, fixed our clothes, cleaned our house, took care of us. That was her role. Georg was a breadwinner – seldom involved in the domestic realm. They were two adults doing what they thought they had to do. Marry and raise kids. They seldom argued, but that might have been because Barbara did not demand what she might have needed.

Now there was a quality of atonement to the manner in which he tried to care for his wife.

His friends who visited would remark, out of Barbara's earshot, how saint-like Georg was in looking after her.

"Most men his age would divorce her and move on," some would comment.

Really?

Much later I would think of Georg and Barbara when the time came for me to take care of him.

Over at the *Cape Times* I had begun to feel like an extra in a low-budget television series, each episode playing out a riff on a theme: a killing, a hunt, an arrest, no arrest. Somehow, at the paper, we had ended up distinguishing between political and criminal murders, blurring transgressions and taboos.

Criminal killings in Cape Town, murders particularly – deliberately plotted and those regarded as crimes of passion, including "moffie murders" – apparently intrigued readers, as such stories do almost everywhere in the world.

Like everything else in this abnormal society, murder was compartmentalised. Gang killings were, well, gang killings, of little interest to middle-class readers who believed themselves isolated and insulated from the ganglands. Political murder was state-sanctioned violence, so that, too, happened in a realm apparently divorced from everyday white life. Political killings made separate news. These were elevated in importance by accompanying condemnatory editorials, commentaries or analyses.

But it was "common murder" that provided, it was believed, front-page gold. These were what drove sales up, prodding and feeding middle-class anxiety and a notion that while life might seem orderly in the suburbs, although random and unpredictable, a crime like murder could happen there too. "Could this have been me?" was perhaps the unconscious morbid traction.

It was while Georg and Barbara were locked in a painful new embrace in their Durbanville home that I was to find myself finally free of the crime beat.

Late afternoon one of my contacts (well, Paddy the police radio eavesdropper) called in a murder. Paddy recited the address over the audible crackle of police radios. It was No. 1 Amanda Street, Amanda Glen, Durbanville. This was my parents' address. I calmly thanked Paddy and immediately called the SAP media officer on duty to confirm it.

"Ja, it's right. How the bladdy hell did you find out, man? Anyway, see you there," said Captain Van Rooyen breezily.

A senior officer was usually dispatched from the media head office in Cape Town to deal with the little swarm of reporters who would inevitably all be rushing to the scene, tipped off by the promiscuous Paddy.

As I grabbed my notebook and bag, I called out to Robin Parker on the news desk that there had been a murder and that I was going out to cover it.

"I think it might be one of my parents!" I shouted, rushing past him to exit through a back door that led down a stairwell to the garage in the basement.

Robin looked up wide-eyed, his mouth moving silently like a carp as he struggled to find a suitable or appropriate response, but I didn't wait to hear what it was.

I raced along the N1 with the most astonishingly detached thoughts rushing through my head.

I wonder if it's Dad or Mom. And I am not letting any of the other journalists into the house. This is my scoop.

I postponed feeling anything until I had turned into Amanda Street only to spot Georg standing in the driveway outside our house.

(Oh god, it's Mom!)

I leapt out of the car, now propelled by real anxiety and shock.

"What happened?"

"It's terrible, Marianna. Ze neighbour zere in Amandel Street vas murdered inside ze house. Zey sink it vas ze gardener."

Amandel Street. Had I heard Paddy incorrectly? The two streets did sound the same.

The relief I immediately felt was soon overwhelmed by my need to scoop *Die Burger* and other reporters who I knew were on their way. I was here first. Time to mop up.

Back at the office later, Robin summoned me to the news desk. He ushered me into the glass bowl of the editorial conference room behind him.

"What the fuck was that?"

"It's fine, man, it's over. I thought it was one of my parents," I tried to reassure him.

It was time, said Robin, for a break. I was moving to the Arts department.

"The Arts department! But I'm a cultural philistine!"

"You'll learn."

It was Barclays Bank and the Enquiries counter all over again.

In the long run, however, I had been given a gift. The Arts department would lead me to what has remained a great love, the theatre (and music, photography, film, fine art). Being an arts reporter was the perfect antidote to the years of blood, guts and horror. The arts would eventually come to restore and nourish me. But at the time, recognising how little I knew, I plunged into educating myself.

The change of pace and the exposure to the brilliant creative minds grappling with the society we lived in felt like an extended holiday. The Arts department opened the door into a magical creative realm where the chaos and pain of life outside was somehow pummelled and shaped into something else, something new, something transcendent. It was where meaning was made of the meaningless.

Through this new "beat" I came to see acting greats like John Kani and Winston Ntshona in seminal "protest" works like "The Island" and also their enduring collaboration with Athol Fugard, "Sizwe Bansi Is Dead". I watched a young Mbongeni Ngema's "Asinamali", writer-director Barney Simon's various dazzling creations, including "Black Dog-Inj Mayama" and "Born in the RSA". I watched the visual and literary genius of theatre makers like Marthinus Basson. I listened live to the music of Vusi Mahlasela and Louis Mhlanga, Amampondo, McCoy Mrubata, Johnny Clegg and Sipho Mcunu's Juluka, Jennifer Ferguson, Amanda Strydom, Johannes Kerkorrel, Koos Kombuis, Brenda Fassie, the Genuines, Duke and Ezra Ngcukana and many, many others. And I met, in person, the man who had brought sanity into my young life in Pretoria, Pieter-Dirk Uys, in various of his performances throughout the 1980s. I had a ringside seat to the creative explosion that occurred in the midst of the terrible repression. It left an indelible impression and love of the arts. Later many of these artists were to become friends.

As the year wore on Barbara still made no progress. She refused to try to walk a few steps, even with her right leg clamped in a plastic brace for support and a medical walking stick offering further security. Her doctor eventually recommended she be placed somewhere where she could receive intensive and constant care and stimulation. It was hoped that here, removed from the debilitating emotional loop between her and my father, she might regain some strength both mentally and physically.

The Chris Heunis Home in Somerset West was a two-storey building, its exterior reflecting the soulless institution it was. My father sold the house in Durbanville and moved closer to his wife. Albert spent large chunks of time "out in the field" as a budding geologist chipping at rocks and stones and would visit whenever he could. Georg bought a small cottage around the corner from Barbara, where he settled in with his two tiny dogs – Dolfie (short for Adolf) and Paisana (vaguely Italian for "hail, countryman") – whom he enjoyed walking in the local park. Dolfie, however, met with a swift and bloody end shortly afterwards when a Giant Schnauzer, which belonged to a fellow German resident, mistook the smaller dog for a rodent and shook him, snapping his neck instantly.

Georg would visit Barbara daily, playing endless rounds of the Portuguese card game Bisca with her and feeding her bite-sized, thoroughly processed chicken nuggets dipped in a sweet chilli sauce. With time, Barbara seemed to overcome her fear of walking and managed, with the aid of a Zimmer frame, to slowly pace out the passage outside her bedroom door, Georg walking patiently beside her.

It was clear that it was better for both of them that Barbara remain there, that this was to be her new home, but Georg could not bring himself to make the decision. So I made it for him.

"Dad, you are still healthy, you're young and you're around the corner from Mom. You can come and see her every day and stay as long as you like. You will have some respite from it when you go back to your own home. Mom is safe and warm and cared for around the clock. Maybe later, if she gets stronger, she can come and live with you again."

Barbara listened impassively as I explained. I asked her not to resist the physiotherapist and speech therapist and at least to try.

"When you can walk and move around a bit," I told her, "you're coming home."

But she never did. She settled into a tedious life of institutionalised routine. Up in the morning, sit in the sunroom, play cards, drink tea, eat chicken nuggets, ask to go to the toilet, watch some TV, shower, get wheeled back into your communal dorm.

Did she feel contained and safe here, leading this small life? Barbara had always been anxious in public. We'd often have to locate emergency buttons on escalators in shopping malls when she would suddenly panic as she stepped onto one of the moving stairs. Journeying into Cape Town, she would need to stop off every 20 minutes to use the loo.

And so it was that both Georg and I comforted ourselves that Barbara made the choice now to remain a patient in an old-age home. It was a place with which I became intimately acquainted.

The daily routine would be disrupted occasionally when some do-gooder would arrive and pound the piano in the sunroom, hoping to entertain the "old folks". It was either that or they were forced to play Bingo or carpet bowls. There was some occupational therapy too and Barbara managed to weave a handbag with her functional left hand, which she proudly presented to me on my birthday.

Mostly, though, she sat and waited.

I was able to relieve my father most weekends and at first, I hated it. I resisted it with every fibre of my sometimes hungover being.

The 40-minute drive to Somerset West from Cape Town was not without its own risks and hazards. The N2 had for years been the locus of random protests, with stones, bricks and even petrol bombs crashing through car windscreens. The criminal element, ever receptive to opportunity in chaos, set up the occasional ambush – laying chunks of concrete across the highway and attacking those motorists who were forced to slow down to avoid them.

Early one Saturday morning a hairdresser returning to Cape Town had been severely beaten and robbed in one such highway robbery. I knew I had to travel the same route a few hours later and that if I didn't do it, I would always be consumed by fear.

I called Georg to tell him about the attack.

"Dad, there was an attack on the highway last night."

"You must buy a cheap blanket and a pair of safety goggles," was his response.

"Um . . . why?"

"Well, ze goggles are to protect your eyes if ze windscreen shatters and if a petrol bomb comes through and you catch fire zen you must stop, jump out, wrap yourself in ze blanket and zen roll in ze sand. If you vant more safety, zen buy a motorbike helmet and wear it in ze car."

This all sounded perfectly reasonable and I immediately set about procuring Georg's suggested counter-criminal measures. Driving through later in the day, I was much comforted by the blanket neatly folded on the passenger seat, even though the skiing goggles I had managed to borrow from a friend when I could not find a pair of safety glasses were a tad uncomfortable.

That neither Georg nor I had thought to avoid the stretch of road until matters had cooled down is testimony to our shared temperament that when there is a problem you simply find a solution.

Years later when I recounted this story to a visitor to South Africa, he shook his head in disbelief.

"What?" I asked him.

"That was your father's response?"

"Ja. What should he have said?"

"Um, maybe don't come or perhaps let's get out of this mad country?"

Neither thought had crossed our minds.

Visits to Georg and Barbara continued through cycles of political and criminal violence.

As I learned to surrender, I came to understand the value of these encounters with my mother. Learning to let go of what I felt or needed from her and just to be in the moment, open to it all. I brought news from friends left behind in Pretoria, cheated at cards, tried to take her out for a walk or just sat holding her hand while we flipped through photo albums. These hours became a meditation of sorts where I thought of nothing but what was happening in the moment.

I also befriended many of the people who lived in the home. The dapper Mr McGuyve, in his 90s, who would insist on wearing a suit every day. The disturbingly cheery old lady who suffered from Alzheimer's but who seemed thrilled, each new dawn, that she had found a pair of slippers next to her bed which seemed to fit her perfectly.

"It's amazing. I put my feet in and they just felt so comfortable as if they were mine," she would tell me.

When I enquired as to what it was she did before she became old and marooned here, she replied, "I don't remember, but whatever it was, it must have been fun."

Oh, the blessing of spending oblivion in such high spirits.

Then there were the two elderly gentlemen who suffered from dementia and who would act out, for years, a routine that could have been a scene from a Beckett play.

"What are you waiting for?" one would inevitably ask the other across the long communal table.

"Whatever's happening next," the other would reply expectantly.

WHAT WAS HAPPENING next on my stage was that I was about to leave South Africa for the first time in 26 years, courtesy of C, the Canadian Writer. By now her relationship with V, Afrikaans Philosopher, had run its course. They had travelled the world, worked as dishwashers in Santorini, and drifted through Europe and North America – each with a backpack and very little money. C, however, had found South Africa fertile creative ground and was determined to make it her temporary home. Ever practical, she had compiled a list of available women in Cape Town she considered "good relationship material".

While we had known each other for over four years and she had been the partner of someone I considered to be one of my closest friends, it had never crossed my mind that we might be perfect for each other, romantically speaking. I had never looked upon her lovely form and thought, Hmm, I'd like to get to know her differently.

There exists an unspoken honour in not hitting on one's friends' partners. I had, in the meantime, had several on-off encounters, none of which could really be defined as serious relationships. Work and juggling the demands of my parents remained my central focus. Generally, I found I had no need for a deep, intimate connection and in fact avoided this. Intimacy, to my mind, was messy and demanding and ain't nobody got time. I was a rock. I was an island.

C invited me out and explained her game plan quite matter-of-factly. I was, she coolly informed me, at the top of the list.

"But . . . but . . . I don't think I am good relationship material," I protested.

She patted my hand reassuringly. "Well, why don't we try and see? There's no growth without commitment," she said.

It was the most original pick-up I had ever heard and the more I thought about it over the following weeks, the more appealing it began to seem. This sober and calculated manner of embarking on a relationship was novel and real. None of this rushing headlong and blindly, driven by lust, pheromones and ill judgement, into a relationship that is essentially a projection, a phantom, a figment of one's own fevered imagination.

These urgent couplings, for as much as they are thrilling and all-consuming, contain the seeds of their own destruction. They are the encounters that end one morning when the most banal habit, the holding of a spoon, the crunching of muesli, becomes overwhelmingly unbearable. It is then that the thin veil of transference rips and fantasy inevitably rubs up against reality and finds it wanting.

There is no subsection in the human manual that sets out exactly how one is supposed to go about having "a relationship". At best, or worst, we model our parents, and mine were not exactly sterling examples of how to commune harmoniously and honestly with a partner. Theirs was a union with much that was repressed, buried and sublimated. A bit like being Catholic. Sure, they stuck it out, but at what cost to their true selves, selves that must have grown increasingly remote and out of reach? Which is why it all cascaded out after Barbara's stroke. Nature, and the human unconscious, hate those rooms in our heads that we neglect or avoid, which is how they fill up with crazy shit which, unexamined, is guaranteed to spill out in public.

To speak out or set perimeters, boundaries, expectations and potential pitfalls beforehand was like preparing properly for a journey, packing thermal underwear or a light raincoat for drizzly emotional climes. And while this might at first not have been a romantic beginning, the relationship with C soon morphed into something wildly exciting, life-altering.

C possessed so many qualities that were indeed deeply attractive. Not only was she gorgeous – something I held against her for no good reason other than stubborn stupidity – she was also delightfully quirky and eccentric, wonderfully independent, dogged, challenging, well travelled and well read.

She had fled the parochial education and existence of her home town, Calgary – sort of Canada's Texas – which was a significant accomplishment for a single woman in her early 20s with no family or connections elsewhere in Canada or Europe. She had been influenced by both the first and second wave of North American feminism, and besides, she had been a topless dancer in Vancouver.

Before leaving her homeland she had thought that Judaism was an ancient, extinct religion that existed only in the Bible. She also did not understand that kitsch was ironic and not necessarily tasteful.

But her world had opened up in the years she had travelled to Milan and Paris to work as a model, one of millions of beautiful young women who made the pilgrimage to these fashion capitals. There she had discovered Henry Miller, Anaïs Nin, Simone de Beauvoir, Jean-Paul Sartre, and Doris Lessing. There she had also fallen in love for the first time with a woman and had later met the irresistible Afrikaans Philosopher. She had lived a life bigger than anyone I had met in my own small world.

And she understood that my world – the world of most South Africans – had been limited; that it had been regulated and regimented by a conservative neo-fascist regime. Apartheid consumed our lives, whether we were its beneficiaries or on its unyielding receiving end. It severed us from the rest of the world. "Out there" was mostly beyond our reach.

What C and I had in common was that we were both writers, she of fiction and me of the less revered journalism. I admired her ability to conjure new worlds and create full-blooded characters and scenarios. I had no such talent or inclination. For me stories existed outside of myself and my job was to be curious enough to find and record them.

While we could not have known or acknowledged it at the start, it was our competitiveness that would, five years later, ultimately serve to be our undoing and the spark of many fiery arguments. Two young, creative minds and the residual narcissism and self-centredness required to sustain this urge are oftentimes not compatible in the long run, especially when both of you are complete unknowns. But in the relationship someone's always on the up while the other is on the down, breeding resentment and, of course, crippling self-doubt, the factory default setting for many creative people.

However, this new relationship developed quickly into a deep, significant and transformative love such as I had never experienced before. And as the vast majority of lesbians across the globe are wont to do, V and C remained good friends after their relationship had ended. V even bestowed her blessing on us, like a latter-day Sappho.

For me, leaving South Africa had never been an option. Many immigrants form a fervent attachment to their new homelands. Like religious converts, we desire to prove our loyalty and create for ourselves collected identities embedded in our adopted geographical space. My entire mental, political and spiritual architecture, no matter how problematic, had been shaped through having grown up a white child in South Africa. I understood the country, or so I thought. It was a part of me and I of it. I could speak, at that point, one of its indigenous languages, its music moved me to dance, its perverse politics had burned itself into my being.

Claiming British, Portuguese or German citizenship had never crossed my mind. Citizenship was and continues to be a political issue, to my mind at least, and I am a South African. I feel no kinship with Britain, Germany or Portugal. I did not understand or belong in these societies and felt no particular urge to do so.

Travelling on a South African passport back then, as now, brought with it several bureaucratic hurdles and challenges. Possessing citizenship of a "Western" nation provided one with a smooth passage through the world. Being a citizen of a "Third World" country or what was and is regarded as the "developing world" is to be made aware of one's essentially undesirable nature. Forms, fees, visas, permits, return tickets, sponsorship letters, guarantees of employment and accommodation, proof of financial status – all of these bureaucratic tags were there. But being *white* and a citizen of the Third World miraculously unlocked the process in a fashion that would not have been as easy had I been a black South African.

"Why don't you apply for your British passport?" C suggested when we first discussed our plans to travel.

"Because I'm not British. I was accidentally pushed out there. I don't feel British. I don't want to live in Britain."

"Don't be ridiculous. You are entitled to British citizenship and it's just a practical matter. You will have access to the whole of Europe and North America without any hassle. And you don't have to live there. Use what you can when you can. Why not?"

I agonised. Should I leave South Africa when the majority of people who lived here could not? There were those who had left on one-way exit permits and who would die in exile; others had made a treacherous clandestine dash across the country's borders.

"Okay then. Travel on your South African passport, but for god's sake, travel!"

I was, in all honesty, afraid to leave. Afraid of the unfamiliar big, apparently free world. Afraid that I might just not ever want to come back. Afraid I would lose myself. Become unmoored, unhinged. Lost.

"What about my parents? My job? And besides, I don't have money."

"Your parents will be fine. We'll find work as we go along. We'll save up and pay off the airfare and money for the journey."

Georg seemed impressed that I had managed to get my shit together enough to finally think of travelling.

"Ja, it is good zat you vant to travel. It is good to see how others live. Perhaps zen you vill come to appreciate vot you haf. But you haf to visit Tante Tuta in Berlin. She vill be very hurt if you don't."

When I informed Barbara I was leaving and was toying with the idea of stopping over in Portugal, she slapped me across the face. Well, that's that then. Suppose not.

It took about a year to pay off the airfare and save enough to survive for at least twelve months, even frugally. In the meantime, I decided to go ahead and apply for my British passport. This was a remarkably un-complicated affair. All I had to do was produce my unabridged birth certificate, which Georg had of course kept safely in his little black steel box.

A few weeks later I went to collect it. It was a heavy blue document –

146

I had opted then for the "jumbo" passport – and it was odd to read the opening gambit in cursive print: "Her Britannic Majesty's Secretary of State requests and requires in the Name of Her Majesty all those whom it may concern to allow the bearer to pass freely without hindrance, and to afford the bearer such assistance and protection as may be necessary."

I felt something of a fraud. I would still use my South African passport, known in those days as the Green Mamba, to exit the country. To this end I had to apply for what was then known as a Schengen visa for the Benelux countries (Belgium, Luxembourg and the Netherlands). Our first stop would be Luxembourg, where the budget airline Luxavia (which was actually a South African airline, Trek Airways, but which became a subsidiary of Luxair in 1971) offered South Africans cheap access to Europe. Because of political opposition most African countries prohibited Trek Airways from flying over the continent, but Luxair, disguised as European, was only too happy to help out.

Resigning from the *Cape Times* was an exhilarating move for me. It would be the first of many subsequent thrilling leaps into the unknown that have always paid off in the long run. With C's network of international friends we arranged temporary accommodation in every city we intended to visit. This was our plan: Antwerp, Amsterdam, London (with a quick interlude in New York), Calgary, Vancouver and then back to London, Brussels, Paris and Berlin.

What I learned was that white people swept the streets of Amsterdam, that "freedom" initially felt completely overwhelming and debilitating, that too much choice rendered me incapacitated, and that not a single day passed without my missing South Africa.

I learned that regardless of my political beliefs, I embodied white South Africa to those who encountered me. And while I obviously tried to distance myself from my country-people, I learned to accept the assumption that I was a privileged, racist arsehole deserving of scorn and attack until I had proven otherwise. There was not going to be any back-slapping or high-fiving just because I said I wasn't like "the rest of them" and didn't support apartheid. To be viewed with immediate suspicion in political circles or feminist workshops was uncomfortable but it prompted a deeper engagement with who I was and what I represented.

I learned that my world had been small, mean and limited. I learned that public libraries were fine resources and I used these in every city I lived in that year to educate myself. I spent most of the twelve months in libraries in a self-absorbed fever, reading everything I could. Marx, Roland Barthes, Chekhov, Trotsky, Biko, Nikos Kazantzakis, Umberto Eco, Wilde and Auden. I studied semiotics, narrative theory, the films of David Cronenberg, the origins of Superman and Batman, the uses of humour, literary theory, philosophy. In the Vancouver public library I discovered shelves of books about South Africa that were unavailable back home.

I found my centre and escape in books. Tons of them. And as much as I had avoided them in my youth, I now consumed them in early adulthood as if they were a cure. And they were. For stupidity, ignorance, parochialism, and a mediocre education. I also spent hours in art galleries, theatres and museums, book and music shops, at anti-apartheid cultural events and feminist workshops. I lay prostrate for months watching British television, astounded by what the public broadcaster had to offer. I watched documentaries on art, history and politics. I watched late-night talk shows where British intellectuals coolly dissected the world.

I learned also that the lesbian and gay community the world over had similar concerns and solidarities. I was part of a much bigger family which existed everywhere, where everyone seemed, miraculously, to dress the same way, listen to the same music, read the same books and locate themselves on the same left end of the political compass.

I learned about Halloween, a ritual unknown then in South Africa. Not having access to a costume or the funds to buy one, I arrived at a Halloween party in Calgary in casual clothes.

"What have you come as?" the host asked, opening the door.

"A white South African."

In Antwerp I was to make lifelong, nourishing friendships which endure to this day. It was here that I was later to meet the "Johnny Rotten of Belgian literature", Tom Lanoye, author, poet, playwright, performer, intellectual, comedian and general mensch, and his partner René Los. Both were to play a significant role in my future life. I was later to find myself bizarrely featuring as a character in a series of original features Tom would write when he came to South Africa in 1994 to cover the country's first democratic elections. I was, for a short while then, world-famous in Belgium.

In 1988 I learned to walk streets at night without a crippling, all-consuming fear. I learned not to lock doors. I learned that women could work as welders and boat builders, that all white men were not sexist, angry and armed, and that you did not need to numb yourself with marijuana or any other substance to deal with life. I learned that freedom felt good and I wondered whether we would ever know it in South Africa. Of course none of us could have imagined that two years later, in 1990, Nelson Mandela would be set free or that even one year later, in 1989, the Berlin Wall would be dismantled, signalling seismic global political shifts.

The wall was still very much a permanent feature of the city when I visited Berlin for the first time on the way back to South Africa at the end of 1988. It would also be the first time that I would meet my German relatives, my father's sister, my aunt, friend to the Goebbelses' au pair, Tante Tuta, as well as my cousin and her husband.

En route from Brussels, C and I had one of our now routine literary arguments. Sharing our compartment, on a train hurtling through East Germany, was a single passenger, a woman who looked like an extra in a Woody Allen movie. Dressed in layers of black with her head wrapped in a scarf, she might have been an East German peasant. The woman remained quite mute throughout the journey, napping most of the way, her head propped between the window and the seat on my end of the compartment.

C sat near the window on the bench opposite ours. She had, as usual, her nose in a book. This one, a biography of Anaïs Nin, had been bought in London before our departure. Travelling light was always a concern and we both made extensive use of libraries, so this book must have been important enough for her to want to lug it along on our travels.

I do not recall how the argument began but it erupted soon after I suggested that Nin was a fraud, that she had sponged off her long-suffering husband, Hugh Parker Guiler, a banker, who trudged off to work each day like a donkey while she languished in Paris pretending to be an independent, strong woman and a feminist. And even worse, Nin had publicly shamed and belittled this husband in her writing. Guiler was later edited out of Nin's diaries at his own request.

I am not sure what the subtext was of my need to pick up on this thread at this specific moment, but it had the desired effect. Furious, C wrenched open the window and flung the book out of it. I watched as it arched across a mediocre grey sky, its pages flapping wildly before coming to land in a desolate, snowy East German field.

My lover slammed the window shut and a strained silence enveloped the carriage. I imagined the book in the field and wondered if someone would find it one day and think how it had come to be there.

Our travelling companion remained utterly silent and uninterested throughout our little drama. She alighted later when the train stopped at an East German station.

By now I had become accustomed to the East German guards who would occasionally board the train checking that those on their way to West Berlin possessed the correct documents and permits. It was a bit like being back in South Africa. Their uniforms, dour demeanour and the barking of orders were familiar. I was unruffled by it all while C was less sanguine.

We arrived in Berlin, and for the first time on this journey I felt as if I had arrived in a city I knew, that somehow all those photographs of its woods, its buildings, its parks and beaches, its boulevards and arches in my father's album provided a layering or a psychic map to the space. In London, Vancouver, Brussels, Antwerp, Paris, New York, Calgary, Banff, I was Christopher Isherwood's camera, "with its shutter open, quite passive, recording, not thinking".

Now here I was in Berlin, my father's childhood home. Berlin, the ruined city that formed the backdrop to all those episodes of *The World at War* I had watched as a child, where my grandparents' once-ruined apartment at 32 Fabricius Strasse, Charlottenburg, still stood. Berlin, once the third-largest municipality in the world, which drew to its salons, coffee shops and cafés some of the greatest intellectuals, thinkers, architects, filmmakers and artists of the short-lived Weimar Republic. Berlin, the most left-wing city of the 1920s, the centre of Jewish enlightenment, the Haskalah. Berlin, home to 160 000 Jews in 1933; in 1945 only 8 000 Jews remained there.

Berlin, with the wounds of the war, the pockmark of bullets and shrapnel on stone, still visible 53 years later.

In 1988 the city appeared to be made up of two distinct groups. The very grumpy and the very old strode defiantly, dressed in woollen hats, long coats and dragging shopping trolleys on wheels, eternally muttering under their breath about the litter, the noise, the graffiti. Then there were the young, anarchic students, who smoked in the streets, dressed like Goths, carried boom-boxes pumping Punk music as they swarmed and lolled around the city's public spaces. This surplus of young people was because many young men fled from East to West Berlin to escape conscription, which was compulsory until 2011, into the post-war Federal Army. And these two generations, pre-war and post-war, engaged with each other in public with naked, open hostility.

My cousin and her husband collected us from the Zoologischer Garten station in the central city. It was an awkward meeting, my cousin struggling with broken English, me with my tongue snagging around rudimentary German while I actually understood every word she said.

We made our way to Tante Tuta's apartment. She had lived in the same three-bedroomed flat since the 1950s when she had married a Bavarian town planner and jazz lover who had died several years earlier. I knew the home from photographs and slides she had sent to Georg over the years. I would recognise the small bedroom that was once the room of her second child, Andrea, a girl born in the same year as I was. Andrea was born without arms, a birth defect from the drug Thalidomide, which was a mild sleeping pill developed in Germany in the 1950s and deemed safe for pregnant women. Andrea didn't survive her first birthday.

Before that Tante Tuta had lost to septicaemia a son, Georg, born in the same year as my brother Albert. My cousin was her only surviving child and her elderly parents doted on her. She was the spitting image of my uncle Franz, her father.

I had never met my aunt but had kept up with the family through my father. They had exchanged slides of all the milestones of their lives thousands of kilometres apart.

The door to her apartment was set back to the left of a vestibule that shielded the apartments from the cold winter weather. We knocked and my aunt opened the door. We looked at each other with that strange recognition those of us who are genetically related cannot deny.

"*Oh mein Gott, du bist eine Thammfrau!*" she exclaimed, before clasping me in a warm embrace.

And then we argued. Immediately.

Being the hospitable German housewife, Tante Tuta had prepared lunch for her guests – with pork as a main feature. I, like millions of other lesbians across the globe, was a vegetarian. I asked my cousin to politely, and I emphasised the "politely", inform her mother that C and I were not meat eaters.

"*Pah. Sie essen kein Fleisch? Das ist lächerlich. Wer kennt sie nicht Fleisch essen – nur Vögel*" (What? She doesn't eat meat? That's ridiculous. Who doesn't eat meat – only the birds).

My aunt was offended and I knew it, but I was not going to budge. I was also not prepared to pick out the vegetables that had been cooked with the pork, as vegetarians were often encouraged to do. I would, I instructed my cousin to inform her, be cooking my own meals during our stay. There would be no compromising. I was going to be very German about it all.

I hugged my aunt, attempting to break the culinary impasse, and suggested we rather opt for Abendbrodt (evening bread, usually pumpernickel) with cheese, pickles and other assorted non-meat toppings. For years I had watched my father eating his Abendbrot off a wooden board at home.

The first night of our stay my aunt gently knocked on the door of the spare room where C and I were to spend our visit, she on a fold-out couch and I on a single bed. Cradled in her arms was a little pile of clothing, a pair of my dead uncle's flannel pyjamas for me and a little frilly nightie for C. Had my aunt known we were lovers? Was she unconsciously playing out some heteronormative scenario in her head? Or did I simply not look like the kind of girl who would wear a nightie?

Each morning, after C, warmly bundled up in a coat, hat, a scarf, gloves and ear-muffs, slipped out early to spend the day writing in coffee shops and libraries – a habit she had cultivated with unshakeable discipline over the years – my aunt and I were left to ourselves. We had got over the food issue and I found the more I tried to speak German the better I got at it. We were soon flipping through old photo albums, my aunt tracing with her finger a map of her journey through Russia as a nurse during the war.

We set up a projector on the dining-room table and viewed a small, tidy library of slides my Onkel Franz had taken of their lives. Then we watched a few old reels of film he had lovingly shot. I noted that my aunt's expression seldom varied in any of the stills.

Tante Tuta had married late, as did many after the war, and had lost two small children as well as her parents. There was no reason to clown around for photographs. You stood with the pram, you turned towards the camera in the kitchen when your husband snapped you cooking, or as you stood decorating the Christmas tree, but with no overt displays of fake happiness. Here I am.

Because Berlin as a city had existed for me mostly in captured images, I was keen to see parts of it for myself, particularly Hitler's bunker. I asked my cousin if she could guide me to its location. I knew that in 1946 Russians troops had blown up the Reichskanzlei in Wilhelmstrasse and that the entrance to the bunker had been located somewhere in its gardens.

She seemed mildly disturbed, replying, "I don't know vere it iss actually. I sink it iss in ze East. But ve don't talk about such sings."

My aunt seemed to blossom in undivided attention and I found I enjoyed her company. The grumpy old lady routine didn't work with me. I had grown inured over many years. Georg cultivated his inner German Grinch – irritable, always right, patronising, impatient – so I was very used to it. In his sister I had been gifted a diluted version of the Grinch and I knew it was all mostly bluff.

Tante Tuta wanted to show me around the Berlin she loved. She took me to the ornate Baroque and Rococo Charlottenburg Schloss, the Grunewald forest, the largest green lung in the city, the Tiergarten park, where we fed swans and drank coffee, ate cake and talked or just sat. I accompanied her to the cemetery to tend the graves of my grandparents and her dead children. She hadn't been there in a while, she told me, and appreciated the company.

We had tea with a woman who I suspected had been an old flame of Georg's (perhaps even the young blonde woman in a photograph inscribed with "Vergiss mich nicht" that I later found among his papers). She remarked in German to my aunt that it was "a pity about the Portuguese", which caused me to shoot daggers at her, understanding the intentional racist sting of the comment.

"You don't know anything about my mother," I mumbled in English, stirring my tea.

I regularly found myself embroiled in several unnecessary altercations with Germans, particularly shop owners while out scavenging for groceries and supplies. Examining the texture or firmness of a vegetable or piece of fruit in Berlin appeared to be a cultural transgression and would trigger a sharp bark to put it down.

"Fuck off," was my rote retort as I continued to fondle the produce.

Alone I navigated the city on foot, visiting museums, libraries and trendy districts like Kreuzberg, where Onkel Fritz had been the Baudirektor before his untimely death behind the desk in his office. C and I also connected with lesbian organisations in Berlin and made one or two friends who showed us around the city's bars and clubs.

Through all my months away I had kept in touch with Georg, writing letters from each city and calling him from Berlin. The letters were mostly rudimentary, written more out of duty than wanting to impart any real information. I withheld my real life for no good reason – that's just what young people do.

After my short trip to New York in April that year Georg had written me a letter in which he'd said: "Glad to hear you liked New York and that you had the opportunity to see some shows. I do not know what made you think that it was the cultural centre of the world or who put these words into your mouth but let me tell you that it is not so. Before you make that profound a statement, go and visit Europe and see what Culture is. As for Broadway shows with Chorus Girls and other musicals, then perhaps it depends on what one regards as Culture. The real Culture you will only find in good old Europe. Some of it has, of course, rubbed off on the Yanks. Na ya, so much for Culture. Everyone must have one's own opinion. When a young person like yourself, for the first time encounters impressions and experiences in any one place, that place will of course imbed itself in one's mind. It is always good to see how other people live and play but in the final analysis they too have a workday Mondays to Fridays."

This culture (with a small "c") C and I were keen to experience. We learned that the top floor of one of the apartment blocks in Kreuzberg housed a popular experimental theatre where a long-running performance considered to be a sort of avant-garde showpiece was still packing in tourists. The title of the piece is now lost but we duly booked and set off through the thick snow to see it.

It was a small cramped space, the audience mostly made up of tourists like us, keen to imbibe local theatre. From the programme note I determined that the lead actor had also written, produced and directed the play. From my experience reviewing theatre in South Africa by then, this did not bode well. But this was Berlin, Germany, Europe, the centre of culture.

The set consisted of a railway line which sliced through the centre of a small stage. On either side were the accoutrements of what appeared to be a station; buckets, a few wooden benches. As the lights dimmed we heard the muffled sound of doors closing and *locking* behind us. There was no escaping, apparently. And then it began. Perhaps the worst piece of theatre I had ever had the displeasure of sitting through. The lead actor/producer/writer/director, wearing a pair of dark glasses throughout the performance, dominated the piece, shouting, gesticulating and flinging himself against props for a good part of an hour.

I could feel myself levitating. I nudged C, but she ignored me.

About two hours into the play, which remained utterly unfathomable to me, the back doors burst open and an actor leading a pack of about ten happy Afghan hounds strode in. Thank God, some relief.

I whispered that we should try to make a dash for it, but just as quickly I heard the lock click again.

When one of them stuck its nose up the other's arse, as dogs are wont to do, I burst out laughing. Loudly.

The actor/writer/producer/director stopped mid-speech. He glowered at the audience, clearly furious.

"*Lachen sie?*" he shouted.

I could feel the Canadian Writer shrink into the seat next to me.

"*Lachen sie?*" he now screamed like a Nazi Gauleiter, scanning the frightened faces.

"*Ja!*" I shouted back.

C dug her elbow into my ribs. "Jesus, Marianne, shut up," she hissed.

"No, fuck him. In South Africa audiences shout back and I can't stand another minute of it. Not another minute."

The actor/director/writer/producer stepped in front of me.

"*Raus! Raus!*" he ordered, gesticulating at the door.

"*Nein!*" I barked back.

He glared at me, clearly surprised at the disobedience, shifting from foot to foot, still waiting for me to make an exit. I sat stubbornly in my seat staring back at him, smiling. I am not going anywhere, fucker.

Afterwards, C hastily grabbed me by the coat and led me out to the street. She had planned to linger and try to connect with the arsehole but it was probably not advisable under the circumstances.

Finally, our sojourn in the big wide world came to an end. One thing I knew was that I was ready to head home. This here, this world, would always be there and I could always return now that I knew it existed.

We spent a magical Christmas and rowdy drunken New Year in snowy Berlin before boarding our Luxavia flight home. We were heading into a hot summer and an even hotter political climate. But at least I was returning home a little less ignorant.

IT WAS one of those years – 1989.

In South Africa a last desperate wave of repression crashed over the country's citizens before the seemingly impregnable edifice of apartheid began visibly to crumble. It was the year the ANC in exile announced in a statement the year of "mass action" and it was exactly that.

Touching down after a mind-expanding year abroad, Jan Smuts International Airport (as it was named then) was a coiled nerve of anxiety and repressed hostility. The airport terminal and perimeter teemed with armed police while cheerless white immigration clerks mechanically stamped passports without the hint of a tourist-brochure welcoming smile. Outside, military vehicles with young, armed, white, sunburned soldiers patrolled the highways.

Had we made a mistake returning? But I could not imagine myself anywhere else.

Within a week I had adjusted to the normal abnormal. None of those instincts required to deal with home had been dulled or eroded by months of relative freedom in Europe, Canada and the UK.

Elsewhere in the world, however, great and tumultuous currents were swirling and they were not unconnected to the exciting rupture that was about to tear up our sunny southern tip of the world.

At the end of 1989 the global political landscape, almost overnight, was irrevocably altered. The Berlin Wall, which had so casually featured as a backdrop in my photographs only a few months earlier, suddenly came tumbling down, signalling the end of the 45-year Cold War.

These events all tilted the political axis of the geopolitical landscape, although, in the eye of the storm, few could see beyond it.

That year stands out for me, more so than the early 1990s which seemed to play out like a high-speed Zip file, with historic events spectacularly folding in on each other, hard to hold onto, difficult to grasp in the moment, but all heady with the taste of promise and freedom.

Viewed in its entirety it was, on the surface, a year of huge mass protests in the streets of South Africa. That was the year of crowds 20 000 strong in Johannesburg, 30 000 in Cape Town, 80 000 in Uitenhage and 50 000 in Port Elizabeth. It was the year when the Peace March in Cape Town saw religious leaders, including the ubiquitous Archbishop Desmond Tutu, Rev. Allan Boesak, Moulana Farid Esack and Rev. Frank Chikane, link arms and lead the crowd.

It was the year of the purple rain – when police put dye in a water cannon and used it on protesters in the centre of Cape Town in an attempt to mark individuals so that they would be easier to identify and arrest afterwards. I was there on that gloriously anarchic Saturday morning and it wasn't difficult to get caught up in it. Along with hundreds of others, including a few confused tourists who had been swept along by the crowd, I found myself bundled into the back of a police truck by a young constable in uniform, whose neck veins bulged from the exertion.

But it was also the year when, behind the chaotic scenes in the streets, the apartheid government was being forced into looking for an exit. In July, the country's tyrannical fish-lipped leader, *die Groot Krokodil*, PW Botha, met, for the first time, the imprisoned Nelson Mandela over a cup of tea at the presidential office at Tuynhuis. By then Botha had suffered a mild stroke but was refusing to go quietly.

In his autobiography, *Long Walk to Freedom*, Mandela later described the meeting thus: "From the opposite side of his grand office PW Botha walked towards me. He had planned his march perfectly, for we met exactly half way. He had his hand out and was smiling broadly, and in fact from that very first moment he completely disarmed me. He was unfailingly courteous, deferential and friendly."

But only a month before that meeting Botha had renewed the State

158

of Emergency for twelve more months and had placed stringent restrictions on the Congress of South African Trade Unions (COSATU). And two months before that, in May, agents working for the apartheid Civil Co-operation Bureau had assassinated activist and academic David Webster outside his Troyeville home. In September they murdered activist and advocate Anton Lubowski outside his house in Windhoek, Namibia.

While Botha was courteously shaking Mandela's hand, his police force was detaining activists, and protest marches or meetings by anyone who was part of the anti-apartheid Mass Democratic Movement (MDM) were banned.

WHEN WE RETURNED home I had few immediate options work-wise, so I rejoined the *Cape Times,* confined once again to the "safe" Arts department. There was no way, however, I was going to miss out on history in the making. You could feel it, a rising sense of a country on the brink. Between sitting in darkened theatres and reporting on art matters, I participated in events where I could, as a citizen, but always also primarily as a journalist.

During the second defiance campaign launched that year, I took photographs at the city's segregated beaches as families from across the Peninsula descended on them en masse in protest. The authorities were determined to stop this peaceful resistance and roadblocks manned by armed sentries were set up on all major roads across the city.

This was the biggest threat to the state, families with children going to the beach?

Young, wild-eyed, white policemen must have questioned the insanity of it all, but they carried out their orders all the same, manning the roadblocks and turning back cars with "suspicious" occupants inside. Protesters who had arrived in buses and spilled out on the city's whites-only beaches were charged at and sjambokked.

On Blouberg beach that morning I started taking photographs, using an inconspicuous plastic Kodak Instamatic camera, as a crowd of protesters – women, men and children – gathered on the beige sand, their fists held high with Table Mountain as a clichéd backdrop in the distance.

Just then police charged and protesters scattered across the dunes. The cops went berserk, lashing out at anyone within range of their quirts. Elsewhere they corralled press photographers and demanded they hand over their cameras before ripping out rolls of film. I slipped away from the melée and headed back to my car. On a nearby dune I spotted a male colleague from the paper, a copyeditor, sitting astride his motorbike, watching it all from a distance, casually balancing his helmet on his knee.

Back at the newspaper's offices I handed my cartridge of film to the pictures editor. These photographs would be the only record of the day and indeed one shot, of raised fists with Table Mountain looming, appeared on the front page the following morning accompanying a lead story of events.

Koos Viviers was the editor of the *Cape Times* at that time. His secretary popped into the Arts department during the course of the morning and said that Koos wanted to have a word with me. I thought nothing of it and made my way to his wood-panelled office hung with portraits of all the white, male editors who had gone before him. Tony Heard, I noticed, was not among the gallery.

He remained seated behind his desk and gestured to a chair.

"Marianne, what were you doing at that protest at the weekend?" he asked.

I didn't understand.

"Um, I am a journalist," I said.

"But you were not on duty this weekend and, besides, you work in the Arts department."

"I participated in the protest as a South African citizen. I agree with it."

"Well, you have to be careful of that. You have to try and stay objective, you know. What happens if one day these people come into power?"

"These people? South Africans? I'm not sure what you mean, but I can tell you, if the cops behave the same way in future, I'll report on it – it's simple."

At that point I realised that Viviers had no idea that the photograph on the front page of the newspaper he edited was mine. I also realised that my colleague on the bike must have ratted on me. Now consider-

160

ably older and wiser than I had been when I first joined the paper, I stood my ground. Picking up a copy of that morning's edition from his desk, I pointed at the photograph and said, "That photograph on the front page is mine. Don't patronise me. I have worked at this paper longer than you have been its editor. If you don't know who I am or how I think, that's your problem."

And then I walked out of his office.

It felt good. But I knew then that my days at the *Cape Times* were over.

Towards the end of that year I would resign once again, and I would never return to formal employment at a mainstream South African newspaper.

In 1989 it was not an environment conducive to women or black people rising up its supreme and influential ranks. Besides, I lacked the ambition for climbing ladders or crashing through glass ceilings. My trajectory, I decided, would be horizontal and not vertical. I wanted a broad range of experience and skills that I hoped would ripple outwards and not upwards.

IN SOMERSET WEST little had changed for Barbara and Georg. While my mother's life was looped into the institutional routine of the Chris Heunis Home, Georg's revolved around his visits to Barbara, cleaning his house and doing laundry, walks with his beloved dogs in a nearby park (he had since acquired two long-haired dachshunds), shopping for groceries, watching German TV (which he found largely distasteful and gaudy) and sleeping. His was a small, contained world and he appeared content with it as it was. By then Albert and his wife and their small son had relocated to Australia and were to visit occasionally over the years.

Georg's was an unostentatious, predictable and static retirement. No cruise ship Kontiki tours, no golfing or card playing or gym going. He had always worried about money and kept notebooks of his paltry daily expenditure as if this would somehow arrest the erosion of his savings and his pension.

Out shopping together, I would suggest that he buy a chunk of cheese he enjoyed.

161

"Vhat? Are you mad? At zat price? Zey are crazy if zey sink anyone is going to buy it."

There comes a time in all our lives when inflation overtakes our sense of the value of money and what we remembered as its purchasing power. Like when a grandparent slips a R10 note into a birthday card thinking it is a fortune. Georg was certain prices were rigged and that if people stopped paying a fortune for everything, prices would drop.

"But Dad, why deny yourself a small luxury like that? It's not that expensive. Treat yourself. I tell you what – I'll buy it for you."

"No," he snapped back.

And that was that. Georg shifted on to the next shelf in the supermarket refrigerator, muttering as he sought out inexpensive meals for one.

Money, for Georg, was always to be spent sparingly and the trick was to avoid all manner of scams aimed at parting you from it. Insurance, for example, he believed, was a money-making racket. He never took out insurance on anything we owned, nor on his or my mother's life. Good investments, he reckoned, were "Persian" carpets and rugs (not so much, especially after being soiled by a succession of dachshunds), defence bonds (totally useless in democratic South Africa), silver one-rand coins (completely worthless), copper paraffin lamps, and oil landscapes and still lifes by obscure Pretoria painters. And the apartment in Senator Park, of course, which Georg had subsequently sold after discovering that the entire block had been turned into a downtown brothel and drug den of sorts.

Cars, too, were never worth spending money on.

"You drive it out of ze showroom and already it is worth less. No, if you vant to invest money, buy property," he advised sagely.

Georg knew what he was talking about when it came to cars. After he retired he drove an ancient white Nissan. You service it regularly, you check the oil and water, you park it in a garage and you drive it until you can't anymore, until it is no longer fixable. Because of my father, I get gaskets, side-shafts, crankshafts, pistons, differentials, and brake pads. I know to disconnect the battery if you're not going to drive for a while. I know that one should, ideally, regularly rotate one's

162

tyres so they last longer; and that one should not drive a car to please anyone else but only to get from point A to point B.

In Georg's world, German and Japanese cars were best. Italian cars were too intricate when it came to the electrical work and gave too many problems. French cars were too complicated.

British cars were okay but not well thought out.

"Vhy vould you put a distributor right in front of ze engine and so low down in a country where it rains all ze time?" he said of the original Mini Cooper. And he was right. An old Mini I later bought would routinely splutter and cut out after splashing through a shallow Cape Town rain puddle. (The trick is to secure a plastic shopping bag around the distributor, in case you were wondering.)

Georg was happy about my visit to Berlin and that I had connected with my aunt, his sister, and that we had spent time together. He laughed when I recounted Tante Tuta's first impression, about me being a *Thammfrau*. He was curious to learn about the church in his old neighbourhood, whether I had visited their flat in Fabriciusstrasse and, of course, whether I had been to my grandparents' graves, which had been lovingly tended for years by his sister.

In his letters to me while I was away travelling, as well as when C and I returned to Cape Town, Georg was always mindful to ask me to pass on his regards to her. Only now do I wonder whether he knew that we were lovers. Or did he think we were just close friends, like-minded companions? I didn't think to explore it. Just left it as it was. Another major part of my life – unspoken, unexplored.

Georg watched the unfurling political situations in South Africa and Berlin from a detached distance, like many white South Africans, unsure of the direction events would take, living day to day in a liminal space. Those of us closer to the political pulse wondered whether the state would collapse, if the violence would ever end, whether we would ever be free of it.

My father's real political views, if he had any that were firmly entrenched, were difficult to distil. I was perpetually poised to call him out should I detect any overt spillage of the rabid national socialism which had permeated the society that formed him and which had such close echoes in apartheid. As a child, the only world Georg had known had been dominated entirely by Hitler's Nazi Party and its demand for uncritical loyalty. Surely these ideas and worldviews had to have permeated his political DNA, formed the bedrock of his own worldview?

Georg had been too young to vote in 1938 but, at fourteen years old at the time, national socialism must have influenced him just as apartheid ideology influenced the majority of white South Africans. Influence so penetrating burrows itself like a toxic time bomb in the mind and soul. It can only be unravelled through deep and painful reflection.

On the desk in his study, Georg kept a small brass replica of the head of the German writer, historian, philosopher and poet Friedrich Schiller mounted on a tiny black marble plinth. On a par only with Goethe, Schiller (1759–1805) was regarded as the German Shakespeare. In his prolific philosophical writings he explored, among much else, the question of human freedom and the capacity for humans to "defy animal instincts" and sacrifice themselves for ideals. He came to be regarded as a literary patriot and prophet, musing on the notion of a German fatherland and nation. But he also longed for harmony, for a rejection of French revolutionary violence, for German unity, most particularly in the aftermath of earlier French Napoleonic domination.

Depending on the political currents of the time, Schiller's ideas of freedom could be interpreted differently. While he might have called for greater civil liberties, his ideas, ideals and writings would come to be co-opted by Hitler and the Nazis, who understood the deep cultural echoes of the poet's work. They subverted Schiller's writing, appropriating notions of an exceptional tribal German identity and incorporating these into their warped notions of racial purity and "hygiene". During this period, what was emphasised in Schiller's writing was its heroic, warlike qualities. Goebbels, the Nazi propaganda goblin, declared Schiller a "poetic pioneer of the revolution" who would have joined the Nazis, he claimed, in their atavistic and exclusionary vision.

Which Schiller had Georg read? I wondered. Or was he just like millions of other German schoolchildren who learned his poetry by heart? I did not bother to ask, and he had no inclination to tell.

I waited for my father to reveal himself. I tried to read between the

164

lines or unpick casual references he might make. I could not separate the man from the politics I thought he embodied. Back then, I could not see past it all and it coloured my behaviour towards him, and my ability to love and see him as a man, my father.

That he had chosen to marry my mother, who would have been regarded in Nazi Germany as inferior, and that in doing this Georg might have dared to dilute the great Teutonic lineage and create a cosmopolitan family, completely escaped me. Cosmopolitanism was anathema to the Nazis who – like apartheid nationalists – abhorred the "mixing" of "races" or "nationalities".

I always broached any subject with Georg with my guns facing outwards, which is something I regret. I seldom gave him the benefit of the doubt when it came to political matters, just as today many white South Africans, regardless of their *Weltanschauung*, are viewed with suspicion, as they should be, myself included, until they prove otherwise. And even then, we remain suspect. Just as I could not imagine my father escaping the forces, spiritual, emotional, political and economic, that had shaped him, so too will white South Africans be viewed with suspicion. This is the burden of history.

While Georg moved through life unaware of the privilege of his maleness and whiteness, he was never overtly sexist, anti-Semitic or racist, which was confusing to me. One of his closest friends in Pretoria had been Uncle Julius Epstein, who was Jewish.

Aside from thinking that Americans were decadent and that the Western world was a plutocracy – political jargon common to the pre-war Communist International, Nazi Germany and Fascist Italy – there was nothing really to situate him firmly to the left or the right of the political spectrum.

I always expected more of an outward manifestation of what I believed crouched in his head and heart. Perhaps a secret tattoo of a swastika or a Nazi uniform concealed in a cupboard. How could one find nuance or subtlety when one is forged in such hellish fire? How could one, or *could* one even, ever escape the contagion of it?

The United States, Georg maintained, was an oligarchy, a view that has sort of subsequently been confirmed by economist *du jour* Thomas

Piketty in *Capital in the Twenty-First Century*. Piketty writes that the US is drifting towards oligarchy where the majority of citizens have little influence over governments, which are beholden to a rich minority.

My father believed that the Bilderbergers controlled world events. The Bilderberg Club, established in 1954, consists of a group of around 150 wealthy individuals of the North American and European elite, who meet annually "to bolster consensus on free market Western Capitalism and its interests around the globe," says Wikipedia.

According to the conspiracy theorists, the Bilderbergers, including proxies from industry, Wall Street, the banks and the media, provide no account of their closed meetings and do not make public any of their plans or what is discussed. Perhaps Georg was onto something. I dismissed it entirely.

While Georg, like most post-war Germans, had to deal with the humiliation not only of losing the war but of supporting a globally reviled genocidal psychopath, he would point out the supreme irony that Hitler had foretold that a New Germany would emerge in his wake. And in many ways it did, just not the Germany the Führer had envisaged.

"Germany might haf lost ze var but ve von ze peace," Georg habitually reminded me.

One example he cited was the label "Made in Germany" on goods produced in the country. Initially this had come about in 1887 when Great Britain charged that Germany had been creating inferior products and sneakily labelling them "Made in Britain". It was also an attempt to encourage British consumers to buy local.

It was the British Merchandise Marks Act that forced Germany to mark all its goods and products, but after WWII the plan backfired when consumers began to associate "Made in Germany" with quality and "cachet", according to Renuka Rayasam, writing in the *New Yorker* in 2013.

The rapid economic growth of post-war Germany, in my father's opinion, also had to do with its superior economic thinkers, Ludwig Erhard in particular, and its workers. While the Marshall Plan to assist post-war Germany was not massive, and the country was paying

166

war restitution in excess of $1 billion a year, it was currency conversion and the abandonment of price controls that led to extraordinary growth after the war. This in the face of the destruction of over 1 500 manufacturing plants as agreed to in the first industrial plan for Germany signed in 1946.

In 1989 Georg was certain that West Germany would soon ensure that the now-liberated East would quickly be "brought up to speed", and while there were enormous differences between East and West Germans, and some open hostility and xenophobia, this would all pass as each "side" got to renew relations.

However, in South Africa in 1989, there was no time to reflect, not yet. In September that year the Nationalist government held a snap and last whites-only election, testing support for FW de Klerk, the newly appointed "reformist" leader of the National Party. It polled 48 per cent of the white vote, a "victory" that was interpreted as a sign that the white electorate was ready for the next chapter, namely, the disbandment of apartheid and the seeking of a compromise with the African National Congress.

That month a significant judicial appeal overturning the death sentences handed down in one of the country's longest-running political trials, the Delmas Treason Trial, which had lasted for 437 days, inadvertently led to the exposure of how exactly clandestine apartheid death squads had assassinated government opponents and ANC activists.

While awaiting trial, the Delmas Four – Jabu Masina, Frans Ting-Ting Masango, Neo Potsane and Joseph Makhura – who were members of an ANC special operations unit, found themselves on death row at Pretoria Central Prison, alongside Almond Nofomela, who had worked for the Security Branch and who had been appointed in 1981 to its assassination squad, located at a place called Vlakplaas and led by Captain Dirk Coetzee.

Nofomela confessed this to his fellow "inmates", who passed this vital information on to their lawyer, Peter Harris. A day before he was due to be executed, Nofomela signed an affidavit detailing the unit's extrajudicial and criminal actions and forcing the then Minister of Justice, Kobie Coetsee, to set up a very public commission of inquiry.

Nofomela's life was spared and his confession was instrumental in exposing the depravity and illegality of the state's response to opponents.

While the commission set about corroborating Nofomela's claims, things in the country began to move remarkably rapidly.

A month later Rivonia trialists Walter Sisulu, Ahmed Kathrada, Andrew Mlangeni, Elias Motsoaledi, Raymond Mhlaba and Wilton Mkwayi were released after 26 years of captivity. This would have been unthinkable only a year before. There was jubilation and celebration across the country as receptions were planned for these iconic struggle heroes' return home. The state was, of course, testing the climate for the eventual release of Nelson Mandela, which would take place the following year.

What it gave with the one hand, it took with the other, and the repression on the ground continued. But the genie was out of the bottle. Freedom was in the air.

In December 1989 over 4 000 people attended a Conference for a Democratic Future at Wits University, which adopted the ANC's proposals for a political settlement and negotiations with the apartheid state known as the Harare Declaration. That same month De Klerk met Mandela for the first time. There was no turning back.

The past was about to become a foreign country. The future was as yet unclear.

IT WASN'T THE BEST place to be when what had to be *the* most historic announcement in South Africa was made. On Friday, 2 February 1990, I found myself sitting munching popcorn in a darkened movie theatre in the Golden Acre in the centre of Cape Town, reviewing some B-grade Hollywood release.

Just down the road in parliament the country's last white leader, FW de Klerk, was announcing that he was freeing Nelson Mandela and unbanning the ANC and all other political organisations. Not only that, but the State of Emergency would be lifted, all political prisoners would be released and various bits of apartheid legislation would be scrapped. De Klerk had crossed the Rubicon that PW Botha had been too afraid to attempt a few years earlier.

Apartheid was dead – well, theoretically at least – and it all happened as I, oblivious, was watching some inconsequential fiction light up the movie screen.

When I emerged into the sunlight I found a carnival atmosphere in the city's streets. Car hooters sounded a discordant cacophony, people were hugging each other and cheering, singing and dancing. Something huge, and clearly joyous, had happened. I had no idea what it might be, but the elation was infectious. It was like stepping into a surprise party. People were so consumed by the moment it was impossible to work out what the hell was going on. Had PW Botha died perhaps?

I pressed through the crowds and hurried back to the newspaper offices, which were only a few blocks away.

"What's going on?" I asked a receptionist at the front desk.

"He's freeing Mandela. Mandela, he's coming out," he told me excitedly.

Learning that Mandela was to be released was, in that instant, for me, a visceral rather than intellectual dawning and it brought with it a peculiar exhilaration. The spontaneous jubilation in the streets of Cape Town I had just witnessed was a manifestation of that same pure excitement. It was a feeling accompanied by an understanding of finding oneself part of a massive and, until then, unthinkable historic moment – a bit like the moon landing.

The newsroom was humming. Phones were ringing and clusters of journalists gathered around talking animatedly about what had just happened. While there had been talk that De Klerk would be making some sort of announcement in parliament that morning, no one had quite expected it would be *this*. There had been false alarms before. It was unthinkable that the National Party would ever go this far, this swiftly.

When I had walked into the cinema the country was one place. When I emerged a few hours later it was already somewhere else.

Wild celebrations reverberated throughout South Africa. This was going to be a weekend of collective partying of note. We were a nation so much in need of good news, of something positive, something concrete, and while the release of Sisulu and other political prisoners earlier had buoyed spirits, this was different. This was *huge*. This was the turning point we had all been waiting for, fighting for. We had grown so accustomed to the fear, hostility and violence in the country that this rupture, at first, made us totally euphoric. It was like taking Ecstasy – all anxieties and troubles momentarily dissolved.

Nelson Mandela, whom we had not seen – *Asimbonanga* – for over 27 years, would soon walk among us. It was like expecting the coming of the Holy Ghost. We had no idea what he looked like. For the first time, "legally", newspapers published sketches of how Mandela might look now, in 1990. Artists drew his face lined, his hair almost completely grey. The last photographs we had seen were of a full-faced, strapping young man, his hair parted, and dressed in sharp suits.

While life continued in the aftermath of the announcement, from that moment it was suspended, liminal. The date of Mandela's release was set for 11 February when he was expected to walk out of Victor Verster Prison in Paarl – where he had been kept for the last few years of his incarceration while he met with members of the apartheid government – a free man.

But even as there was generally a tremendous feeling of anticipation and expectation as the news sank in over the following weeks, there were always the reminders of the ever-present coiled and ominous threat of violence. White die-hards began to talk of war. Some were petrified and began stockpiling food, fuel, water and weapons in preparation for the "revenge" killings they believed would be unleashed by Mandela's release (and would once more be predicted after Mandela's death). For those who knew nothing of the struggle or who did not support it, the announcement must have felt like being plunged through a political wormhole.

Only later, in the years leading up to the country's first democratic election in 1994, would the forces of chaos be fully unleashed as horrific violence erupted. Nelson Mandela might have been free and the ANC might have been unbanned, but there were clandestine forces of all sorts, shapes and allegiances who were determined to halt the juggernaut of history.

But collectively, back in 1990, the majority of the country's citizens knew this was the beginning. Of what we were not yet quite sure.

IT WAS A MAJOR bummer then that my own personal dissolution of sorts came at exactly this point. It had crept up on me. A feeling of treading water, of numb nothingness. And while I could intellectually compute the significance of what was happening in the world, personally I felt more like a collection of gases tied up in a skin. Was this the aftermath of having travelled, of having seen a world beyond my own? Was I worn down and depressed? Was this a form of post-traumatic stress?

Or was it because I was turning 30 and had so little to show for my life? And what was one meant to show anyway?

Wallowing in misery or self-doubt was not a state I wanted to indulge. I thought it was selfish and narcissistic, considering the real misery all around, not of people's own making. How mundane, how bourgeois, how petty and middle-class to feel this way.

What I wanted more than anything was to disconnect from my head and my heart. I wanted to live purely in my physical body. I wanted to do things that would require or demand little or no thought or insight.

Just fucking pull yourself together, I kept telling myself.

"It's called a Saturn return," my white sangoma friend (who was later to explain the significance of the bees outside the funeral home after my mother died) informed me. He was also an astrologer. "Ignore it at your peril," he cautioned.

In astrological terms Saturn returns to the same position it was in the firmament at the moment of our birth when we turn 29 or 30. This, he said, marked a threshold, the beginning of a transition into adulthood and a need to face new challenges and responsibilities. I placed about as much faith in astrology as I did in religion, but there was no doubt that some inner shift was taking place. I was uncomfortable in my skin, my head, my heart.

My relationship with C was painfully unravelling. It was not a dramatic uncoupling but a slow unpicking. I loved C and she had played a significant part in opening up my world, but we had got beyond the first few years of discovery and were now both journeying inward. She had grown insecure about her writing, that illusive big break always on the horizon but no closer. She had penned a play, set in South Africa, which was well received, but it was not enough. I felt there was nothing I could do.

Right then I needed less complication, not more. Perhaps hoping to facilitate the end of the four-year relationship or to escape its complexities, I started seeing someone else. It was not a clandestine relationship and C and I talked about it from the start. I was deeply torn and distressed by the pain I was causing but at the same time exhilarated by the new distraction with all its unrealistic passion and projections. When I was with my new love I forgot about everything, but afterwards, when the truth of it all blew away the fog of infatuation, I hated how I felt and how much I was hurting C. All this emotional turbulence only served to make me like myself even less. And at first I blamed everyone but myself.

I did not know then that our brains continue to develop well into adulthood and that our frontal lobes, that region known colloquially as the command centre, which is responsible for cognition, judgement, sexual behaviour and emotional expression, only finally settle at 25. This is why all over the world, for centuries, various cultures have celebrated a coming of age at 21. Neurologists have now proved that we've always been four years off the mark. In that sense, then, I was only a five-year-old adult. And in retrospect I felt and behaved like one.

C was extraordinarily mature and loving and we tried to remain calm and kind as the "we" tore apart. She had also decided that it was time to leave South Africa and began to make preparations to return to Canada.

Adding to the upset was what I considered to be an even more troubling development. I suddenly no longer wanted to be a journalist. After ten years I saw no future in the profession, if one could call it that, and the idea of working for the *Cape Times* or any other established media house for the rest of my life began to seem predictable and bleak. Besides, after my run-in with Viviers over my photograph on the front page, I had lost respect for the publication. But what to do? These were days before liberating cell phones, laptops, social media or blogs. One's life as a journalist back then was tethered to either a mainstream newspaper or a financially compromised fringe publication. Or so I thought.

On February 11, I stood among the massive throng of people who waited on the Grand Parade in Cape Town for Nelson Mandela to arrive and address us from the balcony of the City Hall. It was a sweltering day. I lived up the road from the Parade and around midday I ambled down the verdant Government Avenue, lined with its old oak trees, alongside the country's parliament buildings.

There was an extraordinary feeling of camaraderie as black and white South Africans gathered together, forming Archbishop Desmond Tutu's "rainbow nation" – a necessary early fiction that served momentarily to distract us from the depths of the real differences and divides that were only to emerge much, much later. On the Parade that day people proudly wore the ANC's black, green and gold, which until recently had been banned and would have provoked arrest.

There were a few incidents of violence on the periphery of the crowd as opportunists took advantage, shattering shop windows and making off with merchandise. Generally, though, everyone stood and waited patiently, singing struggle songs, holding hands. As the afternoon wore on, I decided to head back to my flat and catch up on TV what was holding up Mandela. You never knew – some madman might attempt to scupper it all.

On TV live streaming showed the massive crowd outside Victor Verster and lining Mandela's expected route along the highway. The masses had come out to welcome him back. It was difficult, however, to ignore the banal voice-over by the state broadcaster's correspondent, one Clarence Keyter, and his vapid descriptions of the sun and the lovely landscape. Keyter was clearly way out of his depth. We later learned that he had been ordered by the SABC not to interview anyone in the crowd lest this be viewed as "giving the ANC a voice".

Watching Mandela, tall, regal and self-possessed, wearing a charcoal suit, stride out of prison holding the hand of his wife Winnie was like watching a fairytale come to life.

It was the all-powerful apartheid super-spy, Niël Barnard, who pre-pared Mandela for his release. This man had been key to the behind-the-scenes negotiations between the ANC and the apartheid government. He paid attention to detail (apparently, he had even tied one of Man-dela's shoelaces before he met PW Botha for the first time in 1989). And it was Barnard who had selected what Mandela should wear on his release. The apartheid spy told the BBC's Sue McGregor (in 2009) that the government had not wanted to release the man "in gum boots and an overall . . . somewhere on the Cape Flats but take him to a house to prepare him for the day in which he would be released".

Barnard was to continue to play a key role for many years. As the holder and keeper of many dark secrets, he was a man who had power over many, including many in the ANC. Jacob Dlamini, in his book *Askari*, wrote that in 1994 Mandela asked Barnard to reveal the names of government spies in the ANC but he had refused. These undercurrents were to continue to play out inside the ANC and out of the public view until much later, when they would bubble over during Thabo Mbeki's presidency.

That Mandela looked so much older than we had remembered him brought home just how long he had been locked away, and while he had made sure not to waste these years, the Nationalist government had nevertheless stolen his life, shattered his family and traumatised the country.

There was something biblical about the moment, however. Mandela's smile, which was to become so familiar to us later, his countenance and general demeanour, were very far removed from the thin-lipped (or fish-lipped) angry and threatening faces of so many dour, cheerless Nationalist leaders and politicians who had dominated our lives. He was to be our saviour. In many hearts and minds Mandela already was our president before a single vote was cast.

As the sun set I headed back to the Parade and later, as the light faded, stood listening as Mandela, wearing a borrowed pair of reading glasses, haltingly read out a speech. These small details were lost in the spell of the moment but in retrospect have come to hold deeper significance as a younger generation would begin to challenge Mandela's legacy.

The pragmatism of that generation of older ANC leaders was what was required then. It was, after all, a negotiated settlement and not a revolution, and this would set the path for the country's contested future. The speech that night had been written by a committee and was disappointingly filled with platitudes and clichés which Mandela struggled to read.

We would live for a few more years with clichés and platitudes, and the comforting but precarious stability they brought. Mandela would not, that night, have wanted to speak without the mandate of the party and so he delivered what he was given.

Later, however, he would begin to assert his own voice and leadership. We would come to see his great self-deprecating humour, and also his astute reading of what was required of any given moment.

But that day on the Grand Parade in Cape Town Mandela's voice was still unknown to us. The last snippet captured before his incarceration had been in a TV interview with the BBC back in the 1960s, when he explained the reason for the launch of the armed struggle, and the voice then was that of a young man. Now we listened to a man whose voice had matured, deepened and aged and had developed the measured monotone we would come to know (and many would impersonate) so well.

Mandela almost immediately embarked on an international tour and 1990 whizzed by like a high-speed merry-go-round.

Towards the end of the year C prepared finally to leave. I was heartbroken but knew that there was no other way. I could not expect to have it all.

We drove to the airport in silence. I thought how stupid I had been to fuck this up and also how I was incapable of pushing through this rough patch. As we lovingly said goodbye, I watched her disappear through the airport security gates and began to sob. I cried all the way back to the office. The only time I think I looked up properly, all I could see was a billboard on the highway advertising some dairy product, but I remember the tagline – "Have a ding dong day".

Fuck off.

The last thing I felt like doing was returning to work. I felt like someone had died and I needed time to grieve. Lesbian and gay relationships, because these happened on the fringes of heteronormative life, were an unknown quantity, and considered by many to be insignificant or less meaningful than heterosexual couplings. A divorce or news of a break-up of a heterosexual relationship, back then, would generally be met in the office with a tremendous sense of interest, shock or surprise. Not so my break-up with C. I felt unseen but I was accustomed to it and so I sat gloomily behind my desk and tried to work.

My well-meaning boss at the time had rather inappropriately suggested that Farm Boy, B, and I attempt a relationship – "you are so good together", he said. To those who had little contact with the lesbian and gay community, homosexual relationships were not "real". A frequent response to the reply of "four years" after someone asked how long C and I had been together was "Really? That's amazing!" It is a response that my 22-year partnership still elicits in 2016, although perhaps for different reasons.

176

And so I was alone in my misery. For months afterwards I would habitually scan the interior of the various coffee shops and other haunts C used to frequent, expecting to see her. And each time I would be struck by a searing sense of loss.

There was something about the idea of a free Nelson Mandela that allowed me to contemplate leaving South Africa to find a neutral space to collect my thoughts. I resolved to return to Europe. I had no idea what I wanted to do there, only that I wanted to shed everything – my country, my relationship, my home, my parents, my friends. I wanted no props. I wanted to find myself stripped of everything familiar, all the accoutrements that had accumulated to form my identity. And in order to do this I would have to leave, alone, and see whether I could withstand it all, find out what was inside.

I had never really internalised any roadmap for my life. There was no husband, electrified fence, 2.5 children or an SUV on the horizon. There was no planned career trajectory. There had never been a female newspaper editor, so that was out of the question. I was a lesbian and I wasn't sure exactly where my life would lead. Back then, becoming a mother was impossible. There was always IVF but you had to conceal that you were a gay woman and, besides, being pregnant and giving birth were not conditions I wanted to experience. Equal rights with regard to marriage and every other aspect were not even on the radar at that time.

There were few lesbian role models, not that these are necessary, but when one is invisible they certainly help. Martina Navratilova and Billie Jean King were about the only two highly visible gay women who would immediately spring to mind. Other than that, homosexual men and lesbians were generally portrayed as sad deviants, doomed either to live lonely lives or die from drug overdoses or HIV. We were a completely unknown quantity to everyone but ourselves.

THE DEBRIS was ankle-deep but the knowledge that a large Catholic family had once inhabited the magnificent four-storey Belle Époque house near the Museum voor Schone Kunsten in Antwerp, Belgium, which I was now systematically stripping inside, brought a measure of comfort.

Also there was a fortuitous synchronicity in being offered the opportunity to rip out the innards of this house, an ideal landscape for the personal psychic implosion that I was, worryingly and in retrospect, experiencing as a dispassionate observer. It was as if I were a specimen trapped in a glass slide being peered at through a microscope by some first-person omniscient.

There was no better country to unravel in than Belgium. It was the cockpit of Europe and home to a small and tight circle of friends who would not mind my descent into madness. By default I had learned to speak Afrikaans fluently, audible evidence, I suppose, that the "Afrikanerisation" project aimed at immigrants had succeeded to a certain extent.

Afrikaans felt comfortable in my mouth. The language had moved into my head and was lolling on a couch with its feet up on the coffee table. I sometimes dreamed in Afrikaans. I had always been conflicted. I loved the language but not the people who had forced it on me, who had claimed it as their own and had come to be associated with it. However, understanding and speaking Afrikaans opened a door to one of its linguistic maternal roots – Dutch or, rather, Flemish, in Flanders.

In Antwerp this meant that at least I could communicate in a rudimentary fashion with those around me. It was a dialect that could, in a grocery store and with a few guttural flourishes, pass as something familiar.

It was also Afrikaans that had nudged me towards Tom and René and a friendship that has now spanned more than 20 years. Tom, who first burst onto the Belgian literary scene as an *enfant terrible*, is today considered one of the most significant European authors. Our friendship began over a dinner in Antwerp when I had turned to the South African-born artist Philip Badenhorst, who had fled to Belgium in the 1980s, and said something to him in Afrikaans. Tom, who was seated at the head of the table, leaned in. If he had been a dog, his ears would have strained and tilted in the direction of the shared frequency that filtered through the chatter.

So if I was going to fall apart, I wanted some of these friends nearby. I missed C like a phantom limb. She had been my gentle emotional centre and I had gone and fucked it all up. We had arranged to meet later in the year in Toronto, though, and I was looking forward to it. But first I needed to mend the shattered vase of myself.

At this juncture, I could hardly face myself in the mirror, so Hotel Rasheed (as I had named the house in homage to the Baghdad hotel that had been a target for both the Americans and everyone else during the first Gulf War) was the perfect place to rearrange my internal detritus.

Hotel Rasheed had been purchased by a Dutch writer who now lived in Antwerp. He had grand plans for the house, but first the false ceilings needed to be ripped out, ghastly lime-green-patterned aluminium cladding in the bathroom had to be wrenched from the walls, and thick layers of paint and slack carpeting had to be scraped and lifted off a magnificent wooden staircase.

I took up residence in the only habitable room, a sort of attic on the top floor. It provided a view of the street below and not much else. Each morning I would get up, pull on the same tracksuit pants, top and sneakers, and get to work.

The kitchen downstairs was rudimentary but perfectly suited to a recluse with minimal dietary, spiritual and emotional needs. There was a kettle and a hotplate. A weekly trip to the cheapest retailer, Woolworths (not to be confused with the South African store), would yield tins of ready-made food (curried spinach and chickpeas), a litre of milk and some coffee. Enough to provide the energy required for a fevered demolition job.

At the time Tom rented a small flat, where he could write undisturbed, around the corner from Hotel Rasheed, and some mornings he would pass by and ring the doorbell to check whether I was still alive or just rocking quietly in a corner. I would peer out of the attic window to see him standing beside his bicycle in the street below, his beautiful, concerned, bespectacled face looking up at me.

"You okay?" he would shout up.

"Ja. Fine."

"Okay then. Maybe we can have coffee later if I manage to write enough today."

His check-ins reminded me I was alive, that I was loved. They were all I needed to keep breathing.

I was on a road to nowhere but didn't care. When I wasn't working, the mattress on the floor in the attic became my refuge. My only company was a small, flickering black-and-white portable TV with a wire hanger that served as a makeshift antenna hooked up to a window frame. Through the snowy screen I would absent-mindedly watch moving shapes that spoke Flemish.

The occasional English newspaper would bring the possibility of a job in England, but reading the adverts was enough to induce nausea and instant fatigue. Besides, when I did try and apply for one of them, rereading the application afterwards I found that I had misspelled my own name. Best not then.

Seeking therapy had not been an option. Getting through this was simply a continuation of life as it had always been. Muddle your way through this on your own and hold thumbs that some inner compass will lead to another side, a better side. Georg and Barbara were trapped in their own Hotel Rasheed and would have been of little help to me.

Eviscerating the house enabled me to find a new, physical strength, which made up for what was lacking mentally elsewhere. If my body could powerfully hold it all, perhaps my mind would not drop out somewhere on a tram or on the pavement. I also discovered that I had a capacity to work at a feverish and fiercely focused pace, which was driven partly by an impatience to uncover what the house looked like without the kitsch 1970s decor disaster that had disfigured it. The gorgeous exterior of the house was also as yet unseen; it had been smothered with some sort of grey, spray-on, twentieth-century gravel coating. As I worked, I imagined myself a decorating superwoman freeing the indifferent bricks and mortar from years of impacted dirt, grime and bad taste.

About five months into the renovation a reassembling gradually dawned, together with a realisation that a world existed outside the dust heap on Admiraal de Boisotstraat. Like a game of Tetris, I could see the blocks slotting into place and gradually I began to feel ready to abandon Hotel Rasheed and try to face the world.

It was not immediately evident, or apparent, that any wisdom or insight had been gained from the renovation/implosion, but an instinctual urge to move on slowly blossomed.

London beckoned. I had also, in the meantime, resolved to return, towards the end of the year, to South Africa. A hurdle overcome.

LONDON. ALOOF, COSMOPOLITAN, seemingly indifferent. Perfect terrain to try out this newish, albeit loosely held, self.

A bed was found in the spare room of a townhouse occupied by a fervent feminist lesbian couple I had known in Cape Town. While I had hoped to venture out on my own, it was inevitable that I would be drawn into various social arrangements and soon I found myself tagging along.

A rather famous American feminist author and psychotherapist, who was also considered to be a leading authority on lesbian sex (in fact she was known as the "goddess" of lesbian sex), had been invited around this time to tour the UK in the slipstream of the release of her latest book. I, of course, had read none of her books. My friends, who were seriously connected in feminist circles, had read all of them. They had also been asked to chaperone the author during her London tour.

And so it was that they were tasked with collecting her from a flat near Kings Cross station for a talk she was due to give somewhere in the city. My friends drove a 1960-something VW camper van, orange, and the Sex Goddess, with a cascade of blonde curls and distinctly "femme" dress sense (these were key markers back in the '90s), wedged herself onto the back seat next to me.

She was chatty and witty, and I soon grew aware of a low-level flirtation, a hand brushing a knee and lingering, a gaze that locked for a little too long not to hold some meaning.

Her talk that night was about how we needed to live our truths and passions as lesbians. It was also about being butch, femme or fluid and how we could learn to own our sexuality in a world where it was essentially entirely absent or negated in mainstream. Being gay, lesbian or, more controversially, bisexual was to be rendered marginal.

She was engaging, controversial, loud, clever and funny. Very funny. Later I learned that she had once been described as a "psychocomedian". Afterwards, when we dropped her off at the flat, she leaned in a little too close to me and whispered a sultry goodbye, adding, "I hope to see you again."

I didn't think anything more as we drove off, but we had hardly settled back home when the phone rang. It was the Sex Goddess's agent. She had a message, she said, or rather a command. I was to please make my way to Compendium Books in Camden at 5pm the following day where the author would be giving a talk and signing copies of her book.

With a desolate diary, I was up for anything.

I arrived at 6pm when I knew the talk would be nearing its end. A little bell on the bookshop entrance rang as I tried to sneak in unobserved. The Sex Goddess looked up and smiled. I nodded towards the door, indicating we should leave soon. She wrapped up but almost immediately found herself surrounded by a phalanx of dykes wanting to engage. I held back, browsing.

Eventually I approached, leaned in authoritatively and announced, "Sorry, she has to go now." The Sex Goddess collected her bag and we left, two strangers in a strange town.

We hardly spoke on the tube back to the rat hole, where we spent the next two days in bed in our very own version of an SLN Hollywood movie.

182

I had missed physical contact. It was liberating to be with a complete stranger who knew nothing about me. I was a blank slate to her (and myself still at that stage) and could reveal or conceal what I wished. I could not hide, however, that I was South African, which intrigued her. I found it easier to talk about home with someone who knew little about its complexities.

Then it was time for her to leave for home, which was San Francisco. I accompanied her to Heathrow, where we tried to find some privacy in the only available space, the women's loo. We emerged a short while later dishevelled, flushed and smiling, trailed by disapproving and befuddled looks from women fluffing their hair and fixing their lipstick in the bathroom mirrors.

The encounter was surreal, dreamlike, exciting, liberating, warm and memorable. We would have both won Oscars for best performance in a lesbian fantasy come true. It was my very own Erica Jong moment. My zipless fuck.

I lingered in London for a while and moved from a feminist non-smoking, vegetarian household into sharing a cramped house with two smoking, beer-drinking, meat-eating, television-watching, carousing heterosexual male friends, both ex-South Africans who were hanging out and working in London. I hardly noticed the transition, flexible as I am.

The fog of uncertainty soon began to lift and I began to prepare to finally return home, firmly in the pilot's seat but still with no clear personal flight plan. Saturn, having done its job, was moving out of my astrological 12th house and looking elsewhere to wreak havoc on some other unsuspecting 29-year-old. The next time it returned, I decided, I would be ready.

THE TICKING of the clocks was maddening. Georg loved clocks and had always kept four or five of them going, in the same room. There was the infuriating wooden cuckoo clock with its cutesy carved Alpine detail and two wooden cones that dangled off thin chains like a little pine scrotum. Georg had bought it on some business trip or other. Positioned next to it on the lounge wall was a hideous, square, chiming, brass-and-wood pendulum clock with two brass cylindrical weights attached to chains. Every day Georg would gently tug the chains so that the weights were positioned unevenly about halfway up, ensuring that yet another 24 hours would not pass unnoticed.

Then there was the mantelpiece clock. This one was sleek and minimalist, a 1950s model, encased in light wood. Mercifully, it didn't tick or tock because the wind-up mechanism had been replaced by one powered by batteries. There was an alarm clock in the kitchen, along with a wind-up egg-timer and an hourglass encased in a little brass scaffold. There were clocks in the bedroom and the bathroom. Clocks everywhere.

And thermometers – one outside on the veranda, another near the back door and yet another in the lounge. My father had them all – gadgets to control time, foretell the day's climate, all designed to impose some structure within the tiny, hermetic universe of Georg's two-bedroomed cottage.

Every half-hour the clocks would whistle, hoot and chime (once) and then later for each hour they were marking. It was enough to drive anyone, apart from Georg, steadily deranged. Anticipating the cacophony was in itself nerve-racking – one could never doze off in a chair undisturbed, for example. First there was the stereophonic audible ticking and then the striking of the half-hours and then the striking of the hours. Georg found it comforting. The clocks, and his fat dachshund Nina, who had the most fetid halitosis, kept him company.

While the days through April 1994 in Georg's home in Somerset West were punctuated by the regularity of his clocks, this was a month that marked a turning point for South Africa. It also marked a turning point for another country on the continent – Rwanda. In the same month two major twentieth-century events on the African continent took place almost simultaneously – one filled with promise and hope, the other with utter horror.

The early 1990s in South Africa had flown past in a blur. Citizens could hardly hold onto daily events as we hurtled towards the future. Mandela was a free man, touring the world and the country. Agreements and accords were signed, a last white referendum had been held, talks about talks began, and then, finally, the actual talks began at the Convention for a Democratic South Africa (CODESA). Discussion took place in a hangar in Kempton Park, which was loftily named the World Trade Centre. (Later, the venue was converted into the Emperors Palace casino complex, a somewhat fitting tribute to the global economy that was about to shatter world financial markets a few years later.)

Back then, though, between 1991 and 1993, before negotiations and South Africa's first-ever democratic election took place, out of public view the country's National Intelligence Service began a frantic scrabbling to destroy 44 tons of paper and microfilm, wiping out the names of everyone and anyone who had been part of the apartheid spy apparatus or those in the liberation movement who had been co-opted into it.

This void, this disappearance of the names of those who had been responsible for covert and deadly operations – both within the apartheid state and the ANC – would later begin to play itself out destructively in national politics, first at the country's Truth and Reconciliation Commission, which was established in 1996, and later, once Nelson Mandela had exited stage right. The spies and spooks remained and continued to work behind the scenes, establishing a new network.

In 1993 the country had been taken to the brink when Chris Hani, beloved leader of the ANC's military wing uMkhonto we Sizwe and the South African Communist Party, had been assassinated in his driveway in the suburb of Benoni one Sunday morning by a white right-wing Polish immigrant named Janusz Walus.

Outraged citizens across the country took to the streets, marching in protest, threatening to take revenge. The killing of Hani was an attempt to destabilise the negotiations and many whites, already fearing a "race war", believed that it was about to erupt. However, it was a re-gal Nelson Mandela who, for the first time, addressed citizens in a live television broadcast on SABC and thwarted a potential bloodbath.

That the Nationalist-controlled public broadcaster allowed this might have seemed surprising, but in fact there was no other option. This was the moment Mandela – who had not yet been elected to presidential office – stamped his authority and leadership on the country. It was only Mandela who could contain the grief and rage, and he did so in stern, measured tones, reminding the nation that it had been a white woman who had witnessed the shooting of Hani and reported the kill-er's registration number to the police. He warned that a race war was exactly what those who had orchestrated this campaign were aiming at.

Mandela contained the moment. We paused, we mourned, but we resolved to push on.

In 1994 we were naïve and in thrall to Mandela. We believed in what became known as the "Madiba magic" and the idea that we would or could become a Rainbow Benetton Nation. It was Mandela who told the battered and bruised nation – black and white – that we were beautiful and loved, that we were capable of more, deserved more. For now.

Like a benevolent father arriving at the scene of terrible violence and abuse, he metaphorically scooped us up in his arms and told us we

186

would be okay. His was a symbolic leadership. I have forgiven, so you, too, must forgive each other.

The horrors that lurked in graves, marked and unmarked, the nightmares that played out in the minds of those who had been tortured, or that haunted those who were now faced with what they had done, should be put aside (for now), he told us. Nothing should be allowed to taint the "miracle" that was about to happen. We were wounded, tired and afraid, but we were also elated and relieved. We drank it in.

On 6 April 1994, 21 days before all South Africans were due to go to the polls in our first democratic general election, an aircraft carrying the dictatorial Rwandan president, Juvénal Habyarimana, along with neighbouring Burundian president Cyprien Ntaryamira, was shot down while coming in to land at Kigali airport, killing everyone on board.

South Africans, hermetic in our regional existence, had hardly paid any attention to Rwanda and the political currents of the region. We were too caught up in our own drama and, besides, apart from Zimbabwe, Angola and Mozambique, many South Africans seldom cast their minds towards the rest of Africa.

April 7, the day after the assassination, marked the start of a 100-day genocide in Rwanda as Hutus and Tutsis turned on each other in an "inexplicable" spasm of violence, using anything and everything as weapons – guns, clubs, knives, machetes, hammers, axes – to kill anyone and anything that moved.

The images coming out of Rwanda ricocheted across the world: piles of bodies hacked and burned, bloated and rotting on the side of dusty roads, rivers turned red with blood, refugees swarming across the country's borders hoping to escape the insanity.

Georg watched some of it on the news on television. He subscribed to a German satellite service, deeming South African television hardly worth watching. The Germany he witnessed on cable TV was not a Germany he knew or understood, however. He watched the gaudy, loud talk and variety shows, with their tattooed contestants with strange haircuts and dress codes, with disdain.

"Ze problem is zat nobody vants to assimilate," he said one day when I was visiting.

"Who?"

"Ze immigrants, ze Turks and all ze ozzers."

"Why should they?"

"Vell, if you are going to live in Germany zen you must learn to speak German, you must live like zose people in zat country. You must abide by zeir rules and customs."

"So you are telling me that if, for example, you had moved to Turkey, you would have become a Muslim and learned to speak Turkish?"

"No." Georg looked at me. "Vhy vould I do zat?"

"You expect those who move to Germany to do that, so why wouldn't you apply the same to yourself?"

He seemed exasperated by the questions. I pushed a bit more.

"Because you think that Germans are superior," I said. "You think that the West is superior and that everyone should want to be German or British or American. For you it doesn't work the other way around. We come here and we shouldn't become African because this is, in your view, inferior. That is the basis of your argument and it doesn't make sense."

"Ag, you alvays tvist it. It is not zat simple."

"It is," I said as I rose from the lounge chair to make tea. "It is that simple."

Like many of those who watched the genocide in Rwanda on the news channels, Georg could not make sense of the images. They occurred in a one-dimensional realm, devoid of context or meaning. The narrative of what had preceded the genocide escaped him, as it did most who were suddenly forced to witness the Dantean horror on their flickering television screens, Ian McEwan's "evening clinic of referred pain", as he describes it in his novel *Enduring Love*.

Without an understanding of the history of Rwanda, the roles of Uganda, the US and the UK in the tragedy, the genocide was, for many like Georg, a journey into Conrad's *Heart of Darkness*. It only confirmed the view of Africa as uncivilised, brutal and atavistic.

"Ja, well, you see. Zis is ze problem."

"What do you mean?"

"Well, look at it! Look at what zey are doing. Killing each other like savages."

"Savages?"

"Yes, look at it. Just look at it. It is terrible."

"So you'd approve if they did it with clockwork precision then?"

"Vat are you talking about?" he shouted.

"Well, if they gave each victim a number, put them on a train and sent them to a concentration camp, would that be less savage?"

My father looked at me with horror. He knew where the conversation was headed.

"It is not the same," he said.

"Why? Because those who are ordering and doing the killing are not reading Schiller, listening to Beethoven and throwing the ball for their dog when they get home?"

Silence. Just the ticking of the clocks.

1994 WAS THE first time I had ever cast my vote in South Africa. I voted for the ANC and Nelson Mandela. I thought everyone in my close circle would do the same, so had my political tolerance severely tested when I learned that some friends were going to vote for the opposition, the Democratic Party. For purely practical reasons, they said.

"But . . . but . . . how can you? How can you not vote for Nelson Mandela?" I asked.

"Well, the ANC is guaranteed a huge majority and so the opposition needs votes to keep it in check," argued one close friend, quite rationally.

It was not a reasoning I was prepared to indulge then, although my friend had every right to vote for the party of his choice. That's democracy. Later he did tell me he regretted voting for the DP in 1994 because, after Mandela, he could not bring himself to vote for the ANC.

Georg had decided he was voting for Mangosuthu Buthelezi and his Inkatha Freedom Party. Inkatha had a controversial and violent history of collaboration with the apartheid state, which exploited the ethnic nationalism in KwaZulu-Natal. Inkatha had also threatened, until the last minute, not to participate in the elections. "He iss a good chap and he can hold off ze ANC," Georg confidently informed me.

I wondered where he was getting his low-down on the local political landscape. Like so many white South Africans, the extent of his personal experience of the country was gleaned mostly when running small errands to the local grocery store at the mall down the road and little else. He had never attended a political meeting or rally, had never ventured into a township. He hardly interacted with anyone other than those who walked their dogs with him in the local park, yet his opinions were set and firm. It was an echo chamber of ignorant, amplified consensus.

Georg had always glibly dismissed my reports to him of what I had witnessed in the townships in the 1980s. He belonged to that generation of white men who were certain that only they possessed the wisdom, capacity and the right to the correct and only opinion or view of the world. Usually this was reinforced by their lack of engagement with others – particularly those who might disagree – forging a sort of blind insolence that defied reason and debate, even in the face of evidence to the contrary. Later, in 1996, when live broadcasts of the devastating testimony by victims of apartheid who appeared at the Truth and Reconciliation Commission were beamed into homes across the country, the same stubborn denial prevailed.

The months and weeks leading up to the election on 27 April were heady and all-consuming. There were rallies, concerts and mass meetings, a botched attempt by the right-wing Afrikaner Weerstandsbeweging (the AWB) to invade the fictitious homeland of Bophuthatswana during which the invaders were shot dead on live TV, as well as the Shell House massacre, when thousands of Inkatha supporters marched on the ANC's headquarters in downtown Johannesburg.

A month before the elections a new flag for the country was unveiled, which was a hugely symbolic act. The old flag – orange, white and blue, with its three smaller flags, the Union Jack, the Orange Free State flag and the flag of the former South African Republic, approved in 1927 and first hoisted in 1928 – had come to represent white minority rule. It was universally loathed and had to go. A new national anthem for the country, the hymn *Nkosi Sikelel' iAfrika*, now mashed up to include a verse from the old anthem *Die Stem* and with a new English tail tagged on, was also officially launched.

Voting day in my suburb was carnivalesque. A long queue curled for several blocks around the venue, which was a local school up the road from my apartment. I dressed in ANC colours and walked there with Tom, who was covering the elections in South Africa and by then had got caught up in election fever. Entrepreneurial residents quickly cashed in on the pop-up crowd and were selling coffee, tea, cooldrinks and snacks, and while the bulk of those in the queue were white, because of the spatial apartheid of the city, there were enough black South Africans registered in the area to hint at the "rainbow" we believed ourselves to be. An elderly white lady in the queue ahead of me turned and began to mumble something before fixing her gaze on my ANC regalia. Earlier an election monitor had asked me to remove it. Regulations were that no one was allowed to display political colours near voting venues, a rule the vast majority of South Africans simply ignored.

"Everyone in Gugulethu is wearing ANC colours," I informed the election officer. "I'd like to see you trying to tell people not to."

He shrugged and walked off.

It was a day beyond description. As South Africans, collectively for the first time in history, we were free to determine our democratic future. It was a moment few of us could have imagined, but it happened.

Seeing Nelson Mandela walk out of jail and putting my little X next to his face on that ballot paper remain a highlight for me. By then, 33 years of my life had been consumed, one way or another, by the politics of my country. But in free South Africa there was more to come, much more. I would gradually find myself being eased into a century and a world that certainly were starting to feel and look much better than the ones we were leaving behind us.

WE FIND where we need to be by looking for a path. But what if, at first, no one lets on that there *is* a path? What if it is a well-kept secret? Or what if there is no path, no "footsteps", so to speak, to follow in, particularly if those prints, those traces of what and who has come before have been erased, forgotten, silenced, displaced?

What if there is no known way out, no way forward?

Perhaps it is only those of us who feel comfortable in our stability and status, whose histories are apparently not outwardly disturbed, who possess this elusive map and who assume that life, from one generation to the next, will continue without rupture, give or take a tragedy or a war or two.

For many middle-class white South Africans this was the aspirational dream that leaked and bled off the pages of newspapers and magazines with their adverts for banks, real estate, cars, decor, weddings, clothes or whatever else came to represent the Western figment of the isolated and hermetic, happy nuclear family in the suburbs.

A house with a garden (and a pool), access to cheap education, a gap year, university, marriage if you were a woman, a job if you were a man, family, children, comfortable retirement, grandchildren and a memorable funeral with a notice in the classified section and a great eulogy about a life well lived at the end of it all. And of course the photo albums that survive you, proof that you once lived. The Hollywood movie. All the boxes ticked.

Georg and Barbara, in retrospect, did not appear to have such a map or collective vision for themselves or their small family. We appeared to exist in the moment, taking life as it arrived, improvising along the way. As the martial arts expert Bruce Lee said, it felt, to me at least, that we were formless, shapeless like water.

Perhaps this is just how it was or is for everyone. Maybe we all just improvise.

But for me there appeared to be no expectation of my brother and me as children, well, at least no overt articulation of this, apart from my father's suggestion that I learn the hairdressing trade.

Neither Georg nor Barbara ever spoke of looking forward to Albert or me getting married or looking forward to the day they would become grandparents. We were a family that did not celebrate birthdays or other occasions, not even anniversaries or academic accomplishments, with parties or material reward. Neither Albert nor I have a single photograph of a birthday party; and I don't recall ever going to anyone else's birthday parties either. Perhaps this was not a ritual as established as it has become in the twenty-first century, when every milestone from a pre-school graduation to a 21st birthday has been rendered "momentous" and worthy of collective celebration.

There are no photographs of us surrounded by extended family, cousins, uncles, aunts, grandparents, around Christmas trees or dinner tables. Always just the four of us, together but oddly apart.

What held the silence, the lack of engagement when it came to momentous decisions that could determine our future? Was it because Georg and Barbara could not imagine a future? Were they unable to see the landscape because it was not one that had formed an essential part of their notion of self? Was it because there was no common culture, tradition, language or social and professional networks that rooted or bound us as a family or that pointed us in the familiar ruts of our ancestors? Was it because we were strangers in a strange land that never quite felt like home for Barbara or Georg? Like all migrants everywhere. Did either of them long for, in their private moments, a home they once knew?

Was everything just lost in translation?

Or was this the collateral damage of growing up in politically unstable climes, in an unfree environment where a personal future cannot be imagined outside of the political? Hitler's twelve-year rule ruined Germany; it had forced its citizens to participate or become swept up in tumultuous historical forces. Salazar impressed himself on the psyche of the Portuguese and the country's colonies for 36 years. In 1994 South Africa had been burdened with over 330 years of imperial, colonial and apartheid history. It was still starkly evident all around us.

By the time I was 33 years old, Nationalist leaders – HF Verwoerd, BJ Vorster, PW Botha and FW de Klerk – had shaped my internal architecture as well as that of everyone with whom I shared this geographical space during that period of history.

Without them, these dour men, there was no me, or at least a version of me.

And then Mandela appeared – a beaming and benevolent colossus.

Mandela, democracy and an opportunity for South Africans to reimagine ourselves and the world we lived in. A once-in-a-lifetime opportunity.

The slow release of the once-palpable and ever-present threat that had permeated everyday life in the country for so long, and for as long as I could remember, allowed, for the first time, the rudiments of a new dream and the possibility of a life to take shape with some goal or destination hovering on the horizon. It allowed the possibility of fashioning a life not always in opposition to intrusive external forces.

But what would this life be? To set a goal you need to pinpoint it on the horizon, or at least know in which direction to move. And at the age of 33 in 1994, I began to feel as if I was treading water, no longer flowing.

And then it happened.

Our meeting was accidental and through mutual friends. It was a complicated but thrilling meeting, resulting in a relationship that has endured, at the time of writing, for over 20 years.

Because the recovered history between these pages is mine, she, let's call her X, will, unfortunately, have to remain present here in her absence. It is not my right to reveal her story, which is now inexorably bound with mine. Be aware, however, that she is woven into every line and was with me on every thrilling step I began to take as a free woman in a free country.

But first, for all of this to occur, I had to learn to be vulnerable, to enter the space without armour, to disarm my psychic guns and find the courage to be real. I had to learn to expose myself to the risk of being seen, not as I had been seeing myself, but reflected through someone who loved and understood me. Someone who was and is able to withstand and dismantle all the props I had used just to keep moving.

From the start of the relationship X brought with her a vision of a future I had never contemplated or thought possible. She wanted children. It was not negotiable.

"But . . . but I don't think I will be a good parent . . . I am too selfish, too preoccupied, emotionally ill-equipped. I am a lesbian, we are not supposed to procreate," I protested.

I had never felt the urge to be a mother, had never thought of some ticking biological clock. Besides, I could hardly look after myself. I lived alone in a small home and led a life in which most of the needs on Maslow's hierarchy were vaguely satisfied. It was enough.

I continued to work as a journalist, I had a mattress on the floor, a music system, a great couch and a small bar fridge stocked usually with a litre of milk and ground coffee. My culinary needs were elementary and I ate on the run. I had a great circle of friends and I had freedom. What more did a woman need?

I had successfully managed to avoid ever moving in permanently with a partner, including C. This way, I reckoned, a relationship remained untainted by the banal currents of everyday life. This way one avoided bickering about who took out the trash, who didn't wash the dishes, who left the towel on the bathroom floor.

There was and is no blueprint for how to live life as a lesbian and therein lay the freedom. One could move fluidly between worlds while still keeping one's own world private and safe. X, however, was uncompromising and, try as I might to maintain and continue this bachelorette way of life, the ultimatum arrived. Either we move in and do this properly or we don't do it at all.

I surrendered.

We talk our children into existence. Some of us don't, which is fine, but generally the idea that we will procreate and have children is a firmly entrenched one in most societies. It is how we survive as a species.

That first conversation in 1994 about children was to linger like a blank bubble in a comic strip waiting to be filled in. But back then I hoped it would float off in the ether and be caught by some other couple's whispering and longing for a child.

IF GEORG THOUGHT anything about my now-regular visits to him accompanied by the same gorgeous woman every time, he said nothing. What did he think? And did he ever wonder why I had never introduced him to a man who might have been a potential son-in-law?

I would find out later, much later, but for now this significant development in my life, my new relationship, became part of the familiar silence about everything else that mattered, possibly to us both. It was just how it was between us. Our bond held simply because I had been a part of Georg's life for over 30 years and I was his daughter. A stranger in many ways.

Our conversations were seldom personal. It was the political, history and the past that kept us talking, arguing, connecting or creating a further silent chasm.

During an idle conversation over tea one sunny Sunday about his time as a prisoner of war in England, Georg casually remarked that fellow prisoners had cornered suspected homosexuals among the captives and had flung them from a first-floor window. He told the story matter-of-factly, with neither disgust nor glee.

I stopped mid-sip, horrified at the admission. It should have been my moment. I should have spoken up then and said something like "Well, then you would have had to throw me out of the window too", but I didn't.

It was too painful to confront and so I buried it, along with many other oblique slights I thought I had heard over the years. I did not care enough then to confront the personal. I was not ready for that battle, not yet.

When it came to my father, I chose, when I could, the larger canvas of the political as our battleground.

Barbara, on the other hand, I suspected, might have known or understood, but she couldn't speak, so my secret was safe with her. Years before, on a rare visit to a home I shared for a short while with Garbo, Barbara had cast a keen eye over everything.

I had made sure to remove all evidence of the relationship, taking down or hiding photographs of happy lesbians gathered around a dinner table or me and my lover beaming, arms draped around each other, on a rocky beach.

Barbara inspected the house, running her finger along a shelf or tabletop checking for dust, no doubt to test whether any of the pride she had taken in maintaining our home had rubbed off on me.

To disguise the true nature of my relationship I had separated two single beds in the spare room we had been using while a leak in the roof over the main bedroom was being repaired. Barbara walked in and surveyed the beds.

"Where you sleep?"

"Here, in the one bed," I said, standing behind her, arms crossed, wishing she'd walk out of the room.

"And your friend?"

"There – on the other bed."

"Now whya you donta push da beds together?"

I was taken aback by her suggestion and have always wondered if this was her way of letting me know that she knew.

But I would never find out.

AFTER THE ELECTION in 1994, South Africa set about finalising its new constitution. At the CODESA talks before the elections, all of the parties had agreed to 34 constitutional principles that would later be included in the final constitution, which is considered now to be one of the most progressive in the world.

A technical committee had been tasked with grappling with legal complexities and had turned to international human rights documents to find precedents. However, no international document formally or specifically afforded equal rights for lesbians and gays or offered protection from discrimination on the grounds of sexual orientation.

It was a contentious clause and it was opposed by some political parties and many ordinary citizens in South Africa, which is an essentially conservative, patriarchal, religious and homophobic society. Intolerance of one sort or another was woven into the psyche of the rainbow nation. The apartheid state had criminalised same-sex relationships.

Opposition to the specific inclusion of the sexual orientation clause would eventually be challenged by LGBTIA+ activists (although there were only LGBT ones at that point), who lobbied furiously for its inclusion. Activists mobilised across the country, gathering thousands of signatures. For several weekends a table was set up in the Cape Town nightclub Angels with activists convincing clubbers to sign. An indication of how fearful many of us were was the response to being asked to support the campaign.

"I don't want my name to be made public" and "Will my boss find out?" were some of the comments and questions shouted over the thumping music.

The addition of "sexual orientation" in Section 9 of the constitution and the equality clause was supported by the African National Congress, and in 1995 the constitutional committee accepted the technical committee's recommendation that these words be included in the final constitution.

At the time, television panel discussions, talk radio stations and news programmes devoted much airtime to debating the matter, usually with bigots and homophobes dominating, calling in to spew what felt like a sewerage pipe of hatred. Shows would inevitably begin with the provocative "Should lesbians and gays have equal rights?" or "Should lesbians and gays be allowed to adopt?", which would inevitably attract those responding to the hidden bias of the question.

A less superficial debate might have been elicited had the topic been framed differently. However, a question like "Why is it important for gays and lesbians to have equal rights?" would have required hosts to challenge their own prejudice or undertake research about equality in relation to South Africa's oppressive past. This was a matter that many in the ANC understood and it was because of their unwavering support that these rights were finally adopted.

Listening to an afternoon talk show one day while I was working, I stared at the radio in disbelief as one listener called in to offer the opinion that "homosexuals should die by lethal injection". The comment struck me like an unexpected blow. Hearing it articulated so glibly while the host seemed at a loss for words in challenging him was depressing. But I was to learn in time that the country and its citizens would have to learn a new language and way of engaging about many issues, including issues of race and class. It is a process that continues and that will do so for years to come as we navigate ourselves out of the intellectual quagmire bequeathed to us by apartheid. But in that moment it felt deeply personal and painful, even as I recognised that the airing of views such as these was part of the process.

Talk about "moffies", homosexuals and "the gays" seemed to follow me whenever I was in earshot of a radio or TV and in fact seemed to come up every time I visited Georg. Georg spent much of his time alone at home with either the television blaring in the lounge or a radio on in the kitchen or his bedroom. While I acknowledged that this was his way of connecting with the world and keeping up with current affairs, I hated that he didn't switch it off when I visited. It felt disrespectful, but it was not an issue worth arguing over.

Considering his comment that day about throwing homosexuals out of a window, I'd find myself reflexively flinching when a snippet of a discussion, where the word "lesbian" always seemed to be articulated two or three decibels louder than the rest of the conversation, would drift between us. I dreaded my father idly picking up on it, what opinion he might offer in an unguarded moment, and hearing directly that he might agree with the homophobes and bigots. In these moments I would try to distract him, usually by suggesting that we move outside onto the veranda.

I had wanted X to meet my parents so that she could survey part of the emotional landscape that had shaped me.

This is what we internalise when we are marginalised. We become marginal or create a community of our own where we are safe. I had been pleasantly surprised travelling the world to find an alternative family in the lesbian and gay safe spaces that existed in London, Toronto, New York, Berlin, Vancouver and Antwerp. It was a world that was unequivocally ours, mine. From the dykes on bikes to the drag queens and all the shades in between, this was, I thought, my global family. I could navigate the "straight" world out there, but straight people had little insight into my world, our world, and I preferred it that way. To gain entry, they needed me. But few were interested or curious enough to ask about it.

Society in South Africa was only just beginning to "see" the LGBTI community and hear our stories, but we were, back then, a long, long way from being fully accepted. I hated simply being tolerated or viewed as a freak. During one of the first Pride marches in Johannesburg, a rabid group of Christians, literally thumping their Bibles, walked alongside the parade shouting that we would burn in hell. As we marched past apartment blocks in downtown Johannesburg, residents hurled bottles at the defiant gay and beautiful crowd demanding our space.

Navigating new freedoms would take some getting used to. And the greatest freedom – becoming a parent – was yet to come. Somehow I had entered a brave new world. This world, one I could never have imagined as a child, had slowly been taking shape since that first space trip by Yuri Gagarin in April 1961. It was our desire and our rush to the moon that facilitated the development of new and spectacular technologies that would in many ways come to shape the twenty-first century and the way we now live, for better and for worse.

My work as a journalist had expanded after I moved from the *Cape Times*, and I gained experience in weekly and monthly magazines. By then, though, the job had become mostly a means to an end, a way of earning a living, and I hated the stifling routine of being in an office. Journalists, I believed, belonged not behind desks but out in the world.

My foray into women's magazines was unexpected. At the time

Jane Raphaely, the formidable doyenne of publishing in South Africa, understood that the country was changing fast and that her publications needed to provide readers with new views on the changing vista. Jane wanted to engage with some of the weightier matters that had become part of the national conversation, things like political rights, women's rights, and health rights, and she recruited several unlikely hard-news journalists who had been shaped in the cut-and-thrust of daily newspapers. We were to interview returning exiles, do in-depth features on the new constitution and find human interest stories that reflected the exciting changes.

The transition from grimy, untidy newsroom to the quiet, genteel hum of women's magazines took some adjusting for me. Because the magazines were monthly, the pace was also much more leisurely – too leisurely for my temperament.

Those of us who had spent years reporting out in the field often stood out at boardroom meetings where the beauty, fashion, food and decor editors would present their offerings for the coming month. It was the first time I came to learn a certain "magazine speak", like "navy blue is the new black" or "30 is the new 20".

But no matter how trite or insignificant we might have viewed this traditional content, this was an environment in which I was to learn more about the nuts and bolts of publishing than anywhere else. Jane was a generous if eccentric boss and it was up to staff to learn from her vast and considerable experience in the field. It was here, for the first time in my working life, I found that my opinion counted or at least seemed to matter. Jane would glide into one of our glass-panelled offices carrying a mock-up of the magazine's next proposed cover.

"What do you think?"

"Um."

"Do you think this barker works?"

"Um."

Veteran journalist Pippa Green had been employed as a features editor on *Cosmopolitan*, one of the magazines in Jane's Associated Magazines stable. Pippa had spent years in print reporting on trade unions, labour and politics, and she now found herself in what must have felt like Xanadu. A stickler for accuracy, Pippa was soon to learn that women's magazines existed in a parallel universe.

It was her job to edit all of the features that appeared in the magazine, and she found herself having to deal with copy from the magazine's beauty editor, Nicolene Strydom. Nicolene was a law unto herself and an expert on the multimillion-rand beauty industry. Reading her copy, Pippa began to underline, in red, several quotes about a specific beauty product and its apparent capacity for miracles. What had concerned Pippa were the generous statements and quotes that peppered Nicolene's copy. Strolling into the beauty editor's office, permeated permanently by the subtle and gorgeous aroma of the perfumes and cosmetics that were locked in a cupboard, Pippa asked Nicolene who it was that she had quoted in the piece.

"Myself," Nicolene replied confidently.

"But you can't do that," protested Pippa.

"Yes, I can," said Nicolene.

It was clear that different rules, standards and norms applied in this world.

Meanwhile, my relationship with X was deepening. We had come through the fog of the first few impassioned years to find that we shared what was most important, a common worldview. In surrendering completely and committing to the relationship, I had agreed that we move in together. The tiny third-floor bachelor flat had become too cramped for both of us and my protestations that living together was the kiss of death for a relationship were simply ignored.

Earlier on, X had ordered me to get rid of the mattress on the floor, put up curtains, remove the shelves made of bricks and planks, and stock the fridge with proper food and not just coffee and milk.

Later I found a comfort in this domesticity that I had so vehemently resisted and it soon became routine. About three years into the relationship we moved from the small flat into a larger, two-bedroomed one on the second floor in the same block. Creature of habit that I am, I had refused to move to another location and, besides, the apartment block was populated with an eccentric collection of residents whom I had got to know. We felt like fictional characters in Armistead Maupin's

Tales of the City. Most of us were single. There was a sprinkling of elderly tenants who would invite us for strange Eastern European dinners and one or two residents who would occasionally go off their medication and cause havoc, tossing furniture and books from their flats or shouting in the dead of night.

It was the kind of urban living I had always dreamed of. My 20 years in the suburbs had rendered me incapable of living in any space that reminded me of its forced neighbourliness, the smell of braais. I wanted noise, traffic, sirens, late-night drunken street brawls, parking attendants and the anonymity that came with big-city living.

The first adoption by a lesbian in South Africa took place in Johannesburg in 1995, but it was only in 2002 that couples could legally adopt a child. Before this, couples were forced to decide which of the parents would be registered as the legal parent.

Announcing the first adoption, a spokesperson for Johannesburg Child Welfare, Marionka Manias, had told a local paper: "A two-parent male and female family is a much better role model for a child. Ideally, we would want to place babies with families broadly reflective of society. This does not mean we will prevent other people from adopting a child."

This was a heteronormative trope that was to continue deep into the twenty-first century and Manias's language and sentiments were reflective of the times. However, the adoption by the unnamed lesbian was a victory that opened the door for other gay and lesbian couples to begin to think about starting their own families. Of course, this wasn't the only route to becoming a mother. IVF was always a possibility but specialists were reluctant back then to treat single or lesbian women. Many women, however, were able to conceive this way by concealing their sexual orientation.

I had managed until then to keep the not too insignificant issue of children safely on the periphery of our lives. Instead I found myself suddenly the co-owner of a dog. This turned out to be a small black-and-tan abandoned dachshund with one blue eye. We named her Sugar. Sugar would very quickly test our parent potential as well as our capacity to look after something other than ourselves.

I had grown up with a series of dachshunds and knew the breed well. They are clever dogs but neurotic, highly strung and notoriously needy and yappy. We had not seriously thought through the consequences of the new responsibility as we drove out to the suburb of Bellville one night to collect this new addition to our lives.

Sugar had belonged to a family who had relocated. She was about six months old and clearly frightened and confused by the unfamiliar smells and sounds of these new people carrying her around like a small rugby ball. Returning home with the puppy on my lap in the passenger seat, I realised we were totally unprepared. Not only did we live on the second floor of a block of flats but we also had no idea what to feed her.

We soon learned and began to take turns teaching Sugar to use the garden downstairs. For the next few years we would regularly carry her down two flights of stairs, rain, wind or shine, sometimes at 2am when she whined to be let out. Both of us had full-time jobs and had not thought of what we would do with Sugar while we were at our respective offices. At first she accompanied me to work but it soon became untenable. Sugar hated being left alone and so we decided to get her a companion, Snowy, whom we fetched from the SPCA. Now we had two dogs to carry down the stairs.

Sugar and Snowy became an integral part of our lives and accompanied us on walks around the city, to the restaurants we regularly frequented on Long Street and on occasional visits out of town. They were smuggled into theatres and cinemas when they were puppies and later, when they grew too large to conceal in a basket or bag, we left them happily chewing hooves in the flat. Sugar and Snowy were to remain part of our lives for the next 20 years; later several more dogs were added to our canine family.

Perhaps I should have realised then that my reluctance to discuss children had inadvertently and unconsciously led to this collection of hounds. Who knows how many more we would have ended up with had X not insisted a short while later that the time had come to start a family. But that was still a little way off then.

Whether we know it or not, we are all ultimately attracted to people who somehow reflect – both the positive and the negative – the primary objects of our affection, our mothers and fathers. In that sense I had been drawn to the warm and enveloping love of a partner who loved me unconditionally. It is only when you can be your real self with a partner, when they understand that the self-serving, narcissistic, hurtful and infuriating Doppelgänger who emerges from time to time is just one complex layer of many, that love can deepen and mature or, in the worst-case scenario, sour.

It is not that a social self is somehow counterfeit; it is the armour we need to face the world. But manifesting this can be exhausting. We hang up the cloak of our social selves in our private spaces. I found a space relatively successfully, to inhabit all these selves without inflicting too much collateral damage.

IT WAS THIS internal architecture, these hooks and barbs of a lifetime that nestle in the psyche and that lurk, generally unseen unless we go looking for them, that I most feared in relation to becoming a parent.

The truth of Larkin. They fuck you up, your mum and dad.

Even worse, Georg, Barbara and I had all been contaminated by toxic political ideologies that threaded through the essential architecture of our personal bonds. First a mammoth excavation had to take place. No child should bear the brunt of a self unknown and unexplored. The baggage is only ours to carry and we ought not to pass it on from one generation to the next, in an endless cycle of referred pain. But we do.

But where to find the tools? Therapy?

I had, by then, begun to freelance as a writer – I had indeed begun to write my first book – which plunged me into a precarious financial position. X was now a student with a part-time income, so we lived frugally.

While I was content with working only in the present, there was a larger plan being hatched in our household. And while I might have been oblivious to the course that was being charted it gradually dawned on me that I was merely a *marinero* while X was actually the *capitan* on the good ship La Bamba. The Mexican folk song is about a dance and, in order to perform "one needs a bit of grace/a bit of grace for me, for you, now come on, come on".

Georg had never visited any of the homes I had lived in over the years, apart from the bachelor flat he had bought and had rented out to me in his Dickensian experiment when I first started working at the *Cape Times*. Since then, he had turned down all offers and so it was up to me to drive out every weekend to Somerset West. Sugar and Snowy would accompany us, which, thankfully, resulted in long walks with Georg and his dogs in the park instead of the muted tea-drinking conversations in his smelly, clock-ticking, television-blaring lounge.

While Barbara's health had not improved, she was generally well, apart from the odd infection or bout of flu. My parents' routine remained unaltered, as did mine on the weekends. Cards, chicken nuggets, nail clipping, one-way conversation, visits to the toilet, and then a wave goodbye through the window from my car parked in the street. I wondered how long my mother would suffer. She had no choice but to endure it.

I had forgotten her voice, her thoughts, her little quirks wielding the English language. I could hold onto an emotional outline of that mother, but over time this nuanced memory had been replaced by this sad, beautiful and gentle woman held captive by her body. I had not really mourned this partial death in the aftermath of the trauma of dealing with what was left behind.

Sorting through papers during our move from the small flat, I had found two letters, written by my brother, that my mother dictated to him years earlier. It was a habit I had initiated when he left for the army and these were her letters to me while I finished my studies in Pretoria in the early 1980s.

"I have your picture on the wall and one that is broken and I hang it on the wall in my bedroom. This house is very empty, you are my sunshine. Without you this house is no life. I hope this year passes quickly and you back home with your nonsense again."

I could imagine her stranded at the new house in Durbanville after having cornered my brother, who was probably home to study for an exam, and begging him to write to me.

"You realise this world is only one mother. Never mind how bad your mother are. You must be good for my sake. Don't disappoint me everything."

And then the familiar admonishment that friends were never more important than one's mother.

"Don't mess your time running about. Your friends don't give you what you need, iss jus talk shit. I wish the one year pass quickly because I miss you so much. Never mind. Please write and donta be lazy. The next letter tell me all your problems. I don't want nonsense like you all the time. Never satisfied anyway. I hope you understand what I mean. Please be satisfied what you have. I wish I be like you."

I MET THE NEWS of my mother's death, that evening in 1997, with relief – for her. Between the first loss, after her stroke, and the years of lingering afterwards, it was impossible to find a way of experiencing real, deep grief at the final loss.

Clearing out her locker after the dramatic scenes the night before, when my father had sprinkled the Lourdes water over her corpse while her room-mate urged us to hurry up and get out, I found a stash of several articles written over the years with my byline.

My father had never spoken to me directly about my work. He never mentioned that he had read something in the *Cape Times*, perhaps even a lead story, on any given day, or any of the magazines I had worked at. He could never bring himself to say he was proud of me or that I had done a good job. He was just not capable of offering unconditional praise. Perhaps something in his German upbringing had prompted him to believe that children should not be praised, that the will of a child needed to be shaped and broken so that he or she could deal with the reality of the generally harsh blows of life.

While I might have unconsciously continued to long for his approval, the reality was that he was never going to acknowledge any of my successes. It is a lesson I carried with me into adulthood. I have learned to live around it and not discard it completely. In many ways a grain of truth is buried in this notion. The world does not owe us anything and our achievements, in the end, can only matter to ourselves.

The ever-present fear that I would or will be exposed as some sort of fraud is my father's gift that keeps on giving, his lasting legacy. But I am not alone in this. Many of us carry this destructive seed.

What it did do was prompt a need to try to do the best I can with any given situation, particularly related to work. In this realm I became my greatest competitor and enemy, restless, never satisfied.

Barbara's exit from life had been as low-key and as unremarkable as her life. I mourned for the life she didn't get to lead and for the suffering she had borne so stoically for fourteen years. She deserved happiness and I comforted myself with the thought that she had, at least for some time in her life, found a measure of this. Much of it was located in my brother and me. We were what she had lived for.

While Barbara's death had freed and released Georg from the drudgery of a fourteen-year routine, he seemed, at first, at a loss. He had structured his days and his life around caring for Barbara and his visits. Now he was alone.

There was no need, as is often the case with a death in a family, for Georg and me to reconfigure our relationship. It had found its own peculiar rut outside of Barbara's existence anyway.

And so when I learned, about two years later, in 1999, that Georg had met and befriended a local widow, I was overjoyed. He had been alone for so long. Finding a new companion might prompt a second wind, I thought, and open a new and exciting chapter of his life. I hoped this person would provide the happiness that seemed to elude him.

Georg had always been intensely private and I could tell he was reluctant to discuss this new blossoming relationship. He did, however, introduce us to the petite widow. She was in her late 50s and had long, dyed black hair. She was nothing like my mother. And she was Jewish.

I set aside any thoughts about how a Jewish woman could possibly contemplate having a relationship with a man who had grown up in Nazi Germany and who had been a pilot in Hitler's Luftwaffe. Before she met my father, the widow had been married to another old German who had retired to Somerset West. I had met the man once, in fact, while I was visiting Georg. He was an obnoxious, patriarchal, rude brute and I had disliked him instantly.

The widow was not a self-possessed woman. She was timid but coquettish around Georg. She fussed over him and seemed comfortable in the stereotyped role as the "woman of the house". It was a quality I knew my father appreciated. A woman who knew her place.

I wondered how Georg would cope with the demands for intimacy, not necessarily physical, but emotional, but I was certain that as two mature adults they would work through it all.

The widow moved in temporarily with Georg. I noticed that they did not share a bed or a room. Georg had moved into the smaller of the two rooms while the widow ensconced herself in the larger room with the en suite bathroom. She soon began redecorating the house. "Feminine touches" began to appear – floral prints, scatter cushions on couches, frilly curtains at windows where there had been blinds, colourful rugs, scented candles.

She seemed cautious of me at first. She appeared to be circling me, sizing me up, trying to fathom the nature and depth of my bond with Georg. I am not sure if she viewed me as a potential rival for his affection, but I secretly wished her the best of luck with that endeavour.

It was the widow who had pointed out to my father that his daughter, me, was . . . ahem . . . different.

How old was I and why had I never married? Did I even have a boyfriend? And who was this woman who came with her all the time when she visited him? Had he asked her? "I think you should," the widow said. "You will be surprised."

And so on a subsequent visit, no doubt having been forced to think about this possibly for the first time in his life, Georg broached the subject.

X and I were seated outside on his shady stoep around an arrangement of plastic garden furniture. The widow had dressed the cheap table up with a starched white cloth and had set cushions out on the chairs. She busied herself quietly in the kitchen making tea when Georg uncharacteristically got personal.

He said that the widow had suggested to him that I might be a lesbian.

"Why didn't you tell me?" he said. "Are you?"

X and I shot each other a surprised look. I was happy not to be dealing with this on my own.

"Why didn't I tell you? I'll tell you why. You sat here on this very stoep

211

a few years ago and told me how you had flung homosexuals from a window in the prisoner-of-war camp. I am not a masochist. Why would I tell you the truth if this is how you feel? You are a homophobe."

The widow emerged from the kitchen, carrying a tray of tea and elaborate German pastries, clearly keen to witness the outcome of what might be about to erupt into a spectacular family drama.

"I was just telling my father why I didn't tell him I was a lesbian," I said as I reached for the teapot. "I think you might understand why." And then I repeated the story about the prisoner-of-war camp to her.

The widow seemed disappointed, but made no comment. She took her seat, where she remained a silent observer.

I had expected to feel embarrassed by a personal revelation that we had not spoken of all of my life. But instead I felt triumphant, victorious even.

I knew Georg would be incapable of interrogating the issue in any more depth, no matter how desperately curious he might have been. It was just not in his nature. And I frankly thought that he did not care enough to learn or understand who I really was.

So we sat there in silence, the four of us, nibbling cakes and tinkling our spoons in our teacups. And then we left.

I so wished that I had planted a bug in Georg's house so that we could have eavesdropped on the conversation that followed our departure.

As we drove home, I felt a weight lifting. It was a sort of relief not to be living a lie anymore.

Here I am, take it or leave it.

THE LUNCH was surreal. A circular dining-room table was draped in a cloth with subtle prints of the Star of David on it. In the centre, between the baubles, lacquered pine-cones and sparkly Christmas crackers, stood a nine-branched Hanukkah menorah with lit candles.

The widow's "outing" of X and me had had no obvious fall-out. Georg never mentioned it again and neither did I.

Scraping my chair closer to the table, I scanned the bookshelf for Georg's brown paper-wrapped copy of Hitler's *Mein Kampf.* I was certain it had travelled with him.

Georg and the widow had moved out of his house by this time and back into the house she had once shared with the old dead German. She had rented out the house while she moved in with Georg but found his cottage too small. So here he was, dogs and all, having rented out his own cottage in the meantime. The old German brute had died, of some mysterious ear infection, in a bedroom down a long parquet-floored passage just off the dining room where we were about to tuck into an assortment of heavy German Christmas dishes.

It was strange to see this new version of Georg. He was engaging, skittish even, and seemed to have shaken off the chronic lethargy that had weighted him for years. I did not know this man. He appeared to have been given a new lease of life. To see the widow perched on his lap with her arms around his neck was the oddest sight. I had never, ever seen Georg hug my mother.

As Freud would have it, Hitler came up during the conversation.

"Don't mention that man here," the widow said.

"What man?" Georg looked up, genuinely surprised.

"Hitler, Dad, Hitler," I leaned over and hissed through gritted teeth. What was the strange psychology playing itself out here?

Surely Georg, while it manifested in subtle ways, carried within him the seeds of the most virulent anti-Semitism? He was part of a people, a nation, a tribe, a generation responsible for genocide on an industrial scale. Even as a boy he must have witnessed at least the beginning of these pogroms in Berlin, where the term "Final Solution" had been adopted at the Wannsee Conference in 1942. This was not an event that existed only in history books to him. He was there!

During other visits, I had broached the subject. "Dad, you must have known," I said.

"I had no idea, no idea," he would say, looking uncomfortable and shaking his head.

"But did you not see people lining up at stations to be deported to Auschwitz, Bergen Belsen, Belzeck, Buchenwald, Dachau, Treblinka – all the other camps?"

"I only vonce saw a man dressed in a striped blue uniform vorking along ze railway lines," he replied.

"And what did you think to yourself?"

"I sought he vas a prisoner and ze criminal. He vas shovelling coke. Zat is all I remember."

It was clear that Georg had not been able to engage with the meaning of the horror of the Holocaust or the role of ordinary Germans, whether they stood by and mutely watched it without speaking out or whether they actively participated in exposing Jews, their neighbours, possibly their local pharmacist, doctor, lawyer or the violinist in an orchestra. He might have been one of those "harmless" Germans, who were just oblivious to it all, but still – surely he could not, in retrospect, pretend it didn't happen?

When it came to understanding and dealing with the meaning of the Holocaust, Georg seemed to have "split". This is a common psychological defence used to repress or deny thoughts that might cause a psychic rupture. It requires a willingness to confront your shadow, and face and integrate what you find there to create or shape a more realistic, whole and healthier self.

For Georg this might have been too risky. A precarious sense of self, even if contained by old, rusty scaffolding, remained preferable perhaps to precipitating the implosion of the entire edifice of a false self.

This psychological state was one that would later come to plague many white South Africans. There were many who after Mandela's release and the TRC were adamant. "We didn't know" or "We never supported apartheid" were claims that would be made over and over again. Apartheid, I would have thought, was hard to miss. All around us lay the sprawling townships of the dispossessed who cleaned our homes, cooked for our families and looked after our children. While the evidence was in plain sight, the majority of white South Africans were blind, indifferent or inured to it.

This split became increasingly evident when Georg reminisced about his childhood in Charlottenburg. At the turn of the century there were over 100 000 Jews in Berlin, many of whom lived in districts like Charlottenburg, Wilmersdorf, Schöneberg. By 1945 only 8 000 Jews remained in that city. Those who survived were either married to non-Jews or in hiding.

One afternoon Georg spontaneously recounted a story about his youth.

"Zere vas a family, ze Finkelsteins, who lived a few doors down from us. I remember so vell coming home from school and smelling ze aroma of baking. And I vould alvays go zere and Mrs Finkelstein vould give me a cake or a biscuit."

He grew silent and stared out of the window at the garden outside.

And then.

"I vonder vat happened to ze Finkelsteins?"

"Dad!" I shouted. "The Holocaust happened to the Finkelsteins! The Holocaust!"

My father winced and closed his eyes. What was he thinking? He didn't say.

We left a short while later. There was no conversation to be had. But the afternoon had unsettled me deeply.

215

"What the fuck am I dealing with?" I ranted on the drive home. "Who is he? *What* is he?"

And why the hell did I care? Why did I not just excommunicate myself, remove myself from the toxicity of it all?

In that moment I loathed and resented my father and everything he represented.

I felt I needed to warn the widow. Surely her history must have included relatives who had been victims of the Nazis? But she and my father were adults. I could not assume that this was an issue they ignored and did not discuss. Surely they had?

Whatever the strange alchemy between them, I was relieved that Georg had a companion who could share his remaining years and in some way relieve a responsibility that would have been mine. I could concentrate my emotional energy on my own relationship without it being sapped by Georg. Perhaps now he would even do some travelling and begin to enjoy life a bit more.

And so it was one afternoon, while I was writing, that the phone rang. It was Georg. He sounded upbeat. He was calling, he said, to inform me that he was going to marry the widow. It was merely a practical arrangement.

"I need someone to look after me and she has agreed. And also so ven I die she can get my pension vhich vill help her out."

There was no need for him to ask or tell me but I thanked him for the courtesy. He had my blessing, I told him. But the real reason for the call was that Georg had wanted to run past me the small detail that he was going to transfer his life savings, around R100 000, to the widow.

"Well, then, I suppose you have called because you'd like my opinion on this."

"Vat do you think?"

"Well, I think it might be a bit early to do something so drastic . . ." I started out.

I didn't even know the woman's surname. She was still a stranger to both Georg and me.

"Why don't you just leave her all the money when you die? Why give it to her now? What is the urgency? I think it is a bit too soon, and if

216

you are married you might as well spend it together. So, if you want my opinion, which you clearly do, I think it is a bad idea."

He thanked me, said goodbye and I replaced the receiver. The call had unsettled me. I thought it was very odd. I immediately picked up the phone again to call my partner at her office to tell her about it. And then I heard a two-way conversation I was not meant to hear. The widow had been eavesdropping on a phone extension in the house. She and Georg had clearly continued the conversation after I put down the phone.

This was the first snippet I heard, in German.

"You see, I told you she wants the money," said the widow.

I felt as if I had been pencilled into some bizarre cartoon strip in which I had no agency. What the fuck was going on here?

"Ja, vell, zat is not going to happen," I heard Georg reply.

I was devastated, not only at the suggestion that I would have wanted his savings (a paltry amount I hadn't even known existed) but that Georg had drawn me into this tawdry mess. Most devastating, though, is that he had thought I would be capable of such venality.

I quietly replaced the receiver and sat shell-shocked behind my computer.

No.

This could not just be ignored.

I decided to confront him.

I called his number.

Georg answered and I went straight there.

"Dad, the next time you call me to discuss family business candidly you can tell me whether anyone else is privy to the conversation."

Silence.

"Well, I just wanted to hear for myself," he eventually said.

"Hear what?"

Clearly cornered and embarrassed, Georg veered off topic, deflecting the subject. "Vhat do you care? You haf never cared. You haf left me all alone all zese years!" he shouted.

"That is untrue and you know it. I don't know what you are doing right now, but I want to tell you that you have hurt me deeply. Offended me. I cannot believe you would think that I would be interested in your money. You asked my advice, I gave it. I don't even know this woman's surname."

"Vell, I am going to do it."

"Do it. Do what you will, but until you apologise to me I cannot see you again. You must understand that I am serious about this."

He ended the call abruptly.

That was it.

I sat there stunned. One minute I was quietly writing and the next I had been plunged into an emotional maelstrom I could not have imagined heading my way.

What to do?

It felt unfinished.

So I wrote a letter to Georg, carefully choosing each word. I reiterated that he owed me an apology. I told him that I loved and respected him for the manner in which he had cared for my mother, but that what had just happened between us was unacceptable. I accused him of being weak and spineless.

"Until I receive an apology from you, I am severing contact. I love you. If you need me, you know my number," I signed off.

I faxed the letter to him, watching as it stuttered through the machine, and imagining it spewing out at the other end in Somerset West. I wondered what Georg would do. Would he have the balls?

And then I curled up on my bed and wept.

MY FATHER and I did not speak for a year. In that time I learned to live around a perpetual dull sadness. Georg could not bring himself to apologise. He was too proud or stubborn or cruel. He was not adult enough, not emotionally fully formed, and I let it go. For the first time in my life he was not a centrepiece. While Georg was never far from my thoughts, my weekends were my own now and I gradually began to appreciate this.

I tried to remove all physical traces of him in our flat, placing photographs and small gifts he had given me over the years in a box I stashed at the back of a cupboard. My brother was in Australia, and he and I

218

had fallen into a familiar silence about family matters. Albert had visited us once or twice while out on business or passing through, but telephone conversations across continents are always awkward and stilted. News of his life and mine was rudimentary but I did discuss with him this unexpected development. There appeared to be no resolution for now, so we left it at that.

And then towards the end of the year the phone rang. It was the widow. My father was in hospital, she told me in her halting, broken English.

"I found him vis a gun und he vas doing to shoot himself," she informed me.

It was hard to care.

"You must come here now. I am leaving for Germany and he cannot be on his own."

You have to be kidding me, I thought to myself. What the fuck?

"I don't care what you do. Zat man is mad. He had my cats put down ven I vas in Chermany zis year. You must fetch him from here ven he iss back zis veek. I haf put his dogs in ze kennel."

I drove to Somerset West with a rising dread. I was back in the cartoon strip, which had now morphed into a dark graphic novel.

The widow led me to the bedroom where her previous husband had died. Georg was a gibbering wreck, a shadow of his former self. He was thin, delirious, his jaw quivering, his eyes glassy. He lay curled up in a foetal position, apparently unaware of his surroundings.

Even so, it was hard to summon any sympathy.

I told the widow that I would come and fetch my father in due course and I got back in my car and drove home.

I discussed possible solutions with X.

Put Georg on a plane to Australia? Probably not.

Move to Somerset West to look after him? Definitely not. Under no circumstances was I going to do that.

The best option would be to find a way of accommodating him closer to our home, but where?

Taking Sugar and Snowy out for a wee in the courtyard, I noticed that a bachelor flat on the ground floor was vacant. I could not imagine Georg in my intimate space, but I thought I could deal with him two floors down, where I could keep an eye on him. I made enquiries and learned that the flat was available. I signed a short lease, hired a bakkie and collected furniture from Georg's home. I chose familiar objects – his bed, a chest of drawers and a bedside table. I took some framed photographs of his parents, my grandparents, and other odds and ends that would render the strange flat more familiar.

With the flat furnished I drove out to Somerset West once more, this time to fetch Georg. He was mute the entire journey and he was unsteady as I led him along the passage to the flat at the end of the ground-floor corridor. He seemed oblivious to it all. I put him to bed and called my house doctor. She diagnosed a serious depression and prescribed anti-depressants.

There was really no time to consider or digest what was happening. I lay in bed that night thinking about this wizened old man alone in the flat below.

And so began a three-month routine of nurturing and caring for someone who had hurt me deeply. The only way I could hope to manage this was to enter the space with a blank slate. When I went downstairs to bathe or feed him I would leave all my feelings at the threshold.

It was a rite of passage of sorts. Living in the moment.

But in this way I was also able to see my father's humiliation and vulnerability and I felt sorry for him. I saw no point in reminding him of what had happened between us, nor that he was the author of the situation in which he now found himself.

I relied on my memory of him caring for my mother to care for him during those difficult months. He seemed disorientated, often asking me who and where he was. He said he could see faces in the ceiling plaster. Occasionally he would be seized by a sudden panic. I would reassure him and tell him that everything would be okay.

As the anti-depressants began to take effect he slowly surfaced. To get him to eat, we bought his favourite food, sauerkraut and sausages, from a local German delicatessen.

The financial strain of working as a freelance writer and paying for two households worried me, but there was no way out. The emotional strain was exhausting. There were times alone in the kitchen when I was washing up after serving Georg breakfast, lunch and supper that I resented being reduced to a servant. Fuck feminism – here I was washing dishes, sweeping and cleaning, all in service to a selfish and demanding old man.

I would leave my seething for when I was back home upstairs.

Three months into Georg's convalescence, he regained his mind and his physical strength. Still we did not talk about what had happened. I was weary of Georg. Something had shifted for me and it would take, in the end, a long time to heal. I never completely trusted him again.

The urgency now was that Georg had, I learned, indeed handed over his life savings, as well as his house in Somerset West, to the widow. They had got married, as he had informed me on the day of the phone call. Now he had nowhere to go.

By the time the widow was due to return from her trip to Germany, where she had been visiting her daughter, Georg was healthy enough to drive to the airport to pick her up, and I told him to do so. It was his responsibility, I informed him, to undo what he had done and to find a way of recovering the loss, at the very least, of his home. There was no way I could help him financially. I had done my part.

By then my brother Albert had been apprised of the depth of the catastrophe. I know he intervened and that Georg managed to buy back his house, but until today I do not know how.

My father's three-month stay in the flat downstairs had plunged me into debt and there was no way of recovering any of the money. But on the day after I had dropped him back in Somerset West, I found an envelope among the mail stuffed in my postbox. Inside was a royalty cheque for a book I had helped write for the exact amount I had spent on recovering Georg from the brink.

I KNEW IT was coming. We were trudging along a path through the lush forest that carpeted a flank of Table Mountain behind a house we had just bought when X mentioned children again. This time I detected a distinct urgency to her tone. This was not idle conversation. It was heading for an outcome.

By now we had weathered seven years and we had come to understand and navigate the different strengths we each brought to the relationship. When it came to making big decisions, let's just say 'twas not I who usually took the lead.

I had a tendency towards seeking light-footedness, an unencumbered life which could be packed up in an hour if need be. I recognised it as a sort of fugitive mentality that may or may not have been passed down through some ancestral epigenetic or past-life memory (if one believed in such things). Perhaps a roving troubadour or a forest truffle forager lurked in a chromosome begging to be given expression. Or maybe a hermetic monk or a criminal on the run.

In any event I had successfully managed to dodge the topic of children or at least deflect it in those seven years. During that time we had travelled, acquired two more dogs and begun to build our respective careers. I had hoped the issue would have been forgotten by now.

While we, in theory, as gay and lesbian people were guaranteed equality in the country's new constitution, various existing laws still remained to be challenged, laws that still excluded same-sex partners from enjoying full equality, particularly in relation to pension funds, medical aids, civil partnerships and marriage, as well as joint adoption. But it would be only a matter of time before we, like everyone else, would enjoy the full protection of the law. All around us a society was being shaped that I could not have imagined growing up in South Africa and the world outside.

At some point in the twentieth century, it appeared, we, as a species, had gained a measure of wisdom. We understood that smoking was a health risk and not a health benefit, that the sun could cause skin cancer, that we needed to eat healthily, and that we should wear seatbelts in our cars. We learned that the 1950s Western ideal of the family and suburbia, of white male economic domination, was unjust and untenable and that there are a myriad other ways in which human beings experience kinship.

I am not sure exactly when this tipping point arrived but it had been part of a process borne along by the civil rights movement in the US, feminism, the struggle against apartheid as well as other struggles that had slowly shifted the locus of power, maybe not completely but just enough to begin to challenge the status quo.

And to my mind, while these rights, this equality that is an essential part of existence, were non-negotiable, it did not necessarily mean that we, as queer people, had to become like everyone else. It did not mean that we had to replicate heteronormative paradigms or marriage, which of course has its roots as a business transaction assuring male property rights.

As lesbians we had been offered an exit, a way out of this age-old, predictable procreational dance.

And who wouldn't want this freedom?

Of course the concept of marriage had evolved and been transformed over the years but I still regarded it as a blueprint for all that was outdated. Humankind would be better off re-imagining completely the idea of partnership and family, but preferably without me having to participate.

This I drew on as we talked and talked. On strolls through the forest and parks, over dinner, with friends, or any opportunity to broach the subject. I was, quite frankly, terrified at the prospect of parenthood.

I was like a scratched CD. "Please don't make me do it. I'll be a terrible parent. I'm selfish, impatient, immature. I don't think I have it in me."

I had also had direct experience of living with babies, toddlers and small people. I had once, for some time, shared a home with two friends who had a child. The chaos, drudgery, the demands and the responsibility of it all had completely overwhelmed my friends. I had seen it close up. And while I loved children, other people's children, and the wonder, magic and honesty they brought, I still could not imagine being a mother myself.

Few women who hanker after motherhood are aware of the realities and demands they will be faced with. The notion is so deeply embedded in cultural tropes that it is impossible to think through the gauzy dreamworld conjured in magazines. If we told each other the truth, people would stop procreating. I had seen the physical ravages exacted on new mothers at work. I had seen them age visibly after the arrival of what they had been told was "a bundle of joy". And while post-partum depression is certainly real and terrifying, it also has much to do with the shattering of a myth.

"You're romanticising it all," I whinged. "You have no idea what it is like. It's horrible and once you commit to it there is no turning back."

Now that was a line in the sand.

I was 39 years old, and while I might have passed in public as a fully fledged adult, I was far from it. For me life was about removing obstacles, not going out and deliberately finding and placing them in my path. And children, I thought, were an obstacle. You could not pack them in a backpack and move on.

But there was no turning back. Until then I had been so vehemently opposed to the idea that I had not allowed myself to entertain or even think of it.

And if we were to become the parents that Larkin said would fuck up our children, then it would mean that at some point I was going to have to unpack myself and try to ensure that this did not happen, that I did not pass on any considerable baggage I might, at that point, be unconsciously dragging around with me.

That meant dealing with the meaning of Georg, Barbara, our family

224

and the internal arrangement of mental furniture they had placed there. While I might have shifted a chair or a couch over the years, the rooms were essentially intact, their doors closed shut. Having children would force me into them.

These vital concerns were furthest from my mind at that point as I wrestled with the immediate idea of being part of a new family, my own family. I had no clue what kind of parent I would be or if, indeed, I was even capable of drawing on any maternal instinct.

There was one thing, though, of which I was certain. I did not want to agree to becoming a parent or part of this new family if I viewed it as a compromise. I had to come to accept it fully on my own. I could remain childless and never know what I had missed. We could, like so many lesbian couples across the globe, grow old with our dogs or cultivate some hobby or interest that would see us travelling the world (it would have to be on the cheap, though) or growing our own beets. But then again, was that all there was?

The more I thought about it, the more a yawning chasm stared back at me. But would it be fair to fill that void with children? Is this why people had children anyway – to secure an idea of the future? And was my inability to clearly envisage a future as a mother linked to my very practical acceptance, throughout my life, that having children would be impossible. Would my thoughts have been different if I had been able to imagine it?

The point was that I wouldn't know any of these things until I became a parent. That way I would be able to compare apples with apples. A life before children and a life with and hopefully after they had grown up, beautiful, well adjusted and leaving to make their own lives.

As I contemplated all of this, I gradually grew more excited at the possibility of something I had never before imagined. It began to feel as if we were preparing for an adventure, perhaps the most important one in my life.

But how would we go about it?

While I believed that adoption would have been our first option, we did allow our thoughts to roam into the realm of other possibilities, and these turned naturally to the two men in our lives who we reckoned would make great fathers – Tom and René. If they donated sperm, our children would have two mothers and two fathers on two continents. Things were looking good. This way our children would also benefit from the investment of four parents.

We hadn't yet broached the subject with Tom and René but decided we would do so on their next visit to South Africa.

We invited them to dinner. Both of us looked with new eyes at René, who is a tall, strapping, handsome blond, and Tom, a short, flat-footed intellectual giant, as they stepped over our threshold that night with a silage of Calvin Klein's Obsession drifting behind them.

Later we ambushed them in the lounge. We were careful to make eye contact with both of them lest either one feel excluded.

"We were thinking, you know, that we might be ready to have a child," I began. "And we were wondering whether you might like to make a donation towards the project."

I perched on the couch watching them like David Attenborough observing a scene out in the wild. I could sense that the idea appealed instantly to Tom and his healthy ego. A gentle smile tugged at the corners of his mouth as he must have conjured the scene in his mind's eye.

"Look, you wouldn't have to have anything to do with raising the child. We'll do that. But we couldn't think of anyone else we would like to do this with," I pushed.

René, the realist, immediately grasped the reality and not the fantasy of the plan and was about to speak when Tom interrupted. "Well, if you're thinking of using my sperm, I don't see a problem."

"Absolutely not," said René.

"But why?" Tom asked.

"I don't want to be a father and I don't think it would be a good idea for Tom to be one either."

"Well, you might be right. He does have flat feet," I said. "But René, why not? It might be wonderful."

"Absolutely not."

Then "You're right," said Tom, and that was that.

We were not disappointed. The conversation simply eliminated one option. I was relieved. With the issue safely out of the way, we spent the rest of the night fantasising about the phantom children that could have been.

"What would we do if they were heterosexual? How would we know how to raise them?" asked Tom.

"Well, they'll probably be straight. I mean, our parents raised us and we turned out fabulous gays, so it can be done," I said.

Adoption it would be. This was the option that felt most natural. I could not imagine another human being emerging from my womb. The idea just felt too strange, too weird.

We discussed our worries and concerns. Would it be fair to expose our children to the prejudice or judgement of others who might not approve of who we were? And then the most important consideration of all: could we possibly, as two white people, raise black children or equip them with the armour required to move through life?

Would we ever truly be able to understand how our children would experience the world as black people? Would we be able to gain enough knowledge and wisdom to scour ourselves of our own racial constructs and do no collateral damage?

These were major considerations that would, in time, prove extremely challenging when our daughters finally did come home, but at the start of this journey we could not imagine what these might be. For now, it was all a practical matter. The nuts and bolts of how and when.

I was ready.

I had recalled hearing a fairytale or a myth about a society somewhere sometime where women who had wanted children would sing them to life. The idea appealed to me and we both found a suitable space where we sang our first child to life.

Merely singing beneath a tree, of course, was not going to yield results. Results were going to require a mountain of paperwork and meetings, all of which would still have to be arranged. These preparations soon came to dominate our lives.

Because I am afflicted with a debilitating propensity for lethargy and procrastination when it comes to dealing with bureaucracy, from here on the captain of the household steered the ship.

T HE RIFT between me and Georg, which had continued to drift like an invisible iceberg between us, made it easier to inform him of our plans. Georg had moved back into his old house in Somerset West and had slipped predictably and comfortably into the melancholy rut that cut through his psyche.

Three years had passed since the debacle. His little tango with the widow had not only left him materially poorer but also brittle and irascible. The experience had apparently brought no new wisdom, insight or humility. He wore his pride like an impenetrable shield.

I knew there was nothing that would alter his state of mind and so there was no point trying. I had my partner, someone I loved and who loved me. This was my hazmat suit against Georg's toxic edges.

I grieved the absence of a loving, extended family who could share the news that there would soon be a new addition to this family, but our own excitement, joy and anticipation, shared by some of our close friends and X's family, buoyed me and made up for the lack elsewhere.

Georg had given us a set of keys to his house – one of his precautions should something happen – and I would use these to let myself in when I visited him at weekends. I was careful always to ring the door-bell beforehand to alert him that I had arrived. If he was not napping in his bedroom, I would be sure to find him in the lounge watching German television. He seldom greeted me at the door and seldom betrayed any emotion. Was he happy to see me? Was I intruding? I had no way of knowing.

I had resolved to connect with him regardless, choosing, when I felt strong enough, to ignore his lack of response either way, attributing it to his depression.

The television, as usual, was on in the sunny lounge, drowning out the possibility of any real conversation on the day I told Georg about our plans. I prepared coffee in his grubby open-plan kitchen while he sat slouched in the low armchair in front of the TV. I shifted in behind the circular Art Deco dining-room table that had once belonged to my grandmother in Berlin. Georg's expression was stony and unyielding.

"Dad, we're going to adopt a child."

Silence. Then, "But you don't eat properly."

"How do you know?"

"But you are too busy."

"What do you mean?"

"You never answer your phone."

All of these decoded as "I think you will make a lousy parent". It was not unexpected but I wasn't going to let it slide.

"I'm not sure what you mean. Are you wanting to say that you don't think I will make a good parent?"

Silence.

I spoke into the void.

"Look, I am not telling you this to get your permission or your blessing. I am simply here as a courtesy to inform you that it's going to happen."

I could see he was irritated at having to think about this right now and would have preferred to be left in peace, his mind vacant while some hearty German talk show played itself out on the large screen.

More silence.

"But where will you get this child?"

"Through Child Welfare. It is a process and we have already started it."

He bought time by patting the chair beside him, summoning his fat long-haired dachshund, Nina. She struggled up and settled on his lap. His expression was inscrutable.

"A white child?"

"No, a child."

I would have given for some contraption or device that could ₃ thoughts or gauge his feelings in that instant. Then I interrupted ₂ver reverie was playing itself out. "I have only one thing to say. 1 ₐ.n happy for you to be in the child's life but if I detect any hostility, any racism, anything that threatens him or her, I will remove the child from your orbit. I will continue to visit you and have contact, but I will not tolerate any bigotry."

Georg sat quietly for a few minutes. Then he heaved himself up out of the armchair and shuffled over to the bookshelf.

What now, I thought to myself.

He pulled out an old *Reader's Digest* atlas, put on his reading glasses and reached for the magnifying glass on the coffee table next to him.

"What are you doing?"

"I vas thinking earlier zat I wanted to look at ze map of Ukraine vhere Tante Tuta vas a nurse in ze war."

The war. The war. The war.

Georg was about to become a grandfather and the only way back into the conversation was to talk about Hitler.

It was Turkish Cypriot psychoanalyst Vamik Volkan who coined the term "perennial mourner". Georg, I came to understand, fitted the bill exactly. It describes a state where individuals become "stuck for years or even a lifetime – unable to let the lost person or thing go".[6] These are people, many of whom have survived a trauma, who, while they do not develop depression, are doomed to an existence of perpetual mourning or melancholia. This helped me to understand Georg. He was mourning in part the loss of the country he grew up in, the country that shaped him, but also a country which came to represent the worst of human behaviour. Other losses encapsulated in this geographic loss were those of his father, whom he never saw again after the war, and his mother.

Georg circled this history like a dog in a basket, turning and turning, trying to create a psychic nest but never quite finding a comfortable position to rest. This poring over maps, this obsessive reading of

---

6 http://www.vamikvolkan.com/Not-Letting-Go:-From-Individual-Perennial-Mourners-to-Societies-with-Entitlement-Ideologies.php.

accounts of the war, and the constant talk of it were "objects" or pathways back to this loss, this dislocation of his self.

And so the only way to engage Georg was through the war.

"Did you ever see Hitler?" I asked him.

"One night. I vas very young. I vas building gliders. About 11 o'clock ve finished and I vas valking back to ze U-Bahn vhen I saw a group of men in uniform, standing in a group. Zey vere high-ranking officers. And zen I saw him, ze Führer. He came out of ze Opera house. I stood behind in ze crowd and watched him get into ze car."

"Did you believe in Hitler?"

"Ve all did."

"Did you admire him?"

"I still do today. It is hard for me to believe zat he did so many things."

"And now? How do you feel now that you know?"

Silence.

"Betrayed?"

"Yes. I realise he vas stupid. Zat he did not listen to anyone. In Stalingrad six hundred thousand Germans died. It vas terrible. I must haf had a guardian angel during ze war. I vas in Smolensk retrieving parts of our aircraft zat had been shot down. It vas ze same time. I used to think zat it vas ze people under Hitler who did all zese things, but it has come out now zat it vas him."

Silence. Georg turned the pages of the atlas to the Middle East.

"I dreamed I found two golden fish in my bath," he said out of nowhere. And then, tapping Saudi Arabia with the magnifying glass, "Zey are surrounded, you know. Iran, Turkey, Kuwait, ze Persian Gulf. Zey vill squeeze zem out."

"Who?"

"Ze Americans."

His mind wandered; he was on a riff.

"I haf such strange dreams. Zey all come back to me. Mommy. My father. I saw him ze other night. He just passed through ze dream like a shadow."

Georg was stuck in the past. He had no desire to talk of the future, my future, his future.

I finished my coffee and suggested we take Nina for a walk. He declined. He remained in his armchair as I let myself out.

MOST OF THE couples crammed into the small stuffy hall of a local clinic where Child Welfare was hosting a regular adoption information session were heterosexual. We shifted into a back row, along with two men, who our gaydar had picked up earlier were a couple.

I noticed that while the country's diversity was reasonably well represented in the room, there were no black couples at the meeting, although perhaps it was because of the location of the hall.

During the session, many of the couples indicated that they would like a child who matched their "racial profile" as closely as possible. The journey to adoption, I began to understand, was different for childless heterosexual couples. They often found themselves here after a long and fraught process – after trying to fall pregnant, then tests and more tests, opting for the intrusive and gruelling process that is IVF. And then the grieving for a biological child who was not possible.

A social worker stood at a table stacked with pamphlets and forms and announced that before setting out the bureaucracy of the process, she would attempt to contextualise the reality of adoption in South Africa. "I just want you all to understand the circumstances," she said. While many of us might fantasise that a mother who gave up her baby for adoption might be young, a teenager, or that the child might have been conceived in a moment of passion, the truth was usually bleak and brutal. There were children born of rape, babies whose mothers were addicts or alcoholics, infants born to women who had had no say in their conception and who could not cope with another mouth to feed, infants born to mothers who were HIV-positive, babies who were HIV-positive, babies left by desperate and traumatised mothers in fields, rubbish dumps and public toilets.

There were open adoptions, where mothers could select and meet potential adoptive parents, and then there were children for whom no biological parents could be traced, who languished in hospitals, and who were placed in emergency care, places of safety or orphanages. Some of these children would later be placed in foster care, but many were not.

As she spoke, the reality of life for so many in South Africa crashed into the room – a metaphorical delivery room where our journey to becoming parents was just beginning. So much sadness and loss folded into what we all hoped would be an occasion for joy. The omniscience of historical trauma was starkly present.

"And if any of you were hoping for a white child, your chances are virtually nil," said the social worker, glancing over at the three or four white couples in the room. "So those of you here who are willing to have an African baby, please mark the top of your form with an X, so we know."

Two other white couples, including the gay men and ourselves, asked for the forms we had handed in earlier so that we could add our small "X" at the top right-hand corner.

While vulnerable children in African societies were often taken in by relatives or absorbed into extended families, there remained a taboo when it came to adopting unknown children, the social worker continued. The department was working on trying to change this. However, she added, officials usually prioritised placing children within adoptive families who were closest to their culture and heritage (a euphemism for race). "The further away you are from these criteria, the lower you will rank on the list."

I leaned in and whispered to X that this would place us at the bottom of the pile.

The ultimate aim, said the social worker, was to place a child in a loving home and it didn't matter whether you were rich or poor. The wait for a baby could take anything from a few months to a few years. And in the equation, in the triangle that was the biological mother (or parents), the potential adoptive parents and the child, it was always the needs of the child that were a priority.

"But if you are prepared to take a black baby boy, you won't wait long."

This was, she told us matter-of-factly, because so few people wanted these baby boys.

We shouldn't be doing this, I thought to myself as the meeting dragged on into dusk. It didn't feel right. I was torn between believing that we needed to find a way of becoming part of something, a movement, a mission, to make life bearable for vulnerable women and children, and being overwhelmed by the sheer size and scale of the problem.

By 2001 the HIV/AIDS epidemic in South Africa was a national crisis. The country had the highest number of new infections in sub-Saharan Africa and the peculiar response by President Thabo Mbeki, who questioned the link between HIV and AIDS, exacerbated the epidemic. His Health Minister, Manto Tshabalala-Msimang, stalled on implementing vital antiretroviral programmes in the public health sector, which resulted in an alarming spike in new infections as well as millions of deaths.

Already the epidemic had left around 500 000 children orphaned or vulnerable. The state was completely unprepared for the devastation caused as it raged on, decimating thousands upon thousands of families. Some politicians refused to acknowledge and manage it.

"So it is up to you to decide," said the social worker. "Are you willing to take a child who is the product of a rape? A child who is HIV-positive? A child whose mother is an alcoholic or drug addict? Think about all of these things until our next meeting."

I left the meeting depressed. That the gift of motherhood would come at such a great cost to others felt overwhelming.

We spoke on the way home and almost through the night. Would we be able to raise a son without a father? Was the lack of a father, for a boy or a girl, that much of a catastrophe? There were so many single mothers raising sons in South Africa that the lack of a father did not seem like an immediate priority. We would involve those male role models in our lives, we said.

We agreed that we did not mind the sex of the baby. A baby is a baby until society decides it is a boy or a girl and begins to socialise the child into the ritualised performances of masculinity and femininity. We would deal with whoever arrived.

For now we needed to begin work on our "profile". This is a booklet, with photographs and text, Child Welfare presents to mothers seeking to give their babies up for adoption. They are given several profiles to choose from.

"I am not sure that anyone would want their baby to be raised by two women, by lesbians?" I offered.

"Why not?"

"There is so much prejudice and misunderstanding. Why would a mother choose us over a heterosexual couple?"

"You don't know that. What if a mother was happy to have her child raised by women?"

It was these and other essential questions that we grappled with as we sat together in our lounge, tracing figures from a beautiful children's book about the Mexican artist Frida Kahlo with which we were preparing to decorate the bedroom we had set aside for our child. As we traced and painted each tiger, each little unique creature, each smiling little skull or watermelon, it felt as if we were decorating our own womb to receive this baby who would soon, we hoped, enter our lives. But before that could happen there were things to be done.

Apart from filling in even more forms, we were also required to undergo a series of face-to-face interviews with a social worker and host a home visit.

The forms were detailed. They included sections on religion and on whether either of us drank or had used any drugs.

I didn't see why I needed religious beliefs, but we wanted a child, and this was the system. "Secular Buddhist", the best I could come up with, seemed to satisfy her.

And then the section about drugs. While I had never been arrested or convicted on any charge, I had spent much of my youth smoking weed and I wasn't going to lie about it.

"I'm going to say yes here," I said. "I don't want to lie about anything."

Torn, I called a friend who was a social worker and asked for advice.

"Don't feel bad about it," he said. "Just say no."

So I did.

We prepared a "show book" of our lives for the mother who would be giving up her child.

We filled its pages with photographs of us with our dogs, of our home (inside and out), of my partner's family, her mother (who would be our child's grandmother), her sister and brother and their children, our child's cousins, all smiling, happy, welcoming. Between this we wrote to the mother, telling her why our home and our family would be ideal.

I tried to, but could not imagine, the pain and anguish of the mother who might be flipping through these portfolios of potential adoptive families with their fat, happy lives, and having to decide which of them to choose. Would she read the faces of those who would become the family of her unborn baby? Would she find some succour or comfort in their expressions?

To be placed in this position must be unbearable. Surely no mother reaches this point without considerable agony. Would she, for the rest of her life, I wondered, think about her baby, how he or she might have grown, who they would become? How could she not?

Whoever she was, she would always be a part of our lives. Every birthday, every Mother's Day, she would be there. As would the child's father. The absence, their absence, would have to be held not only by them, but by our child and ourselves.

Slowly and imperceptibly, the rhythm of our lives had begun to alter. While, before, a myriad of ordinary currents had consumed us, now the baby occupied our hearts and minds, and already the physical confines of our home.

We were expecting, although if you strolled past us in the street or in a shopping mall, and saw us fingering tiny baby outfits, you would not have known.

With the forms filled in, the profile done, the room prepared, it was time for the next big hurdle – our face-to-face interview with the social worker.

We were ushered into a waiting area to wait our turn in the interview room. This was to be the first of two or three interviews. We were both nervous and, to distract ourselves, flipped through the magazines that were stacked on a table. At the top of the pile was an old copy of *Fairlady*, one of the magazines I wrote for. It also just happened to be one where the cover barker shouted out that a story inside would argue two points on the legalisation of marijuana in South Africa.

Needless to say, the story was mine. In it, I recalled, I happily admitted that I had smoked weed and expressed the strong view that it should be decriminalised.

"Oh my God! Look here," I whispered. "Do you think they've read it? And now I am going to lie in the interview!"

I immediately wanted to throw up. My palms were sweaty. I needed a drink of water. I needed to lie down. I needed to sleep. I needed to run away. Just get the hell out of there.

I shifted the magazine to the bottom of the large pile, hoping that no one would ever read it. And then it was our turn.

I was immediately struck by a huge printed copy of the constitution of South Africa that was pinned up on a board behind the social worker's desk. It calmed me down. The reality of the constitution and the rights it afforded me, as a lesbian, and us as an adoptive couple, were tangible and concrete.

I had undertaken that day to dress in a fashion that would not feed into any assumptions about us as a couple. I wore a pair of jeans and a neat white cotton shirt. I had also thrown on what I considered to be an accessory, some or other necklace that hung from a rack in the bathroom. My partner wore her usual skirt and top.

The interview seemed routine and rote until we got to the question of religion. The social worker held our completed form in front of her and peered at it through her reading glasses. She seemed satisfied with my description of myself as a "Secular Buddhist", because she asked no further questions about religion.

And then a few minutes later I caught a question that at first I thought I had misheard. In fact I believed for an instant that I might have had a slight stroke or that my nerves had got the better of me and I was hearing things.

"Which one of you is the man?" asked the social worker.

I could feel the tension rising. This was the one red rag that I could not ignore and X understood that it might trigger a dangerous slide into belligerence on my part.

"I am really not sure what you mean," I said facetiously, with a gesture that encompassed us. "We are both women."

"Well, perhaps this might help you," I said calmly, politely. "If either of us sees a spider in our kitchen, we call a friend."

Not only was this a brilliant riposte, I thought, which subtly undermined the absurdity of the question, but it also contained a reply. If the social worker had been looking for a "man" in the relationship, now she would understand that neither of us fulfilled this role. I could hear the little wires sizzling in her head.

Meanwhile I was almost genuinely puzzled. What had she meant? Surely she knew that the question she'd asked was inappropriate and stupid? Surely she had dealt with enough lesbian and gay couples to understand that generally we did not replicate a heteronormative paradigm in our relationships.

I seethed quietly – at the ignorance and insult.

Perhaps what she may have actually wanted to know unconsciously was how we had sex. The Freudian trip-up.

After this interview, we were scheduled to do two more: separate one-on-one sessions. While my partner would remain with this social worker, I was booked with a volunteer social worker from the UK who was assisting Cape Town Child Welfare with their horrendous workload while she conducted research.

I later learnt that the social worker had decided that I was "the man".

She had probably made this expert snap assessment because I wore my hair short and preferred jeans. She lacked the imagination to think of us outside the narrow confines of her own understanding of male–female dynamics. She was not alone. We were often asked which one of us was "in control" or "head of the household". Even children who visited were so steeped in this power dynamic that they would ask, "Which one of you drives?" or "Who does the house belong to?" We grew accustomed to the questions and always found unique ways of either confounding or educating, depending on our mood.

The volunteer social worker seemed much more professional and not consumed with merely ticking all the right boxes. She conducted an in-depth interview with me, asking about my relationship with my parents, my father in particular. She asked my views on discipline, on education, and on religious instruction.

And then she deviated from the process to ask whether we had considered a child who might be "older" – by which she meant a baby up to seven or eight months. These were children who had slipped through the cracks, whose biological parents could not be traced and who existed in an official limbo.

"I don't have a problem with that," I replied.

I found it peculiar that this option had never been offered to adoptive parents at any of the information sessions we had attended so far and I asked my social worker why this was.

"They are just swamped," she said.

She told me she volunteered at a place of safety nearby where there were hundreds of babies who were never considered for placement. Child Welfare were just too busy to process these children for possible adoption. They concentrated instead on mothers who approached the organisation seeking to give up their babies. And then she said, "I would like to suggest that you and your partner visit the place of safety and see for yourselves."

BACK HOME, exhausted and emotional, I told X about the discussion. I said that I was really concerned that a mother might not choose us over a heterosexual couple. "Why wait, if there are children ready to be placed?" I said. "I think we should explore this."

We contacted our social worker, who seemed mildly annoyed by our request. It would mean additional work for the already hard-pressed small team that dealt with adoptions. She also seemed acutely aware of the power vested in her to make this life-altering decision and I resented having to tip-toe around her lest we should offend or irritate. But we had a goal in mind and that was all that mattered.

"I'll look into it," she promised.

A few weeks passed and we heard nothing. What should we do? Should we call to find out? Would she be so annoyed by our impatience that she would scupper the attempt if she felt her authority was being overridden or questioned? Having to second-guess her response only irritated me further. She was a state official and she was paid to do a job.

Two months passed and still we heard nothing. We decided not to push, to leave the matter in the hands of bureaucracy.

Three months, then four, then five – months, we were acutely conscious of, that were vital in the life of a baby needing a placement, where crucial developmental issues, bonding for example, should occur.

Ours, I realised, was an open-ended "pregnancy". There was no nine-month time limit. The ETA of our son or daughter was unknown.

We made one last call to find out whether the social worker had made any progress with our request. "I'm working on it," she said. "There might be a child who is ready. I'll let you know."

Might? Maybe? Perhaps?

Eight months into waiting we decided it was time to have a baby shower. It was a happy event and it made it all so much more concrete and real. So far we had decorated the bedroom with our Frida Kahlo drawings and bought some clothes. We had set up a cot we had inherited from my partner's sister.

A dear friend of ours hosted the party at her home. I had never been to a baby shower in my life, and now here I was at my own. It felt like a parallel universe.

We left laden with everything we needed, from a push-chair to a camping cot to changing mats and bath toys. As we exited, we untethered one of the helium-filled balloons we'd been given and watched as it floated up, up, up, until it became a pinprick in the blue sky. The balloon was our flare to the universe, our shout out to the currents of life.

We're ready. Come, baby, come.

Exactly nine months later, the social worker called.

At least if you're physically "with" child there is some prior warning – contractions, breaking water, belly kicks, time to calculate maternity leave, although there was little chance of that as we were both self-employed.

One moment we were pottering around the house childless and the next we were parents. While we expected it, of course, and it was always going to be sprung on us, no matter how much you try and prepare you just can't.

"Your daughter is ready. We just need to finalise a few documents before you can collect her. But if you like, we can go to the place of safety and you can meet her in the meantime," said the social worker on the phone.

After the phone call we ran around the house whooping and screaming, propelled by a rush of adrenalin and whatever other chemicals the brain releases in moments of extreme joy and confusion. Two of the dogs scattered while the other two ran excitedly around us in circles, clearly believing all this excitement could only mean one thing – a walk.

At the age of 42 I had become an accidental mommy. I found myself in a place and in a time in which this significant miracle, the gift of parenthood, had been made possible. All work commitments immediately faded into insignificance, as did the rest of the world out there. Everything was telescoped and compressed into a single concern: our daughter.

Our social worker asked if we could pick her from her office en route to the place of safety where our daughter – just using the word was strange, new and bizarre – was being cared for. She also asked whether I knew the area in which it was situated, as she had never been there before herself.

It was a sunny Thursday morning when we picked her up and drove to the place of safety (such a celestial-sounding location), which turned out to be a shabby brick, one-storey building with an overgrown garden, tucked behind rows of houses in a nearby township. I had expected the social worker to have arranged with the staff at the centre to meet us but they seemed unaware of our visit. The sounds of children's voices and cries drifted through the corridors where whiffs of institutional food being cooked somewhere hung heavy.

A large, officious but polite matron in a uniform eventually appeared and asked us to follow her to a nursery at the back of the centre. We were unprepared for the scene that greeted us. Rows and rows of cots. There were at least ten children, some tiny babies, others standing clutching at the railings, all of them needing attention.

In one corner two nurses hunched over a baby being bathed in a plastic bath.

The social worker left us in the middle of the room while she went and talked to the two nurses. And there we stood, surrounded by children, some staring at us, and others, like the two beautiful, emaciated little girls who shared a cot, straining over the railing reaching out to be picked up. We could not resist. Next to them was a newborn baby wrapped tightly in a blanket who cried deep and soulful cries. I wanted to pick up and comfort the child and hold the two little girls at the same time. I looked around for someone who could help but there was no one.

A nurse noticed us fussing.

"She's hungry. Don't worry, we'll feed her soon," she said, glancing at the crying baby.

"And these two little girls?"

"Their parents died, but they are very sick."

242

It was devastating. I could feel a sob rising and tears searing. Crying would just upset everyone, so I turned and quickly left the room. I felt like a coward. Who was I to weep? I stood in the passage outside, reeling.

I wanted to go home. I wanted to unsee what I had just seen. I wanted the heavens to open and make everything okay for everyone. How could we parent only one child? What about the others? The cauterised bubble of our lives popped, pricked – gone. So much pain in that small room and embodied in tiny bodies.

The social worker emerged.

"Your daughter is ready for you."

And then we saw her. She was the baby the nurses had been bathing. A little round bean with huge brown eyes. She was beautiful and she was ours. Layla. That is what we had decided to name her. Layla, born in the night. Layla, gift from the universe.

The social worker placed the baby girl in my arms. We were strangers to her but she stared at us calmly, intently. I leaned in over her and she smiled suddenly and then clutched at my nose. I wanted someone to beam us immediately out of that nursery and into a safe private space. The magnitude of it all was overwhelming.

The two women who had been caring for her were smiling broadly.

"We are so happy. She is our little star here," said one.

The social worker's voice cut through the moment.

"I just wanted you to meet her before we finalise everything. She's not ready to go home with you yet. She still has to go to hospital for a final check-up and we need to get an order of the court releasing her."

"You mean we can't take her now?"

"No, afraid not."

It was impossible now that we had met our daughter for us to think we would have to leave her there for the weekend or even longer while Child Welfare arranged for the hospital visit and the final legal requirements. How long would that take?

"Depends on our schedules and if we can get a vehicle."

"Can't we take her to the hospital?"

"I suppose you can. Fetch her tomorrow, but you have to bring her back here immediately afterwards," said the social worker.

We wanted to spend as much time with Layla as was legally possible and immediately began to press for the process to be finalised. It was agonising to think that she had to spend more time in the place of safety when her room at home was ready. Now that she was real, here, in the flesh, we could not bear not to be with her. The need was visceral. But the bureaucratic machine had to be assuaged. Feelings were not part of the equation.

Handing our daughter back was excruciating but we consoled ourselves with the knowledge that she was in a space she knew and with people who had already cared for and loved her for at least six months. We arranged to collect Layla early the following morning for the required check-up at the Red Cross Children's Hospital.

Afterwards we felt shell-shocked. We dropped the social worker off and decided to gather ourselves in a coffee shop nearby. Our only preoccupation now was the little person we had just met and who would soon be coming home with us for good. Her face, her smile, her little hands, her being – these things, this whole, this child filled our emotional vista.

But we were both unsettled, out of kilter and suddenly extremely exhausted. As we prepared to leave the coffee shop, we realised that in our rush we had forgotten our bags and so could not pay for our coffees. We phoned a friend who came over and paid the bill.

We returned home and called friends and family to tell them the news.

Georg was, as expected, underwhelmed.

"Well, good luck then," he offered.

I recognised his now habitual undermining tone. He was so unhappy within himself that he was unable to be happy for anyone else. I clung to the hope that someday he would snap out of his self-pitying misery.

We fell asleep thinking of Layla in her cot and the next morning we rose early.

Layla was dressed in an awful green dress and two flimsy, government-issue disposable nappies. We had been concerned that she might be afraid or upset at being removed from her familiar surroundings, but from the start she faced us and every new experience with a sense of intense wonder and curiosity. She fully engaged with the world, taking

244

it all in. She smiled when she saw us, which was a relief. How would we have comforted a crying, unhappy baby?

One of the care-givers handed Layla to us.

"Um . . . what does she eat?"

"I think she has had a bottle this morning," the carer offered.

"But what if she needs a feed? We might have to wait at the hospital."

"Don't worry, she will be fine."

Layla was remarkably calm. She watched as we struggled with the complicated buckle on the child seat (it would take us months to work it out). I sat at the back close to her, stroking her head and talking to her while my partner navigated through the early-morning traffic. Suddenly the enormous responsibility of driving with a child in the car was all-consuming. Was it too hot? Our car was old and unsafe. We needed to buy another car immediately, we agreed, one with side-impact bars and airbags. We needed sunshades.

"Careful, drive slowly! Watch out for that arsehole on the left! Put your flicker on."

Layla kept smiling.

I realised I had used the word "arsehole" in front of *the child*. We'd have to be toning that down a bit. Years later Layla would ask me casually, after she had learned to talk, of course, what exactly an "arsehole" was and why they always seemed to make an appearance only when we were driving.

"Mommy is an arsehole for calling other people arseholes," I explained.

The Red Cross Children's Hospital is one of the biggest and best in the country. That morning even before 8am mothers with babies on their backs were spilling out of taxis and buses at the entrance. Inside the corridors bustled with doctors and nurses, while patients and their carers sat on long wooden benches waiting, waiting, waiting.

We wandered through the maze and eventually found the doctor who was named on the form we had been given. All this time Layla didn't cry or wriggle as we took turns holding, cuddling and kissing her, waiting for our names to be called out.

And then an unfamiliar sweet smell seemed to envelop us. It sort of came from nowhere and hit me right in the nostrils. Well, it came from somewhere, obviously. Layla's nappy.

"But we don't have anything. We don't have nappies, we don't have a bottle. What are we going to do?" I panicked. It should have been an early warning that I would soon become one of *those* parents, the 0-to-panic-in-less-than-60-seconds ones. But we were not to know that quite then.

We found a nurse at a work station who immediately offered to find some nappies, a bottle and formula in case Layla was hungry.

We were so ill prepared. Why hadn't we thought to bring a "baby bag", which would later become a permanent accessory? Were we even capable of parenting? We didn't even know what to feed her. We were both such thoroughly undomesticated women.

I was yet to discover that you grow into parenthood. There is no switch that trips when a baby arrives. There is no instruction manual. Although there are books you can read – and once read, instantly forget – but the truth is there is simply too much to absorb. For me, becoming a mother was a gradual dawning, a process of extracting something deeply remembered. It was as I scrabbled inside myself that I began to recognise faint traces of my own mother. I discovered a treasure trove that Barbara had deposited and left there for me to find in my own time.

We owed it to Layla, this child who had enabled us to be parents, to be the best moms we could possibly be. We were going to try not to repeat the Larkin poem.

Layla, sweet-natured Layla, endured the doctor's prods and pokes with the same sense of sanguine curiosity she displayed at everything else that unfurled or unfolded around her.

Having bonded during the hospital visit, we found handing her back to her care-givers for the long weekend unbearable, but it had to be done.

Three days later, on a Tuesday morning, on 7 October 2003, we finally brought Layla home.

We had brought a white Babygro with us to the place of safety and dressed her in it. She smiled when she saw us again, which was so re-assuring. As before, we struggled again with the darn clasp on the baby seat. Layla shot me the most magnificent smile, which I managed to capture in a photograph, and then we headed off home.

We got out of the car and settled her in her push-chair. As we wheeled it to the front gate, where our four dogs had congregated excitedly, she laughed out loud at the wagging tails and flapping tongues.

Soon our house was filled with flowers, cakes and visitors who had come to welcome Layla home. Her granny, cousins and other friends passed her around. Everyone beamed with delight and Layla, sweet Layla, took it all in.

And then she fell asleep and she slept and slept and slept as we hovered over her cot in her quiet peaceful bedroom, monitoring every breath.

"But SHE'S an infant!"

Georg stood looking down at Layla, his new granddaughter, as she lolled happily in her portable baby car-seat the first time we carried her over his threshold.

"But of course, what did you think?"

"Well, I thought the child would be a toddler, someone who could walk around," he said. He stared at her for a further minute or two, before turning and shuffling back to his armchair in front of the TV.

I hoisted Layla onto my hip and she gave Georg a gummy smile. I saw his face soften.

"She's a very beautiful little girl," he said.

Silence.

"Now vhat about your vork? Who is caring for her?"

"We are. We both work from home so we're flexible. And she's not too demanding at this stage."

"Vell, I just hope you know vhat you haf let yourself in for."

Don't, I told myself. Don't rise to the bait.

I wondered whether Georg would have offered the same advice, or rather non-advice, had I been heterosexual, married and had given birth. Knowing Georg, he probably would have.

We soon learned that any outings needed to be constructed around Layla's routines: food, nappy change, a nap, nappy change, some playing, nappy change, a walk in the push-chair, food, nappy change, bath, and then hours of rocking and singing while she resisted falling asleep.

248

My attention now was on Layla and not Georg. While she was with me, I didn't have the energy or the inclination to try to read his moods and wants or deal with them.

I asked Georg if he would like to hold Layla. He had always enjoyed the company of small children and I wanted to gauge whether he was capable of, for once, rising above himself.

I placed Layla in the cradle of his arm as he sat in the chair. He looked at her and pulled a funny face. She laughed. He liked that. Then he sang a little German song to her. She liked that, too, and she stretched out her hand to grab his nose. She did not care that he was a grumpy old fart. She didn't know. He let her press his nostrils and he made funny nasal sounds. Still Layla smiled.

Soon Georg was bouncing her on his lap, singing another old German song, about a horse.

What was going on inside this brittle old man? I wondered. He seemed to have surrendered to the moment. It was the first time in a long time that I witnessed him smiling.

"She really is a little sweetie. Who vould not vant zis child? How can it happen?"

"We can never know the pain of how she came to be here," I told him.

He said nothing as he held Layla, leaning in to blow a strawberry on her forehead.

In that instant, Georg, without the carapace of injury, perceived hurt and collateral damage of life, was the kind self I sometimes glimpsed. It was still there. It had taken a child to unlock it, and now that I had seen it, I was determined that we would work our way back towards it, whatever it took.

My father's other grandchild, Alex, my brother's son, was growing up in Australia. Georg had seen Alex on a few occasions before my Albert and his wife had left South Africa. At the time there was no discussion about what this meant, no long goodbyes, no regrets. Nothing. It just was. This is what people do. They come, they go. We are left alone.

And typical of our strange family dysfunction, my father didn't seem to feel the need to keep regularly in touch with his grandson.

The fracturing of his own family, his sister and mother left in Berlin while he uprooted himself and moved across the world, was still playing itself out here and now, two generations later. My mother had also severed all contact with her family.

Even now, my brother and I, although I think of him often, remain dislocated, solitary molecules. I often wonder: does he see me as I see myself? Do I see him as he sees himself?

But now I had my own primary family, new roots spun and holding me tightly, safely.

In becoming adoptive parents I had no idea, at the start, just how much curiosity and ignorance we had opened ourselves up to. It became immediately apparent from some of the bizarre and oblique ways people would ask questions, perhaps a bit like our social worker who had wanted to know which one of us was the man.

Ultimately, the most difficult adjustment was not learning how to be a parent but suddenly finding ourselves clearly clocked in public spaces as a lesbian couple with an adopted child, a black child. Before that we were just two older white women in the crowd. Unremarkable, unseen, unnoticed.

Mostly people asked because they were curious. We were still an anomaly. We had, as an LGBTI community, been mostly unseen, apart from when newspapers would send photographers out to capture the most outrageous moments at gay pride marches. We were not shaping the narrative; it was being shaped around us, around crude stereotypes of dykes on bikes or fags in heels.

Now here we were, not wearing flamboyant costumes and not riding bikes. We were pushing a stroller with a baby in it.

"I don't understand," became my standard reply to questions I knew masked another.

"Who will change the nappies?" someone in the family asked.

"Who's going to be the mother?"

"Both of us."

Most children, later in life and if they can afford therapy, only have to undo the damage one mother is capable of serving up on the side, while our children would have two. Perhaps the shrink would offer a discount.

In the first few weeks after Layla's arrival we would both dash to change her nappy or bathe her. We'd stand for a few seconds arguing about whose turn it was while Layla patiently sucked her thumb or played with her toes.

Our first and most important lesson, however, was learning how and what to feed her and when. Our kitchen morphed into a small laboratory with sterilising equipment, measuring spoons and various baby bottles lined up on counters. If you didn't know any better, you might think we were cooking up crystal meth.

I soon adapted from being someone who would swing home with one bag of groceries, usually containing filter coffee and a few nibbles, to someone who could negotiate a huge packet of disposable nappies clasped between my arm and upper chest while carrying at least four shopping bags in one hand and Layla, strapped in her car-seat, in the other. I learned I could close the boot of the car with my head and that feet were not only made for walking but also activating the collapsible stroller.

It was exhausting.

The social worker and the carers at the place of safety had been rather vague about Layla's diet.

Was she on solids?

"We're not sure," was the reply.

We had been given a large tin of government-issue formula when we collected Layla, but that was it. After gulping down her first bottle at home, Layla had projectile-vomited a stream of curdled gunk. She did this after almost every feed. Something clearly was amiss or we were doing something wrong. We read up and phoned our friends with children.

"Switch to soya," one of our friends advised. The curdled gunk was a sign that Layla might be lactose-intolerant. We did and soon she was sucking contentedly, keeping down her bottle and gaining weight.

Layla had learned at the place of safety to fall asleep on her own, soothing herself by sucking her thumb. At first, around 7pm after her bath, she would easily "go down" by herself. And while this might have been glorious for us as parents, we felt that Layla needed to feel contained and held, and so we undertook to hold, rock and sing her to sleep, undo what had not been done.

Layla, of course, loved this so much that instead of falling instantly asleep, she would now lie in our arms – depending on whose shift it was – and stare at whichever mom was doing the singing and rocking. She went from a baby who slept instantly to one who now took at least an hour before her eyelids grew heavy and she dropped off.

"Go to sleep, go to sleep, go to sleep," I would sing and chant while little Layla offered in return a penetrating but gentle stare.

It was during those hours sitting with her in my arms, bathed by the gentle yellow glow that beamed out of a baby dragon lamp, that I began to discover unmapped internal landscapes, places I could not have dreamed I would reach had this soul not entered my life. The key to unlocking the door to this vista, beyond the superficial self I had come to understand, was internalising the immensity of being responsible, in full, for another human life.

In those quiet times Barbara became more real to me than she had ever been in life. In the darkened room I found my own mother again. She had not died. There, with Layla in my arms, Barbara lived even more vividly. I found fragments of someone I had lost, took hold of a maternal thread reaching across time and silence. Whoever had handed Barbara those treasures was there too, and the woman before her, and the woman before that.

And then this memory.

"Closa your eyes, Marianna. Whata you see?"

"Nothing, Mommy."

"Whata you mean nothing?"

"It's just black."

"Well, I can see da circus."

"Really? The circus?"

"Yes, a beeg, beeg, beeg tent. Red and white with da clowns and lions."

"I can't see it! I can't see it!"

"You can. You musta look. You musta look carefully and you will see."

And I did.

We embrace to be embraced, wrote JM Coetzee in *Age of Iron*. "We embrace our children to be folded in the arms of the future, to pass ourselves beyond death, to be transported."

In that room Barbara was transported back to the future.

Going out in public began to feel as if I no longer belonged to myself, as people tried to make sense of us.

Puzzled garage attendant: "Who are this child's parents?"

"We are."

"Oh, I see."

Woman in queue: "Is that your child?"

"Yes."

"Did you adopt her?"

"Yes."

"You are doing such a wonderful thing. She is so lucky."

When to engage and when not to became a skill. When to refuse to answer, when to change the narrative.

"Actually, *I'm* lucky. Because of her I am a mother."

Toy-shop owner: "Did you adopt her?"

"Yes."

"Is she coloured?"

"Um . . ."

"I can see this child has got some Malay in her, look at those beautiful eyes."

"You think so?"

"I can see it, man."

"Oh, okay."

And then those who knew no boundary.

Another woman in a queue in a grocery store: "Did you adopt her?"

(No, I froze Bob Marley's sperm.) "Yes."

"Does she have HIV?"

Sigh and eye-roll.

We became adept at predicting what would come and formulating standard replies.

Our lives changed as we adjusted to the triangle that we had become. We also learned to deal with how the world came at us. We had to take our space and just be, surround ourselves with an aura which hopefully would insulate us from the stares and the questions.

We celebrated Layla's first birthday at Kirstenbosch Gardens with a few family friends. A few days later she took her first steps, to much whooping and clapping. One tooth had popped through by then, but that was it. Sometimes we wondered if she would ever have a full set, but discovered that some babies just cut late, and Layla was one of them.

Georg phoned on Layla's birthday to say he had bought her a teddy bear. I was overcome by the small gesture because I needed him to be an arsehole. We drove through to see him. He fetched the little brown bear from his bedroom and gave it to Layla. She smiled, clutched the bear to her chest and then bit its nose.

"She has a disarming smile," said Georg.

We named the bear Georg. We still have him.

Georg had put on weight and the colour had returned to his cheeks. Now that Layla could walk, our time during my visits was taken up keeping her occupied with puzzles, stacking cups, and an old chicken that was once mine and that Georg had kept. Georg cleared a space in his dining-room cupboard for Layla's "things". Every now and again I would find Georg on the carpet with Layla, playing with her. I wondered if he was conscious of the lightness this child had brought to his spirit.

FOR ABOUT two years there were just three of us – my partner, myself and Layla.

What I do recall?

Layla's first words were "hello, gorgeous" and then shortly afterwards "dog", "hair" and "pear". Flowers were "lada". She said "out" when she wanted to go into the garden and "up" when she wanted to be picked up. She called her little electronic piano "poppin". She said "Oupa" whenever she saw Georg. He would smile and kiss her then.

She loved broccoli, pickled fish and tomatoes, and grunted if she enjoyed her food.

She laughed a lot, more than she cried.

She liked to dance.

She liked books.

She loved music.

The dogs irritated her.

She ruined my brand-new laptop.

She loved Barney (even I loved Barney).

She liked to sleep with us.

She liked cuddly toys and her dolls – especially Rosie, the only black doll we found in a toyshop wrapped in cellophane and stashed under a shelf stacked with little white dolls with cupid lips and housed in lovely boxes. I had taken issue with the shop manager because there were no black dolls (apart from sweet Rosie hidden away).

"They prefer teddy bears," he had said.

"They?"

"Black people."

"Maybe if you stocked some black dolls, people would buy them."

"I am not going to just stock black dolls to make a point."

"And these rows and rows of pretty white dolls don't?"

"Huh?"

Layla also loved a creepy doll that had mysteriously followed me into adulthood. I had never loved or taken care of her. I had cut her hair short and she had gathered dust for years in a cupboard. Barbara must have held onto the doll and passed it on to me. I became convinced the doll had a mind of its own. How had it stuck so close for over 40 years, through travels across the world, and many moves to communal homes and flats?

Layla held her tight and kissed her. Finally, dolly found a little girl who loved her.

At times I felt as if I was living with one of the Marx brothers.

Just before Layla dropped off, one night she shouted out "cucumber".

I realised I loved Layla so deeply it was scary.

I found a poem, "The Cradle Song", by Yeats, wrote up the last verse and put it above her cot.

"I sigh that kiss you

For I must own

That I shall miss you

When you have grown."

We heard about a "moms and tots" group in the neighbourhood. This was a good thing, people told us. Here local mothers gathered with their babies and stimulated the shit out of them. Because of our work schedules we agreed my partner would go to the first part of the playgroup and I would relieve her later.

I arrived at the double-storeyed Victorian home with its moist, spongy lawn littered with jungle gyms, hula hoops and small plastic motorcycles, and found my way through a side door, following the sound of children's voices. In a sweltering garage I spotted around eight mothers, all white, seated in a circle singing and clapping with their toddlers in front of them.

I was suddenly overwhelmed with a feeling of intense claustrophobia and dread. The room began to spin and I had the urge to flee screaming. Layla picked up on my distress and began to tear around the garage. I was aware of disapproving glances. The woman at the centre of the playgroup was in the process of setting out the rest of the afternoon as if it were a small-scale military invasion.

We were to move from this room to another, where the toddlers would paint for five minutes. Then we were to shuffle into another venue where the children would play with clay, and then another where they would take turns at using a variety of rocking, turning and twisting apparatus to help with their midline. I felt a migraine begging to erupt. Nausea, blurred vision. No more, out now!

I excused myself, picked up Layla and we made a dash for the car.

We would not be going back, I told mom number one when I arrived home, needing to lie down in a darkened room to recover.

As Layla grew, and considering she had been such an easy baby, we soon began to talk about our second child, a brother or sister for her. We chuckled privately about friends or others who complained of colicky babies, post-natal depression and the desperation of sleep deprivation.

"I mean, really, they're such pussies," we agreed.

My only condition was that this time we would do it through a private adoption agency. While many of our friends had had extremely positive experiences with Cape Town Child Welfare, I had felt somewhat battered by the process, the lack of resources, the having to tip-toe around officials who wielded enormous power, of having always to be on my "best behaviour" just in case we "slipped up" as a same-sex couple.

I did not want to be asked again who the man was. I did not want to lie about my religious beliefs or any other beliefs, for that matter. I did not want to feel uncomfortable in my skin, my being. Georg could handle that task all on his own.

And so it was that I called a private agency. My first sentence to the social worker was "We are a same-sex couple, we have a daughter and would like to adopt another child. Do you have a problem with us? Just be honest."

We learned that many private agencies were run by Christian groupings who were opposed to same-sex adoption and who refused to place children with lesbian or gay couples just in case we ate them for breakfast. There was no point fighting them; it was just not going to happen.

"Of course we do," came the reply and then laughter, followed by "Don't be ridiculous, of course we can help".

This social worker was clearly so comfortable that she could joke about it. That sealed it for us.

The process this time was extremely rigorous. There were mountains of forms to be filled in, psychometric tests, a home visit and visits to the agency for gruelling interviews. But never once did I feel that we were being humoured, tolerated or accommodated because the agency was legally obliged to do so.

We had expected a long wait, at least nine months, and had hardly had time to prepare for the arrival of a new baby when three months later the call came, on 20 May, that our daughter was ready for us to collect her.

Kenya arrived home at 10am on 23 May 2005. Our lives would never quite be the same.

K ENYA'S "HANDOVER" occurred in circumstances much less traumatic, for me at least, than Layla's. We had arranged to meet the social worker at a McDonald's drive-thru near the place of safety located in the northern suburbs of Cape Town on the morning we were due to pick her up. It was early and the restaurant was buzzing with people grabbing a quick unhealthy bite to eat before rushing to work.

My partner's sister accompanied us this time, which served to dissipate our nerves. The social worker arrived bright-eyed and bushy-tailed, grinning. We followed her in our car to a neat Spanish-style, double-storeyed suburban home with a lawn that leaked casually onto the pavement. This place was so different from the place of safety that had been Layla's home for several months. There was no wall or fence separating it from the street.

An elderly woman with a perfect grey coif and floating dentures opened the door. There was the aroma of cooking inside and the sound of children, babies, floated down the carpeted stairs. The woman gave us a broad plastic smile and asked us to wait in a reception area while she went to fetch our daughter.

Minutes later she appeared at the top of the stairs carrying a small bundle dressed in a shocking-pink little tracksuit. I took one look at our daughter and wept. She seemed confused, frightened and angry. She was a chubby baby with huge cheeks. She didn't smile, at us or anyone else.

We wanted to leave with her immediately but the woman with the dentures insisted that we come upstairs to see where Kenya had slept and to say goodbye to the women who had cared for her. "Oooh, she kept them busy. She's a bit colicky," she said as she padded back up the stairs ahead of us.

We followed, carrying our inscrutable daughter.

The nursery here accommodated only about six babies, some of whom were being bathed and fed. The carers all smiled and kissed Kenya goodbye. We were handed a small parcel which contained her blue dummy, a soft toy and messages that the carers had written for her.

And then it was time to head off home. We had left that morning as a family of three and were returning a family of four. There would be new reconfigurations, triangulations, adjustments. How would Layla respond to her sister? How would we shift the perimeters of the triangle that had shaped around us into a square?

My sister-out-of-law drove while we sat at the back with an expressionless Kenya buckled into the car-seat. I understood that this baby was needing to take in these unfamiliar people who had plucked her from the only home she had known. I longed to tell her she was safe, home now finally with her moms. We had fallen instantly in love and wanted so desperately for her to feel contained, but with Kenya it would take time. And she, and not we, we soon learned, would set the agenda.

We had left Layla, who was now a babbling, busy two-year-old, at home with a day mom, who would increasingly come to play a vital role in helping us to care for our children while we worked in separate offices in the house.

We lowered Kenya in her car-seat so that she could meet her sister for the first time.

Layla immediately smiled and kissed her and then named her "the face", for that was the most striking element of Kenya's being – her face and all it contained, and hid.

I gently prised her out of the car-seat. She seemed wide-eyed and terrified as we walked her around the house, showing her each room, introducing her to the dogs, who by then had realised that Layla was a vulnerable source of food. She had learned to walk around with a biscuit or carrot stick held high so they couldn't snatch it from her.

And then Kenya began to cry. It was not a cry which gradually grew into a wail. It went from 0 to 100 in one second. It was a terrifying cry, a cry of anguish, a cry of confusion. Her little fists balled tight. I held her close to me and went and sat in the lounge, where I rocked her and sang to her.

Still she cried.

Inconsolable.

"What's wrong with her, Mommy?" asked Layla, clearly deeply concerned.

"I think she is scared, my darling."

"Don't cry, baby," said Layla to her sister.

But she did. For four solid hours while I held her. She finally fell asleep, exhausted, still shuddering from the effort.

I felt so helpless. Was she in pain? Did she need medication? Was she uncomfortable? Hungry? Angry? Scared?

Unlike Layla, Kenya revealed nothing apart from her distress. Layla was concerned for her new sister and it was profound watching her trying to console her. Kenya would stare intently at the little smiley face pressed close to her. And then she would cry, again.

"It's okay, face," Layla would say.

Her first night home I slept with Kenya tightly bundled in my arms. She was a restless infant. Her hands constantly moved, kneading a little blanket, and she sucked her dummy as if her life depended on it.

And so it was that Kenya introduced us to the altered state of permanent sleep deprivation. Severe sleep deprivation. Whereas Layla could and did sleep through the night, Kenya did not sleep for longer than 20 minutes. Deep in the quiet dark she had night terrors, which manifested in blood-curdling screams until, with a jolt, she would rouse herself.

We were beside ourselves with worry and fatigue. Nothing seemed to help. Kenya cried before a feed and afterwards. She cried when we bathed her. She cried when we picked her up or put her down. She cried when we rocked her and sang to her.

One morning around 3am, exhausted and trying to console Kenya,

I felt Barbara's presence strongly, and then the comforting words "You can do it, you can do it" floated spontaneously to mind.

Dealing with Kenya's almost daily distress was exacerbated somewhat by Layla's apparent obsession with her baby sister. She would not leave her alone for a single minute. If she wasn't stroking her cheek, she would be climbing into her cot to lie with her. She kissed her all over, bit her lovingly, insisted on bathing her.

The first time we saw Kenya's gummy smile was one afternoon when Layla exuberantly burst into her bedroom after a very short afternoon nap. For Layla, the world was a joy and an adventure, a place to be explored and discovered, devoured. She loved the sun and the rain; she loved the dogs, her toys, music. She loved us. But more than anything she loved her sister.

And soon, slowly but absolutely surely, Kenya began to thaw. She no longer napped with her fists balled and gradually began to sleep on her back, her arms outstretched. Kenya smiled not when we wanted her to, but when she felt it appropriate.

Georg – Oupa – had fallen in love with Layla and he received Kenya with the same visible display of joy. When we went to visit him now, he greeted us cheerily at the door and had always made sure to buy something for each of his grandchildren, usually chocolate (which we disapproved of, initially). He would bring out his collection of strange hats for their amusement, and crouch on the carpet in his lounge and play with them, doing a puzzle or stacking cups.

Soon he began to look forward to our visits and would regularly phone to ask how we were and when we would be coming.

I couldn't help wondering how Georg interpreted what had shifted inside himself, whether he could feel it. Did he recognise that part of him which these children had seemingly helped to unlock and restore?

One afternoon he tried to articulate, although he was not aware that this was what he was doing, how he had come to internalise his grandchildren, his black grandchildren.

It was then that the convoluted and twisted logic of a mind that had been shaped by blunt prejudice, attempting to work against itself, was laid bare. His explanation was as shocking as it was astounding.

261

"You know," he said, bouncing both children on his knees as he sat in his armchair, "I haf noticed since 1994 zat black people look different now. Zeir skins seem to be lighter and zeir heads are different. Smaller. Rounder."

As they left his mouth, entered my ears and sizzled around my brain, I let each word settle.

Incredible.

Georg had used the prism and ideology of eugenics to interpret an emotion. In order unconsciously to internalise our children he had had to make them "whiter".

The tragic power of political collateral damage. It lurks inside the folds and membranes in each of us. Until we know it, it stands guard at the portals of understanding.

I undertook, in that moment, not to unpack with him what he had just said but to perhaps pick up the conversation later.

Around eight months after Kenya's arrival we began to feel as if we were surfacing, albeit barely, for the first time, from the aftermath of an earthquake. Kenya had shifted the ground irrevocably. Now, finally, we understood all those near psychotic, sleep-deprived parents of babies who do not sleep. I felt as if large chunks of my brain had been turned to goo, gone, like data on a corrupted hard drive, never to be retrieved again. But then again, the shutting down of old control centres there drove me into other regions of the 10 per cent of our brains experts say we use. Thank God, then, for the other 90 per cent, for it must have been there that I drew sustenance to place one foot in front of the other.

This was a rite of passage I could not have predicted or known. I came to the conclusion that there is a reason we don't pass this information on from generation to generation. It is this aspect of parenting that would surely stop us from procreating – this and the price of disposable nappies.

Kenya possessed an extraordinary power. She knew what she wanted and what she lacked and she was not afraid to make these known. She was stubborn, uncompromising, funny, infuriating and extremely attuned to the emotional frequency of any situation. She could instantly pick up when we were distressed, for example, and we had to learn to contain our own anxieties in order to deal with hers. She was teaching us how to parent her. Three months after she arrived home she smiled at us (and not Layla) for the first time. It was a breakthrough. As more time passed she began to mellow and trust us and herself. She allowed her brilliance to shine, and when it did it was dazzling.

In the meantime, we had undertaken to send Layla to nursery school. She was two and a half and ready for the stimulation, growth and socialisation the environment would offer. It was important for us that she attend a school where the majority of the teachers (not just the assistant staff) and children were black, and that it was a school that embraced diversity. This was Cape Town in 2005 and there was only one school on that list close to where we lived that stood out.

Chameleon, in the suburb Sybrand Park, started by Sue Bailey, had gained a reputation as one of the most progressive pre-schools in the city, and it had also been recommended to us. Sue had started a small school in a garage in Pinelands in 1995, a school that had an ethos of "anti-bias" education where the focus was not only on the children but parents and staff as well. Differently abled children were welcome there, too. From the moment we walked in, Chameleon just felt right.

As the day approached when we would take Layla, there I began to suffer terrible separation anxiety. We had never left Layla anywhere before, never mind a pre-school 10 km from our home. But she was ready and it was time. I spent the entire first day lurking in the corridor, classroom and dining room trying to stay out of everyone's way. The teachers and Sue were wonderfully accommodating of me, this anxious parent, but it was clear Layla enjoyed every minute, including her mid-morning nap.

The following day Layla was excited to go to school and, after being stuck for an hour in early morning rush-hour traffic getting there (and another hour trying to get back home), I was able to return home knowing she was safe and happy. But I did spend the rest of the day staring out of my office window, wondering whether she was okay. She was.

From the start we were both aware of the enormous responsibility of being white mothers raising two young black women in post-apartheid South Africa, where centuries of racism and structural inequality shaped the experiences of the majority of the country's citizens. There is something to be said for the US Association of Black Social Workers' position that black children should not be placed with a cross-racial adoptive family. The Association was vehemently opposed to this, believing that identity grew around three levels – physical, psychological and cultural. A 1972 statement by the Association claimed: "Ethnicity is a way of life in the United States and the world at large." How were we, as white South Africans, going to be able to socialise our children to move through the world as black people when we ourselves had never had to encounter the world this way? We could not know what it means to be black in the world and while we might have believed that we ourselves were "woke" or conscious, we could never experience life through our children's eyes. We had no idea what awaited them, but it would not be long before we would begin to find out.

This was going to be a challenging process, and it would require from us constant vigilance and exploration – mostly of ourselves. Our children would have to know and understand not only the country's past and present but also the history of negritude. How could we prevent our children from being assimilated into a worldview largely shaped by Western liberal democracy when we ourselves were products of this? We knew we needed to root our children firmly on the African continent in our own country, South Africa – but how to do this?

The challenges were immediately apparent, not only in procuring toys such as dolls that looked like our children, but also in finding nursery rhymes, songs and stories that were indigenous and in African languages. Chameleon had curated a CD of lullabies and other children's songs from South Africa; at that time it was the only such CD available in Cape Town. Music shops had racks of CDs filled with children's music, but none of it was local.

The same applied to children's books and television shows. While Barney the purple dinosaur, a crafty early pusher for monotheistic faith, certainly included an extremely diverse cast of children, the values were all American.

Almost every single TV show featured casts of mostly white children. Back then black Barbies or Brats were rare. Finding anything with black protagonists was impossible, Disney being the biggest culprit with its posse of blonde princesses. Well, okay, there was Pocahontas and Jasmine in *Aladdin* but they were not African. Eventually, Disney did create a black protagonist in *The Princess and the Frog*, but guess what? The black protagonist, Tiana, spends much of the movie as a frog, while the white princess, Charlotte La Bouff, just gets to be a white princess. The film is filled with stereotypes about voodoo and black magic. We took the girls to the cinema to see it and spent much of the journey home discussing what was wrong with the film. This would become the only way we could watch anything exported from the US; we deconstructed it simply and incontrovertibly. Mercifully, the film was lost on Kenya, who took the opportunity to nap and drink her bottle.

And then the question as to which "culture" to expose our children to. Does a child "belong" to a culture? If I had adopted a white child from Romania, would I raise my child as a Romanian?

And what was *my* culture? Apart from being white, I was a half-Portuguese, half-German, recovering Roman Catholic atheist lesbian immigrant. At least I had options, unlike X, who came from a family of several generations of white South Africans, with a touch of Welsh and Afrikaner ancestry.

We decided that the best we could do was firmly locate ourselves in South Africa and to open our children and ourselves to the cultures and languages that surrounded us. We resolved to try to cultivate in them, and ourselves, a love, wonder and respect for alternative ways of being and thinking; to understand how economics shaped lives and limited or expanded options; how global capitalism and the corporatisation of the world scoured us of our traditions, creating a false egalitarian chimera that we are all uniform and our destiny is to consume.

A friend, after I had mentioned to her that Kenya, after two years, still did not sleep through the night, suggested that we perform a ritual to inform her ancestors.

"You have to do it."

"Okay, tell me how."

"You have to slaughter a goat. And you have to do it at your house. You have to brew beer but you can't do it on the stove, you have to do it on a fire outside. I'll give you a recipe. You have to take the gallbladder of the goat and place it in her room. And then you have to use some of the skin for a bracelet."

Oh fuck.

There was no way the dogs were going to leave anything they considered food intact. And I was not going to be able to slaughter an animal myself.

"I'll think about it," I said.

As time wore on and I became dangerously, murderously sleep-deprived, and after one particularly gruelling night, I considered ringing the goat's neck myself if it meant just one full night's sleep.

Interestingly, no one had ever suggested that we perform any rituals for Layla. Her "ethnicity" was less fixed, more fluid. Why would one child require a ritual and the other not? And what if my one daughter was considered "coloured"? What rituals then to culturally acclimatise her?

Without losing sight of the massive challenge, somehow we would have to muddle our way through all of this. But between the weighty matters we got on with parenting.

Part of this process was that I discovered what kind of a mother I was (and am). I enjoyed reading to the girls at night, giving each character in the book a distinct accent – Afrikaans, French, German, Portuguese, Italian. When anyone else read to them, they shouted for the voices. They found a way of distinguishing which mom either of them wanted. I was to be called Nana (Layla named me) or Mommy Nana.

This way we didn't both rush when one of our children shouted "Mommy!"

Later, when a serious discussion was initiated, I became Marianne.

At the age of 44 I get to relive parts of my childhood. I find that I really, really enjoy parks – slides in particular, and swings too. And we go to the Natural History Museum in Cape Town, particularly on rainy days, where we scream and run away from the dinosaurs, and look through the glass at the stuffed baboon and snakes. The museum becomes a regular haunt, one I love. We make up our own jokes for some of the displays. The two grizzly bears become favourites – one

266

bear lying on the floor while the other bares its teeth, making it look like it is laughing.

"Look, that bear is laughing so much he has fallen on the ground," I tell Layla and Kenya. "I wonder what the joke was."

We think for a while. I tell them I know all the old bear jokes.

"Ah, I know," I say. "Knock, knock."

"Who's there?" they say in their little voices.

"Barely there," I reply, slapping my thigh at the ingenuity of the punchline.

They stare at me nonplussed.

"Barely there? Don't you get it? They're bears, man. Stuffed bears! Barely there."

They smile, humouring me. Later, through sheer repetition on my part, they get the joke.

We sit in the Whale Well imitating whale sounds.

Our weekends are spent away from home with the girls, exploring. We find restaurants with jungle gyms, we walk in the mountains and on the Sea Point promenade, we swim in the sea (which I hate), and we go as often as we can to the Company Garden in Cape Town, which is one of my favourite spots.

We drive through the city with both girls lying in the back seat and looking up at the buildings. They have to find the horse head, the elephant in the architecture.

It is as if two delightful guests arrived and never left.

At the best of times, that is.

At THE WORST of times I imagined that Layla and Kenya, along with every other small person on the planet under the age of three, were secretly tuning into broadcasts by Radio Satan. Radio Satan transmits globally at a frequency out of range of the adult ear.

There was just no other explanation for the sheer ingenuity and completely Dadaesque behaviour that both seemed to display and that was specifically aimed at unhinging fragile adult carers.

My work and politics, which had both been such a significant focus of my life, still featured, but my emotional and intellectual devotion had been somewhat domesticated.

But still I had to work. I was a freelancer and, as a freelancer, a day not worked is a day without pay. I found ways to scrape in an income from my writing as my industry crumbled around me, succumbing to technology and a dwindling print readership. My income and work were erratic and I had constantly to think of a new project while in the middle of a usually quite significant one. This was to become a way of life. In the process I learned a range of new skills that would come in handy later, apart from stand-up comedy. That comes in handy all the time even though I seldom do it in public. My children are my best audience and no. 1 fans.

In the early years of parenting I attended so many work meetings so utterly exhausted that at times I looked at the people seated around a boardroom table and could not remember why I was there. But journalism has no sympathy for fatigue or illness. You simply get left behind. It is a job that requires more than curiosity, an ability for endurance.

And it was this that I learned in those early years. No one cared that you were tired or sick, or that you had a demanding father, two children, four dogs and three budgies who needed your attention. You had to just pull on those big girl panties and get on with it, like millions of other adults in the world. Flu, pneumonia, bubonic plague or a migraine would offer no excuse, and I began to appreciate and worship at the altar of big pharma and its ability to mask illness and disease in service to routine.

And Georg was beginning to surface from his years of holding onto and dragging the weight of the centuries. In December 2005 he invited us to his house for Christmas lunch. It was the first time ever that he bothered to celebrate. Before the children, one bleak Christmas, I had arrived at his house with a tree that I wanted to set up and decorate. He was Christian and I knew the season must have meant something to him. But back then he could hardly rouse himself from the chair, to the extent that at times I thought if he did stand up, the chair would come with him, as if it had become a part of him.

This time we arrived to a home decorated with baubles and candles. Earlier, he had given me cash to buy gifts for his grandchildren as he had no idea what twenty-first-century four- and two-year-olds would enjoy. He had bought a selection of very German meats, some sauerkraut, sweet carrots and potato cakes for lunch.

He offered to hold Kenya, who was a hefty little pudding, while I spread the food out on the dining-room table which he had set with a white cloth, a red candle, crockery and silver cutlery. Layla immediately headed for "her" nook in the sideboard and extracted her toys.

I watched as he tenderly rubbed his nose against Kenya's. "Zis is how ze Eskimos say hello *Keeeenia*."

Kenya, unlike Layla, would not smile just to humour him, or anyone else, but she stared at him and then clutched his wrinkled, sagging cheek.

Like Layla, she had developed her own way of pronouncing things: "speedbelt" for seatbelt, which we thought was rather clever; "High

School Nunisal" for "High School Musical", which was the movie *du jour* at some point; "maked" for naked and "high heel chair" for her high chair.

She surprised us with her creativity. From the back of the car one day she suddenly, gleefully, shouted "Epelent!"

"Where?"

"Dere," she said looking out of the window.

And there, sure enough, high up above was a cloud shaped exactly like an elephant.

Our two little gifted children.

I began to look forward to the free association of the learning of the ways of the world and often the girls, just before they fell asleep (well, Layla at least), would chatter away after their bedtime story.

Layla: "Why have you got hair on your fanny? Are you a scientist?"

Me: "No, sweetheart, it's just that I am a grown-up."

Layla: "I am going to be a scientist when I grow up."

Kenya: "I am going to be a hula girl."

There we had it.

We had decided, soon after Layla and Kenya arrived, that we would celebrate Christmas, for the children, of course. After reading Viennese psychologist Bruno Bettelheim's *A Good Enough Parent*, I was convinced. Much to the chagrin of my fundamentalist, secular, rationalist, materialist, communist friends.

Bettelheim wrote that on an unconscious level, the notion of Santa is important to children because this jolly, rotund figure speaks to our most important emotions and that it is through him that children can access the meaning Christmas has for small people (when they are not tuning into Radio Satan, that is).

While the birth of Christ has deep religious meaning to all believers in Christianity, Bettelheim writes that it is Santa Claus alone (and there was such a man who bestrode the earth once upon a time, St Nicholas) who caters to children in a way no amorphous "spirit of giving" could possibly do.

"To exchange presents as a token and symbol of love and goodwill can take place at any time and occasion. But no child believes that Santa

270

brings gifts to his parents and most would think their parents foolish were they to hang up stockings on the mantel for Santa," he explains. He continues: "Fat and jolly Santa, who brings presents for children down the chimney and puts them under the tree, is only for children."

It made complete sense that according to Bettelheim some children might feel that presents received from parents or relatives would somehow make them beholden to these adults.

"But children know they have harboured no negative thoughts towards Santa, and that he expects no gratitude, thus they can accept gifts from him without ambivalence."

I came to understand that magical thinking is only possible when you are little, for too soon the world with its pain and darkness will intrude. And then it is too late.

So each Christmas, until they reached that age when magical thinking becomes dimmed and discredited (until we find it again ourselves), we put out carrots, cookies and milk for Santa and his reindeer. I would leave just one carrot and watch on Christmas morning as both children would rush to the front door to see whether he had been and whether he and the reindeer had eaten what we had put out for them, before they turned in a frenzy on the pile of presents under the tree in our lounge.

These are memories that remain and provide sustenance.

So, too, the memory of Georg, more comfortable in his skin than I had ever experienced him. He had gone to such effort that Christmas buying chocolates and Pfefferkuchen. Even my brother seemed to have, from afar, reconnected with us here perched on the tip of Africa. That year Albert sent me an unexpected gift – a watch.

Having children plugged us into a social circle of other people with children. The childless could not stand the apparent noise and chaos, the stop-start conversation always interrupted by a small person demanding food or needing a nose wiped or exercising toddler lungs.

Socialising happened during the day and at weekends. For many years we would collapse exhausted into bed at more or less the same time as the children. Would we ever go out into the world as adults again, clubbing, drinking, smoking pot and watching the sun come up? For some reason – probably extreme fatigue – it seemed like the worst possible thing anyone would want to do.

Our relationship now veered from arguing about how to parent, with one of us backing down (usually me) to moments of extreme frustration (usually from me) as I tried to find a path through the life of the mind and life in a very demanding physical universe. And I was not always well behaved.

There were times when I longed to have a tantrum as the children did when they were frustrated, or just cry out of sheer exhaustion (because that is what children do, and rightly so).

With two small children to care for we became less and less aware of how others viewed us or whether they were even looking at us at all. They were. But it just didn't matter anymore. I did not think it was my job to explain ourselves to anyone. This was the twenty-first century. Google it.

All too soon Kenya was ready for pre-school and we watched as both our girls would wobble out each morning with their backpacks on, like two little turtles.

I would often collect them from school to find them sporting entirely new hairstyles.

We had decided that we would not tamper with their hair. No chemical straighteners (ever, we hoped). Mostly our kids looked great in their 'fros.

But I knew when someone offered the "Who did their hair?" that it actually meant "For God's sake, white woman, learn how to take care of it".

And so we would find ourselves, the only white people, in hair salons along the Main Road in Mowbray and Observatory. Hairdressers in South Africa are segregated. They shouldn't be, but they are. Our own hairdresser at the time shrugged and said she had no idea how to work with "ethnic hair". I pointed out that our hair was "ethnic" too, but she didn't quite understand.

The genteel rituals of white hairdressers, where you were in and out – if you were me – in half an hour max while you sipped coffee, were not a feature of the braiding "saloons" of Main Road. I learned that doing –

braiding – children's hair could take up to *four* or *five hours* and that it cost half of what it costs to "dress" "white" hair.

I learned also that I needed to cover my children in Vaseline, otherwise they would turn a sickly shade of grey. I learned to condition their hair with olive and other oils and that oil was miraculously absorbed in seconds.

Hair, we came to understand, was political. Hair and variations of skin tone.

Hair is not only a political statement for black women. White women seem unconscious of the fact that bleaching or dyeing our hair blonde is a political statement, for in the world of whiteness, blondes, natural or otherwise, rule.

Lesbians, too, have a thing about hair. We all seem to wear it the same way. In Cape Town a well-known hairdresser would turn out dykes with identical coifs – an added signifier before we could wear our sexual orientation on our social media profiles posting rainbow flags.

The Western ideal of beauty, the standardised generic big tits, tanned skin, skinny arse, white teeth and blonde hair, erased identity as much as a full burka. And whether women tried to accomplish this ideal, or way of being seen in the world, out of choice or to fulfil a religious or cultural notion of womanhood, it still rendered us standardised and invisible as individuals.

Layla did notice that her hair was not like ours and one morning demanded "a pony".

"You want a pony, I'll get you one," I said.

I went out and returned with a hair extension which we attached after I had scraped her magnificent Afro into a bun. Once it was clipped on securely, she spent a few hours flipping it in the mirror, and then she got bored, the fantasy fulfilled.

Georg had the easiest time with his hair, which, remarkably, even when he was in his 80s, had not greyed much at all. It made him look younger than his years. Every now and again he would order me to cut it with the clipper he had bought. But he enjoyed going to the barber and paying R30 for a cut.

Georg seemed surprised that he had reached 80.

"I really don't know how it happened. I can't believe I am 80," he said on his birthday, adding, "I am older than my mother now and my father."

I told him I could not believe I was 44. Neither could he.

"I still remember you when you were little, my menita, my little girl."

And so it was we both understood that in the end, time is all you have.

IN THE GREATER scheme of things – time, space (that place my hero Yuri Gagarin had explored a month after my birth) and the rest of the cosmos – our children are older than we are. As a species, each new generation extends our lineage. And that is why children bring wisdom (if we care to acknowledge this), even when they do so using an internal duct flute – the recorder – at 5am on a Saturday morning.

Until our children's arrival, my life, Georg's life, had been mono-thematic and anhedonic. We trucked listlessly along the same groove, circling the same centrifugal emotional forces. And then it was as if a switch had been turned on in a dark room. And there we were, like moles, exposed and terrified of the light. Surrounded by the debris, the shards and fragments of our histories, guided in some way by the epigenetic traumas and collateral damage that had kept me and my father locked in this embrace, Layla and Kenya snapped back the blinds and opened the windows of our souls. In so doing, what was of no real value, the excess baggage of stupidity, unconsciousness and repeti-tion, was illuminated, albeit dimly at first. Mandela played a part in this too.

Adolf Hitler and Hendrik Verwoerd might have stood as silent conductors of the discordant music of our souls, might have shaped some of the scaffolding of our minds, but it was Mandela and all he represented – compassion, justice and humanity – who pointed to a way out. Nelson Mandela, the symbol, the embodiment of that counterintuitive realisation that, at times, what hurts us can also come to heal us, that is if we make it out alive.

Nelson Mandela, the real man, the human, was as flawed as we all are, but the power of the medicine he brought extended beyond the corporeal. And while political cycles might repeat themselves (owing to our own inability to learn from the past), Mandela's golden thread of enlightenment, as tenuous as it might seem now and dimmed at times by shadows, serves as a delicate filigree of decency that binds.

In two generations Georg and I had moved from a world of stone hearts and bloody minds to one of acceptance and understanding, of equality and a common humanity. What stands in the way, what stood in the way, required the sloughing off of all that was placed there before – history, ideology, privilege – the externals.

And it was what Mandela brought to the little place at the tip of the African continent that enabled me, against all biological odds, to become a mother. It was through his guidance, and the guidance of those who fought with him for that ideal, that the ethos of human rights was ushered in. The ethos which recognises me as a lesbian with full and equal rights. And which in turn allowed Georg Albert Thamm to become the loving grandfather of two black grandchildren.

As Georg and I slowly unwound these outward ties, these forces that had shaped us, we found renewed connection, but the charged wires were still not making full contact. This alchemy would take time.

And Barbara? Where was she?

I dream one night that I am stranded in a landscape I do not recognise. I am in a hotel or a guesthouse. Outside is an overgrown, moist garden. Among the long grass and foliage I find a small grave. It is Barbara's. The headstone has toppled over and her name has been erased, but I know that this is where her ashes are interred. I lift the stone and beneath it find three of Barbara's rings. Her gold wedding ring I recognise immediately – it is the one I removed the night she died. It is the ring my partner still wears. The other two rings I do not recognise. The dream ends.

For days the dream lingers. What does it mean? What are the shiny rings?

I am driving in heavy traffic when the significance of this postcard from my unconscious begins to take shape. The rings represent the "gold" my mother has left me, her love, her understanding, her courage, her unconditional love and acceptance. The two new rings are my children. I find her gold because now I, too, am a mother. But can I hold onto the gold and pass it on with all its lustre?

The thing about gold is that it is a magical precious element, not in terms of its financial value, but with regard to how it came to be. Gold comes from outer space, from the meteorites that have struck our planet over billions of years, settling in faults and natural cracks in the core of the earth. Gold is malleable and can be shaped and bent, but to find it we must mine it, and usually under horrendous and exploitative conditions. South Africa is built on the quest for gold. Gold and other minerals beneath the soil.

My search for the gold in faults that existed in Georg would continue, but we did not have very much time left. In five years he would be dead. In retrospect, it was such a short time, less time than it takes for a laptop or a phone to become obsolete.

In the meantime Layla, Kenya, my partner and I had found our groove as a family.

We lived in, through, around and with each other. We couldn't tell where we started and they end. Instead of sleeping in their own beds, the girls insisted on being in ours. This resulted in a game of musical beds, which continues until today.

I am not to blame for this. It is parent no. 1 who has encouraged this.

I am uncomfortable sleeping with anyone (apart from the odd beloved dog). Too much wriggling, too much sniffling, coughing, wheezing, movement.

Years later, I found refuge in my own womancave. It is my space and mine alone. It is here that I wrestle and cuss and curse, fighting the demands of being a mother and a journalist/writer, a partner to another adult, the owner of dogs and budgies and hamsters and baby squirrels and birds rescued from under tall trees. And when he was alive, Georg. High-maintenance Georg.

As the years wore on and as lesbian and gay people (the transgendered would only become visible later) became ordinary tax-paying, child-rearing drones (as opposed to party animals who like parades) just like everyone else, we thankfully began to move less obviously through the world.

In fact our once-outsider status now provided us, I began to understand, with a certain amount of "diversity" cachet when it came to applying for schools.

Two white, middle-class lesbians (they obviously can afford to pay fees) with two black children (great for our diversity numbers) were high on the list of must-have sections of society. We managed to get into every single school we applied for, even though the girls were still a few years away from having to enter the grind that is the formal schooling system. There, I understood, the magic would be knocked out of them unless we found ways for them to withstand and preserve the onslaught.

It was during this exercise – this quest for a good and balanced education – that the deep, toxic and endemic racism that still lingers in South Africa was revealed in all its crude, subtle and not-so-subtle ugliness.

During a visit to one school in the southern suburbs on one of those Open Days when schools hope to display what they have to offer parents, we came up against one of its most genteel but violent manifestations. There was a festive atmosphere at the manicured and well-resourced school, and little tables with knick-knacks to keep the children occupied while parents snooped around.

Layla and Kenya were oblivious to the undercurrents trapped in the geography and architecture of the moment. Wanting a cupcake, they rushed over to me to ask for change. As I rummaged through my bag, I dropped a shiny coin. Layla stooped to pick it up. Suddenly, from out of nowhere, an elderly white woman appeared. Cupping Layla's elbow, and turning her to face me, she ordered my daughter to "Give that money back to that lady".

An urge to violence, incredible violence, surged through me. I could not find words apart from "That is my daughter, leave her alone".

I fantasised about smashing the woman's head against a brick wall. I wanted my children protected and cauterised from such toxicity – so emotionally and physically present in one apparently harmless old lady's words. But it was everywhere – in the air, in the shopping malls, the streets, the restaurants, where black lives daily encounter vulgar assumption, a negation of self, an intrusion of gross ignorance and perceived superiority.

"Let's get out of here, now," I hissed.

And then began the explaining to Layla and Kenya of why we had to leave. They were less than five years old, and what was simply a fun day at a school provided an entry point for finding a way to prepare them for what might come at them as black people in the world.

"Why are we going?"

"Because I am angry. I am angry at the way that lady thought you had stolen the money because you are black."

The political education had begun. It continues.

And there were many such occasions, too many to recount without a sense of despair, but here are a few.

As the girls came to see through the ignorance of how they might be viewed, not as Layla or Kenya, but as black children, part of an amorphous mass, they too learned to assert and take their space.

As I was dropping Kenya off at school one morning, a mother in a 4x4 (a vehicle my children had learned "makes the world dirty") glided into a parking bay. As the passenger door swung open and her daughter stepped out, the little girl remarked loudly, "Look, Mommy, Kenya comes to school in a car."

The layers in that simple statement are many but I was thrilled to discover that Kenya knew this. Almost immediately she mimicked, in a sing-song, the little girl's voice: "'Mommy, look, Kenya comes to school in car.'"

"Why do you think she said that?" I asked her.

"Because I am black and she thinks I should be walking or that maybe I must come in a taxi."

"Maybe on a horse even," I said as we both laughed.

Yes, my little politician. And, indeed, a while later Kenya did tape self-made posters around the house. A drawing of her face with the words "Vote Kenya" at the top and "She's awesome" at the bottom.

At a restaurant with rolling lawns where children played ball and flew model planes, Layla encountered a child who told her he could not play with her because she was black.

"That boy said I can't play with him because I am black," she ran to tell us as we sat gathered with friends and their adopted sons.

"Do you want me to talk to him and his mother?"

"No, I already did," said Layla.

"What? On your own?"

"Yes."

Layla had assumed the child's mother would be horrified. And she must have been, or at least embarrassed. She gave her the usual reply: "I don't know where he learns that."

Layla, brave Layla, who believes everyone in the world possesses the generous and gentle heart that she has.

Our table at the restaurant did attract surreptitious looks. By now I was a past master at interpreting any look that came our way. This one was, All these women with all these children. Where are the men?

My children (and I) learned that the minute they entered a shop, security guards would follow them. Unable to clock that we were their parents, the guards assumed the worst. My children were and are still watched wherever we go. It is not something any white person will know. The banal regularity of it wears off. My children take their space.

And for a time, while my children might have been wiser and older than me, I was, to all intents and purposes, in their eyes at least, a walking, breathing manifestation of Google +. My daughters thought I knew everything and everyone, and for a while I managed to pull this off.

"Mom, does the sun circle the earth?" Layla asked one day as we drove home from school.

For a split second I could not answer. It was as if I had never been to school at all. There was nothing in that drawer that enabled me to say with certainty that yes it does, or no, the sun does not circle the earth. But there was a vague remembering that we all orbited the sun.

"Um . . . no, the earth and the other planets revolve around the sun, I think" (the last said softly to myself).

Guests to our home included many people whose faces my children saw on posters dangling from outdoor street poles advertising their work. Comedians, musicians, authors. And for the longest time they thought everyone in the world was known or "a celebrity". The upside of working as a journalist in the same city for so long is that it enabled me to cross paths with extraordinary people with unique talents and beautiful hearts and minds who have become part of my karass.

My daughters also forced me to pay attention again to the smaller things in life, those peripheral matters that eventually just become wall-paper, life passing by the window.

One day on the way home from school Layla, looking out of the window of the car, spotted a specimen of suburban graffiti hastily sprayed on the wall of a house near the school's exit. Not the kind of graffiti mural that spray-can artists have created throughout the city, but a crude little bit of in-your-face-fuckers type.

There on the grey wall was a small rendition of an erect hairless penis.

"What's that?" asked Layla as Kenya leaned across to catch a glimpse of it as well.

"That? It's a drawing of a penis," I offered rather matter-of-factly.

Actually it looked more like a mushroom with two tumours instead of a stalk.

"Oh."

Silence.

"But why?"

"Why what?"

"Why did someone draw that?"

Bloody good question. Now whether to give the complex or simple answer.

"It is a representation of the violence and dominance of patriarchy and the military-industrial complex as symbolised by the penis – note the shape of guns and rockets, cigars and golf clubs (at a push) – which in this world carries with it a status it does not deserve."

Well, that was the ticker-tape of thoughts that ran through my mind, but I opted for the simple answer instead.

"Because whoever did the drawing probably likes his penis. And I suppose he wants to shock us or maybe just show it off," I said.

Silence.

I kept thinking about the outline of the cartoon penis as we drove.

Why didn't women go around spraying renderings of their genitals on suburban walls?

And then I thought about it some more . . ..

It's dusk or maybe late at night. No one is around. You find a wall in a great spot – loads of foot and vehicular traffic for maximum impact.

And then you begin. Pshhhht . . . mons pubis. Pshhttt . . . two labia minora. Pshhhtt . . . Pshhhhht . . . two labia majora. Pshht . . .clitoris. Pshhhtt . . . clitoral hood. Pshhtttt . . . urethral orifice. And then lastly to top it off . . . Pshhttt pshhtt pshtttt . . . a lovely crop of pubic hair.

No wonder women don't do this. It would take ages. And in the end it would look more like a spider that had caught a lizard perhaps.

Men scribbled penises on toilet and other walls, I decided, simply because they are easy to draw.

It was around 2007 that Georg's health began steadily to deteriorate. He had suffered from several chronic illnesses over the years, including asthma and spondylosis of the spine. The latter is a narrowing of the vertebrae that brings with it rounds of back pain, which Georg managed with anti-inflammatories and by trying to exercise regularly, walking his dog in the park.

And there was the low-grade depression, the perpetual mourning.

Other than these he seemed relatively robust. He did sleep a lot but, hey, he was in his 80s and retired.

In 2007 the beginning of the decline began. It came with a phone call. I was in Johannesburg on an assignment, covering a DA federal congress where Helen Zille was elected leader of the party. I was staying with friends and their children and we were seated around a noisy dinner table. I missed my own children, who were at home safe with Mommy 2.

"Marianna, I haf no pulse," my father informed me in a voice tinged with real concern.

I stepped outside into the Gauteng dusk to take the call.

"But Dad, you'd be dead if you didn't have a pulse. What do you mean?"

"It is very low. I haf checked my blood pressure and it is not good."

I was due to return to Cape Town the following day and I promised him that we would immediately go and see a doctor. It was the first time I had heard Georg so concerned about his health.

Back home I drove through to Somerset West early the next morning after having made an emergency appointment with his physician. Georg was dressed in a gorgeous light woollen suit and open-necked shirt. The braces with the paisley pattern that he preferred to wear rather than a belt peeked out from under the jacket.

A veritable squadron of doctors occupied a wing just off the Vergelegen Mediclinic, each one dedicated to various organs/parts of the human body; there was a proctologist, a nephrologist, and a cardiac specialist, which was where we were headed. This would be a drain on my father's medical aid, but at least he had coverage.

Georg was always chatty around doctors. He reckoned he understood his body, understood our bodies, as he had always medicated us for whichever ailment we had, including the bad chests that both my brother and I had inherited from him. I asked if he wanted me to accompany him during the examination and he said yes.

I helped him slip out of the suit and shirt and strip down to his underwear. It was the first time I had seen his body this bare in a long while. His skin was grey and thin. Flaps hung below biceps that were once firm.

The doctor, a middle-aged Afrikaans man with a rather abrupt but still polite bedside manner, hooked Georg up to a variety of monitors and pads that were attached with little suckers to his hairy chest. I had forgotten that Georg had a third, small residual nipple on his left side. It had intrigued me as a child, this tiny useless little teat embedded in his hairy chest, which now was greyer than his head.

The doctor stared at the screen as a paper print-out frothed from a machine located near it. He ran the long strip with the scratches that had been made by a graph machine. He said nothing apart from that we needed to shift to another room further down the passage where someone would be taking a "wobble gram", a sort of sonar scan of Georg's heart.

He offered Georg a blue hospital gown which tied at the back. He held onto my arm as we shuffled down a warren of corridors and into a darkened room with more machines.

Georg reclined on the upholstered bed while a young woman hitched him to more machines and there, for the first time, I saw his heart gently, and irregularly, pulsing. The heart that had beaten through those Hitler Youth rallies, when he traversed Europe during the Second World War, when he fell in love for the first time. It was this heart that had skipped a beat one day in a forest somewhere in Russia when a bullet had shattered the mirror he had balanced in the nook of a tree in order to shave. He had no idea of the interior monologue that ran through my head in that moment.

Afterwards I helped Georg slip back on and button up his shirt. He stepped into his trousers and I helped guide his bony arms through the sleeves of his jacket.

The heart specialist was already seated behind his desk, scribbling in a file, when we found our way back to his office. He looked up as we took our seats in front of him.

"Georg, you are in stage D heart failure. I am booking you in now for an emergency pacemaker to be implanted."

"Now?" Georg asked, surprised.

"Right now. You are not going home. You are going straight to ICU."

Georg looked terrified.

"What about my dog?"

"Don't worry," I told him. "I'll take her home with me. First we'll have you admitted and then I'll go and fetch what you need. Your pyjamas, your reading glasses. You tell me what you want."

At that moment he seemed scared and frail. I waited with him as a porter arrived with a wheelchair and he was whisked off to the main wing of the hospital to fill in the paperwork. The weight and the reality of the diagnosis seemed to have stunned him. He asked that I deal with the admissions clerk while he sat slumped in the wheelchair.

We entered the labyrinth of hospital corridors and found our way to ICU, secured behind a locked door that needed a code to let you inside. The nurses seemed to be expecting Georg and bustled around him, wheeling him behind the curtains drawn around a bed. After a couple of minutes a cheery sister emerged carrying a pile of Georg's clothes. She handed them to me, saying, "You can talk to him a bit now. We're taking him in shortly for the op."

"Right now?"

"Ja, he's in heart failure, it's an emergency."

Georg was propped on pillows and seemed to have surrendered to whatever was going to happen next. I sat in a chair next to him and held his hand. Another young nurse appeared, wheeling a drip on a stand.

"Mr Thamm, I'm going to insert this drip. It might be a little bit sore."

"Don't worry," I said, trying to lighten things, "he's an old soldier."

And then, turning to look at me, for the first time he said it.

"Ja, for the wrong side."

Georg WAS READY to be discharged in 24 hours, the pacemaker implanted beneath the skin just below his collarbone. It was remarkable how soon the colour had returned to his complexion. But Georg could not be alone while his ailing heart and body learned to adjust to the renewed assisted rhythm. He had always tended to walk or move briskly. "You have to remember to give your heart an opportunity to catch up with your brain," the doctor told him now.

After collecting a mound of tablets from the pharmacy, we left the clinic. At first Georg seemed overwhelmed by the new medicinal routine, with its specific instructions of pills to be taken at set times in the day. He was, I insisted, to come home with me while he recovered and we had cleared a back bedroom for this purpose, with an accessible toilet for him.

Layla and Kenya were thrilled to have Oupa staying with us. On the first night when Georg removed his dentures to soak them in an effervescent cleaner, they shrieked with delight.

"Oupa can take out his teeth!" Layla rushed to tell me.

"Can I try them on?" Kenya asked.

Georg was a homebody. I knew he was uncomfortable out of his own surroundings and so we did our best to make him feel welcome. At least having him in the back room while I worked in my office at the front of the house brought, for me, peace of mind.

It was also time, I thought, to talk to him about perhaps thinking of moving, either in with us – a matter I had discussed with my partner –

or at least to another space where he would not be alone. Georg refused point-blank to entertain the idea.

"I vill be fine at home. I cannot come and lif here. It is too far from everything."

"What everything? There are chemists here, and libraries, and beautiful gardens where you can walk with the dog."

"No. I like Somerset West. It is my home."

We had not quite reached that point where children can categorically begin to parent a parent and override their authority.

I tried another angle.

"Well, then maybe when you do go home we can just explore what might be available in Somerset West. Somewhere where you will get meals, where someone will be on call if you need them or if you get sick."

"What about my dog?"

"We'll find a complex where you can keep her."

Silence.

But at least we had opened the discussion.

In a week Georg was ready to go home. During his week with us I had often found Layla and Kenya in his bedroom, one lying in the nook of each arm, watching the soapie *Isidingo* on TV. That he looked like a thin, toothless, embalmed mummy didn't matter to either of them.

Each family, each of us as individuals, will arrive at that moment when we are sandwiched between our growing children and our ageing parents and their needs. There is little preparation for this, nothing in the instruction manual we come with.

That it comes as a surprise, as it mostly does, is testimony to how Western culture has fundamentally interrupted a narrative of kinship. In this world, we are encouraged to be nuclear, hermetic, independent units, sealed off from our relatives and their needs. Every man and woman for himself. If you cannot succeed here and provide for yourself, you have only yourself to blame.

We are not burdened with the "black tax" so many newly middle-class black South Africans have to bear, supporting extended family members who for years have been denied an opportunity to build a nest egg or accumulate property or wealth, none of the accoutrements of privilege that enable independence.

But eventually as one force of life, youth, cascades towards us, we must deal with another, that of our parents, who are receding. Georg's parents had both died young; his sister had cared for their mother, my grandmother, as she grew sick, old and frail after the war.

My mother's own parents, too, had died when she was young, so we had no example of this inter-generational responsibility of reciprocal care.

And at the time when Georg cared for Barbara, I had not understood how much it would later serve as an example of how I would need to care for him, nor just how much it would require, physically and emotionally.

Where our mothers (or fathers) once changed our soiled nappies, we, too, would one day need to bathe and clean them when they returned, in old age, to a vulnerable and helpless state. That is, if they enjoyed the privilege and pain of growing old, of being forced to surrender agency and independence. As we hurtle back towards the pinprick that is nothingness, this is what we must do. Relinquish the material things we hold onto that once provided meaning, but that cannot be taken with us.

Georg enjoyed telling a joke about this. The joke is about an old, rich man who died. Afterwards, at his funeral, his relatives discuss his wealth.

"I wonder how much he left?" asks one.

"All of it," someone with rare insight replies.

I could never have imagined, as I tore freely through my childhood and early adulthood, that this would ultimately be a task that would be mine. I had never imagined my parents as old, frail and helpless.

And while the white, Western way is for offspring to leave home as soon as possible, propelled into the world armed with the shield of privilege and accumulated wealth – be it financial, an education, or the mental, physical and emotional well-being a relatively average middle-class life provides – we seldom drill down into what it means to care for elderly and ailing parents.

My peculiar sense of kinship had been readjusted and augmented by my partner's loyalty and commitment to her own family, fractious and oppositional though they might have occasionally been. Through this new family I learned to step out of my feral emotional and physical default position and do what must be done.

As Georg grew older and less vital, he began to talk more and more about his own family of origin, his mother, his father, his sister and his grandparents. Where did we, I, feature in this landscape? I wondered.

It was Proust who wrote that "when we pass a certain age, the soul of the child we were and the souls of the dead from whom we have sprung, come to lavish us with their riches and spells".

Georg slept beneath a black-and-white portrait of his mother and father in his musty bedroom, and he dreamed about them regularly. He dreamed about his work and his now long-forgotten life as a mechanical engineer. He dreamed away life in real time.

"I dreamed again I was in the factory working," he would tell me as I roused him yet again during an afternoon visit.

"Well, I hope you got paid for it."

WHILE GEORG AND I were slowly constructing a rickety bridge – each from opposite sides of the physical, emotional, political and ideological valley that still separated us – it was still unsafe to use. Could, would, either of us ever be able to make our way across it?

For while the children had brought a warmth that had thawed parts of his character, the essence of Georg had remained intact, calcified, clogged, like his veins and arteries, with the plaque of past experience.

It was almost as if Georg was incapable of "seeing" me and of surrendering to a connection that would be uncluttered by our assumptions of each other. And while I had come to see some aspects of Georg as Georg, my melancholy father – Georg the German, the Nazi, the man who had been shaped by Adolf Hitler's Germany – still loomed. Georg the undermining patriarch, Georg the withholding father, concealing his hand of cards. Georg the stubborn and unyielding man.

Soon after he returned home a brighter shade of pink – the pacemaker and pharmaceuticals providing a false sense of physical regeneration – he had a terrible fall.

It was late afternoon and I was, as usual, on a work deadline. The phone rang. It was Georg. He sounded nasal.

"Ach, Marianna, I slipped and fell in ze passage. But I sink I am all right now. But zere is a lot of blood everyvere."

"I'm coming now. Just wait."

I dashed to the car and just managed to evade Cape Town's rush-hour traffic on the N2.

The blinds of his house were drawn and it was worryingly quiet inside. I unlocked the door to find a pool of blood in the entrance. There were signs that Georg had tried to mop it up. Inside his darkened bedroom, while his dog napped on an armchair, I found Georg prostrate on the bed with a bloodied dishcloth bound around his forehead, his mouth open. He didn't rouse. I thought, This is it, he's dead.

I shook him gently and he woke up, confused.

Removing the dishcloth, I found a 10 cm gash above his swollen eye where his glasses had cut into the delicate skin. The flap of severed flesh revealed a layer of fat underneath. This was going to need stitches. His nose was swollen and bruised.

"I'm taking you to the emergency unit, now."

"No, I am not going. Ve can put a plaster on it."

"No. This is serious. I'll help you to get dressed."

And off we went, Georg pressing a clean towel against the wound.

Georg needed fifteen stitches above his eye and was told he had to spend at least two nights in hospital.

It was time to have *the* discussion. I no longer felt comfortable that he lived alone at home.

"Dad, you have to think about moving somewhere where there are people around and someone who can care for you. Why don't you come and live with us, even for a little while, before we find somewhere else?"

"No. I am okay on my own. I can't live vith you. I vill be a burden. I vill be in ze way and you are busy every day viz work and ze children."

"Dad, that is why we have family. You won't be a burden. We have the space and we can find someone to come and look after you when we are too busy . . ."

"No."

After he was discharged Georg did, however, agree to spend a few weeks at our house recuperating. He was uncomfortable, I could tell. He was a loner and missed his privacy and his home.

One Sunday I arranged to call my brother in Australia, so he and

Georg could chat. Georg hobbled to my office at the front of the house to the landline. As he sat at my desk waiting for the phone to ring, he took in the room with its photographs and knick-knacks.

"Vhat are all of zees things on ze desk?" he asked, motioning at the arrangement of awards I had won for my journalism and columns over the years.

"Those are awards."

"Awards? Yours? For what?"

I burst out laughing. It no longer mattered that he didn't know or that he hadn't been aware of this crucial part of my life and who I am.

I offered to get him tea while he waited for the call.

I had been asked to perform a comedy routine at the Darling Voorkamerfest a week later. This was a unique arts festival in the little dorpie where my hero Pieter-Dirk Uys had settled. For several years the festival offered audiences an opportunity to experience artists, singers, dancers, and comedians, performing in the intimacy of people's lounges in their homes.

On the morning it was my turn, I told Georg that the family was driving through to Darling for the festival, where I was due to perform. I had begun to re-explore stand-up, a little hobby I had experimented with earlier around 1994–5.

"You doing comedy?"

"Yes."

"I didn't know you vere funny," he said, sipping tea while seated in an armchair in the bedroom.

The thing is Georg genuinely did not know that his comments might hurt or undermine me. He was simply speaking his truth. He actually had no idea who I was apart from what he experienced in our day-to-day interactions or past notions he had shaped and held onto. The Marianne he thought he knew was the child he had raised for seventeen years and who had then moved out.

In the car en route to Darling, the children cut through the hurt of the moment.

"Is Oupa dying?" asked Kenya.

"I think so," I said.

"When?" asked Layla.

"I don't know."

"Soon?" asked Kenya.

"I really don't know."

"Can we watch?" asked Layla.

And so it came to pass as I had foretold it.

Georg was insistent that he continue to live in his old house on his own. No matter how much I tried to convince him that it would be more traumatic to move him suddenly to an old-age home – oh, okay, retirement village – he stubbornly refused. He had humoured me earlier and had put his name down at a nearby complex, but he failed to inform me that they had called to say that a space had become available. Or that he had turned it down.

Caring for Georg now also involved driving through to Somerset West twice a week in the afternoons to walk his dog. Since his old smelly dachshund Nina had died, Georg had acquired a new dog, Suzi, a young dachshund cross Jack Russell we had collected from a local animal shelter. He had seen the dog advertised in the local Somerset West knock-and-drop and had called to inform me he was ready for a new dog. He was 85 at the time, but I understood his need for companionship and shared his love of dogs.

We drove to the shelter together. It was a depressing, freezing and wet winter morning when we were introduced to an emaciated Suzi in her concrete cage. She was a lovely little dog, young, affectionate and energetic. She would need a lot of attention and exercise, and I worried that Georg might not be able to care for her properly. Suzi was about a year old and I understood, as he cradled her in his arms, that she would outlive him and would one day have to be absorbed by my pack at home.

Georg had a tiny garden which Suzi, in frustration, dug up. He tried to take her for walks but was growing too weak and frail to drive out to the park on his own. And so it was that I offered to walk her twice a week for 30 minutes before dashing back home to finish my work and help with the children.

As the year wore on, Georg began to shrink. He seemed a head shorter and spent most of the day sleeping. He had also lost a lot of weight but he thought this was healthy.

"It is not good to carry too much veight," he said.

But this was not good.

During one of his regular check-ups to adjust the frequency of the pacemaker, the doctor discovered that his kidneys had shrivelled and so off we went for more rounds of tests, Georg convinced each time that medical science would offer a reprieve.

And each time I watched him disrobe and walk with difficulty in the blue hospital gown through the maze of corridors to the various rooms, where almost every part of his body would be scanned, prodded and measured.

And then the inevitable. The day came that he could no longer be alone. He had fallen again and had grown so weak he could hardly get up in the mornings.

It unfolded as I had imagined and so, apart from being overwhelmed by the sheer weight of the paperwork and bureaucracy, I was somewhat prepared.

First the move back to our house while we found suitable accommodation in Somerset West. We had to redirect his mail, put his house up for sale, empty it, remove his furniture (which ended up being stored in my garage), cancel cable TV subscriptions, and sift through years of accumulated documents, notebooks and even till slips.

Then there were the mounds of documents required for his application for a room in the old-age home of his choice. This was a large complex, located in the centre of Somerset West and surrounded by a tall security fence. It was light and sunny, with convivial communal areas and a reasonably sized garden, where those who could still walk could amble between meals, sleeping or playing carpet bowls and Bingo.

Rows of old men and women sat in the sunroom, reading, knitting or just sitting, staring out at an old tree and the birds that flitted about it. There was a communal dining room and residents could expect three regular cooked meals a day. All of them were white, the staff all black.

Another of God's waiting rooms. You do not leave here alive.

Georg's life was reduced to one small room with an en suite toilet. It had a comfortable bed, an armchair, his television, a clothes horse and a table, where he set out framed photographs of his mother and father, one of my brother and his son, and several of Layla and Kenya. These of course provoked discussion among the staff and Georg was proud to announce that they were his grandchildren.

Georg would be using a communal shower down the passage. Because so many of the residents were frail, they needed help with this simple routine, which those of us who are young and healthy take for granted.

It would be, I understood, a period of adjustment, of coming to terms with a massive loss of independence, to say nothing of privacy, and all that had once surrounded him and been familiar – his desk (which was now in my office), his carpets, his own peculiar smells. Georg would soon begin to absorb the new smells of urine and canteen food that permanently hung about the old-age home. After a while he no longer noticed.

I took Layla and Kenya to visit him, where they became the focus of everyone, staff and residents alike. They brought with them a vitality that was distinctly lacking as the old patiently sat out their time. Georg, when he was able to get up and go out of his room, would proudly introduce them, and me, to those residents he had managed to befriend, usually those who shared his table in the dining room.

Layla and Kenya would do cartwheels in the courtyard under the tree, and try to pet the resident cat.

Surely this could not be more comfortable than our own home, I thought, and yet this was what Georg had chosen.

Georg had asked me to take care of his meagre finances – his savings as well as his monthly pension deposits. The amount was not enough to cover the cost of the room in the old-age home and we would later supplement this rental from the sale of his house.

I was extremely reluctant to be saddled with this responsibility and suggested that he employ a local attorney to deal with his bank accounts and various payments to creditors. I was still smarting from his accusation, when the widow was standing by, that I had somehow sought to benefit from his savings. I wanted no room for misunderstanding or paranoia. To avoid this I would bring his post, which had been re-directed to my home address, unopened, for him to deal with. That way he would still feel some sense of control. As it was, he could no longer keep any cash or credit cards on him at the old-age home as these were likely to be stolen, as the matron who ran the home told me.

At the end of our days, I soon realised, all we have left are those things other people are not able to take: the love of our family, our children, our friends, our dogs, and our memories of them; the notion of a life well lived, which will provide sustenance as we think back on it as we exit. How much of a reservoir did Georg have that he could draw on? I often wondered.

At first I dealt with each health setback as if it were the last, but I soon learned that the road to oblivion is paved with many false alarms. There were the months Georg could not get out of bed without falling and hurting himself. This was soon remedied, however, when we real-ised that he needed to reduce the dose of diuretic he was taking to help relieve the fluid build-up on his lungs.

One week I would find Georg too weak to get out of bed and the next he would be up and dressed in the one suit we had taken with us, chatting in the sunroom.

It would only be a matter of time before all his organs slowly began to fail and, unlike an old car for which we could find spare parts, there was nothing to be done about it apart from alleviating any discomfort.

Georg was moved to a room on the ground floor where there were more staff capable of keeping a watch on the terminally ill or the de-mented. The room opposite his was occupied by an ancient man who had entirely lost his mind. He spent much of his time either strapped to his bed or circling the carpet in an adult nappy, which he would pull off after soiling it. The sickly sweet smell would alert us, as well as staff, and a round of frantic mopping, scrubbing and cleaning would take place.

No one ever visited this man as he lingered in limbo surrounded by photographs of people he no longer recognised. Occasionally, when he had the strength, Georg would help his neighbour with a drink of water or pull up a blanket that had slipped off as he dozed in his chair.

Which is better – to be dying, fading away, with your mind intact and fully aware of it, like Georg, or to be completely oblivious to it all, like his neighbour? At least if we are conscious in those last days and months, we can try to find closure and, if we are not anxious or in pain, prepare for the journey to that place we must all go.

But can we ever be prepared?

It WAS THE GREAT Stella Adler, Marlon Brando's acting coach, who provided him with a key to exploring that which animated him with such luminosity on the screen.

"Do not bring anything into the present that does not have the past," she advised him.

It is a truth for life in general, too. Everything we are is, in some way, tethered to our history and we ignore it at our peril. We ignore it actually to repeat it all, as personal and political histories.

And so, we must return here to the beginning, which was also the end.

"Is Oupa dead yet?" Layla would ask as I arrived home at dusk after visiting Georg.

"Not yet."

"Will there be a funeral?" asked Kenya.

"Ja."

"Well, I am wearing my ballet tutu," she announced.

And in that moment all the suffering and pain confined to that small room in the old age-home where Georg awaited death's embrace were momentarily erased.

The day before he died, we said all we needed to say, apart from the one thing I was hoping that he could bring himself to express now that he hovered at the threshold of life.

"I love you, Marianne."

But he could not.

While he did love me, verbalising it was simply impossible for him.

Was it too embarrassing? Too painful? Just not done, even now as we said our last goodbyes?

But it no longer mattered. I had come, through him, through my children, through my partner, through the world I now found myself in, to love and understand myself a little more. That is the best we can hope for.

LAYLA AND KENYA were extremely disappointed that Georg's coffin was closed and that his corpse was not on full view for the handful of mourners who had gathered in the Doves chapel to say goodbye.

Children know exactly how to treat death, not with fear, but with curiosity.

"Can I have his teeth?" Kenya asked as we drove out.

"I think he's wearing them," I informed her.

She seemed disappointed. I did try to imagine her running around with my father's dentures wedged into her small mouth. The very thought of it made me queasy but she clearly had no qualms.

I had spent the week after Georg's death in a sort of formless and atomised secular grief. There was no ritual to stop the tide of outside life from spilling into the fractured, silent and slow arena of my grief. And it was then again that music held me.

I also took refuge in what I know best, writing. This time I composed a clumsy poem:

Natural Causes
He died
they say
of Natural Causes

Natural causes;
a swim in the lake,
a cold beer in a garden,
a kiss in a field,
a marching band,
a stamp collection,
a haircut,

a walk with dogs,
a game of cards,
raising a son,
a daughter,
nursing a wife,
listening to Schubert,
laughing at the Goon Show,
sitting in a patch of sun,
watching a bird glide in an air pocket,
saying goodbye
on a sunny
Monday afternoon
stroking a dog.

IT WAS A beautiful, sunny winter's morning when our family drove out to Somerset West to take our final leave of Georg. The service was simple. The plain wooden coffin with rope handles was draped in a purple velvet cloth. I placed a framed photograph of a smiling Georg, taken a few months before he moved out of his home, and a bunch of white St Joseph lilies on top of it.

I had selected a few items of music to play that I thought represented what Georg meant to me and that he might enjoy hearing wherever he was now.

I played some infuriating German marching music, a clip from Monty Python, and an old German song, *Du sollst nicht weinen*, by the boy wonder Heintje, a sort of Justin Bieber of German kitsch. It was a song that reminded me of my childhood with Georg.

At home I lay in my darkened office while memories of Georg fluttering his hand for me to slip mine into as we crossed a busy road surfaced and unspooled like an old home movie. There was Georg shaving, his cheeks lathered, and Georg wiping and puckering his glistening lips for a kiss. Georg teaching me to drive, Georg taking us to the library, Georg small and frail with his large ears jutting out of his shrunken head like cup handles. Georg shuffling off to the great, unreachable beyond.

But his death also brought with it relief. Relief that his suffering had ended. Relief also that we had both been freed from each other. We built the bridge, we reached each other in a fashion. We both gave it our best shots. We had done the work.

And now I was motherless, fatherless, an adult, and I felt guilty, for the feeling was one of exhilaration and release tinged with occasional sadness.

I was free to be me, away from my father's mortal gaze.

And with time Georg in his greater fullness and complexity began to dawn on me. As I absorbed his life, rummaging through his documents, his photo albums, his Bible with the lock of his mother's hair pressed between its pages, he emerged less gift-wrapped in the outside forces that had shaped him.

The twentieth century and all it represented, all I had found loathsome and oppressive about it, became also less stark, less jagged and dangerous.

I live in a world, an epoch and a country where the potential for individual liberation and enlightenment has never been greater. But the remnants of history lurk all around us.

IN 2013 Nelson Mandela died. It was not unexpected. But still it brought with it the searing pain of loss of someone deeply loved, someone who, for me, came to represent, in many ways, the freedom I enjoy.

Mandela's death drove me to the same piece of music I had played when Georg died, Estonian composer Arvo Pärt's *Spiegel im Spiegel*.

It is a work of great simplicity, composed for a single piano and violin with the endless repetition of small notes, reflected back and forth, back and forth, creating, like a mirror, an infinity of images. It captured for me perfectly the essence of Mandela and what he will always be – a prism, a mirror and a reflection; an essence deeply embedded in our collective consciousness as South Africans, even now as we still struggle "to become".

In a column for the online *Daily Maverick* (where I have now found a home) I wrote: "For those of us who lived through and survived apartheid in South Africa, Nelson Mandela had always been the man who wasn't there. Banished to Robben Island in the winter of 1964, Mandela spent 18 of his 27 years in this isolated prison, both physically and politically cauterised from South African society. The presence of absence."

And now Georg and Barbara, and all my ancestors, are present in their absence. And sometime, hopefully not too soon, I, too, shall become an ancestor, hopefully not a wrathful one.

Growing older is a business not to be resisted but embraced. It really is much more fun than being 13 or 20 or 30 or even 40. After 50 it is only a matter of time, I suppose, before I peer into the window of a shoe shop and begin to find those old-lady sandals attractive. And will there come a day when I drive past a bowling green and find myself thinking, That looks like a fun sport?

My beautiful, talented, clever daughters are on the cusp of adulthood. Yuri Gagarin and the twentieth century that shaped me are as far away as WWII was to me when I was a child. They might ask me one day if I ever met Verwoerd or Mandela and what it was that I did in "the war". I'll hand them this book and smile.

I had, like many South Africans, believed that Nelson Mandela and the ANC had brought freedom to South Africa and, while much has changed and been altered and people are indeed free, I now find myself once again drawn back into a world outside my home. Democracy is a work in progress. It never just is.

And so it is that while writing about the Constitutional Court's finding that President Jacob Zuma violated his oath of office and the country's constitution in using taxpayers' money to renovate his private home at Nkandla, I have to deal with Kenya telling me that she needs a three-dimensional frog for a school project which has to be in "like tomorrow" and Layla needing to recite a long poem she has to learn by heart.

And while writing this in 2016, we have come to understand that South African politics are riddled with as much greed, corruption, venality and self-serving dishonesty as everywhere else in the world, I am also aware of the extraordinary energy, creativity, passion and drive of a younger generation who are pushing the boundaries, dragging us further into the twenty-first century, a place that, ultimately, is far better than the one I survived . . . and lived to tell this tale (of sorts).

In the end we pass through life as it passes through us. The one lesson I learned from Georg is don't wait for happiness to send you a WhatsApp . . . go out and be it.